JUST SAY YES

ALSO BY MIRIAM BROOKS BUTTERWORTH

Celebrate! West Hartford

(an illustrated town history, co-authored)

JUST SAY YES

A Memoir by

Miriam Brooks Butterworth

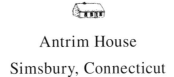

Antrim House
Simsbury, Connecticut

Library of Congress Control Number: 2010936226

ISBN: 978-0-9843418-7-0

Printed & bound by Sheridan Books, Inc.
Ann Arbor, MI

First Edition, 2010

Captioned photographs by Miriam Butterworth, Oliver Butterworth, et al.

Book design by Timothy Butterworth and Rennie McQuilkin

Just Say Yes originally appeared in five spiral-bound volumes entitled
Don't Just Stand There, published by Tim Butterworth under
the aegis of Sugarbush Hill Press of Chesterfield, NH.
His book design has been largely retained
in this composite edition.

Photographs from LIFE magazine on pp. 217-218 (by Lee Balterman)
and p. 221 (by Gerald R. Brimacombe) are by permission
of Time/LIFE, Inc. and Getty Images.

Antrim House
860.217.0023
AntrimHouse@comcast.net
www.AntrimHouseBooks.com
21 Goodrich Road, Simsbury, CT 06070

TABLE OF CONTENTS

INTRODUCTION

PART I: LIVING IN INTERESTING TIMES

PART II: FAMILY MATTERS

PART III: WHAT ON EARTH DID YOU FIND TO DO?

PART IV: THE PAST IS PROLOGUE

PART V: EPILOGUE

INTRODUCTION

I started to write this autobiography a few years after the death of Oliver, my husband for half a century. I supposed I was writing it for my children and grandchildren who might someday want to know something about their early selves and their forebears. But I really was writing it for myself, wanting to relive my life which had been wondrously filled with joy and adventures. In 1994, memories had become a large and pleasurable part of my days, and writing about them was a way of focusing more systematically on the past, to mull it over and take stock. My purposes for continuing became more ambitious the more I wrote. I discovered I was not only gaining some insight into who I was and who I am: I believed I was adding to an understanding of the 20th Century that was coming to an explosive end.

I had a wonderful winter writing Part I. I delved into family records, re-read ancient diaries, hunted up old newspaper articles and reminisced with old friends and relatives. In the process, I created a picture of my early relationships, remarked on the kind of education girls were given in the 1930s, and reported my impressions of, among other things, Germany in the summer of 1938 and Washington D.C. in February of 1940. In subsequent years I wrote Part II about life as wife, mother and teacher. In Part III I tell of being an active observer and often a maker of history – a minor player, of course, but a participant nonetheless, one who learned a lot about the actions and motives, the hopes and fears in my corner of the world. How did some ordinary people in an ordinary Connecticut town respond to Joe McCarthy in the '50s and Gene McCarthy in the '60s? The assassinations of Martin Luther King, Jr. and the two Kennedys? Earth Day and Vietnam? In Part IV, I describe organizing and working against militarism and the arms race, as well as getting to know the turmoil in Central America and our country's part in it. I had several more significant experiences in the 1990s, which I describe in Part V. These include three weeks on the Peace Train to Beijing and the UN's Women's Conference, and an archaeological study trip to Israel. I also catch up with family news.

A warning: since I wrote this book over a span of thirteen years, there may be some inconsistencies in tenses. Sometimes an *is* in the beginning becomes a *was* by the end.

Appreciations: I couldn't have pursued this project without the help and interest of my son, Tim Butterworth. I am grateful. And many thanks to Mike Butterworth for meticulous and time-consuming proofreading and fact-checking.

Miriam Brooks Butterworth
July, 2010

for Bud

whose delight in life was contagious

PART I

LIVING IN INTERESTING TIMES

John Lee Brooks

Douglas, Genevieve, and Miriam

CHAPTER 1

MY NEST IN A BRANCH OF
THE FAMILY TREE

STATION 14

I was born on the 14th of April in 1918, two years before women got the vote, and was called Miriam, a good biblical name for a Methodist. My brother, Douglas, was only 20 months older than I and later I sensed that mother had not intended to have a second child so soon. I was to be the last. We lived in an apartment on Vine Street in Hartford, Connecticut in that April of 1918 but soon moved to Windsor, the next town north. The place I first remember living in was an old, two-story, white clapboard house with a wrap-around porch set back on a slight knoll on the west side of Windsor Avenue, the main road from Hartford to Windsor.

The trolley tracks running from the Isle of Safety 4½ miles south of us in downtown Hartford to the center of our town two miles to the North, were on our side of the street, with a stop, Station 14, on the edge of our front yard. The trolley was a continual source of wonder and excitement with its clanging bell announcing its arrivals and departures, and its grinding hum starting low and escalating to a high pitch as it swayed away along the tracks. It was particularly wonderful in winter when the overhead electric wires were coated with ice. The grooved wheel that ran on the wire sometimes slipped off, creating sparks that seemed to me to rival the 4th of July, and the motorman would have to climb out into the cold and snow to reattach it. Motorman Jim was an added attraction. He always waved to us on his way by and helped us when we rode with him. We made him valentines, May baskets and Christmas presents. We counted him as one of our good friends.

There were several big oak trees in our front yard where Dad put up a makeshift jungle gym. He hung a truck tire on a branch for a swing and a bar on which we hung from our knees and did other acrobatic tricks. We also had a tent for a playhouse and a hammock. Once I was lying carefully in the hammock, nursing a bad sunburn, when the neighborhood bully, Bassett Hunt, dashed into our yard and swung me so high and violently I fell out onto my tender shoulders. It hurt and I'm sure I cried, but the marvel was that Doug punched Bassett, who went home crying too. Doug often teased me and upset my dolls' tea parties and wasn't above knocking me out of the hammock himself, but he could rise to a threat from a hostile intruder.

Dad also had a moment of glory at Station 14. When we first moved there, we lived across the street at Miss Shelly's. I am told (this was before my memory kicked in) that one night a man crashed through the French doors into the living room. A burglar? Dad showed admirable forcefulness, rushed downstairs and confronted him. He turned out to be a drunk who was at the wrong house. Still, Dad had acted like a hero, a status that was short-lived and rare. He was more used to the scorn he brought on himself one windy autumn Sunday when he raked up the oak leaves, lit them on fire (this was before environmental concerns) and then went inside to change out of his good clothes. When he returned, the fire had spread to the meadows surrounding our house, the fire department had been called, and the whole neighborhood was gathering to fight the flames. I remember the firemen shaking their heads in disbelief that anyone had even dreamed of burning leaves on such a windy day.

It was at Station 14 that my school days began. The nearest school was about a mile toward Windsor Center at the top of Stony Hill. It was a little one-room brick building with one teacher, Miss Kelso, who taught twenty or so children from kindergarten through third grade. It had a pot-bellied coal stove in the middle of the room and two privies, one for girls and one for boys. In most weathers we walked to school but when it was stormy, we rode the trolley with motorman Jim. It was also at Station 14 that I had my first boyfriend. There was a golf course, of all unlikely things in that mainly rural town, about a half mile east of Windsor Avenue. We used it in the winter to slide on, bellyflopping off the tees. On one side of the golf

Mims at Station 14

Mims and Doug

Playing with the Ducheneaus

Stony Hill Schoolhouse, Windsor

course was a farm where a family named Schillinger lived, and their oldest son, Johnny, was my special friend. He showed me where early hepaticas, anemones and wild lilies-of-the-valley grew. One balmy summer day while I was playing there, I fell on an upturned pitchfork, tearing a hole high on the inside of my thigh. I remember the worried look on Mrs. Schillinger's face as she carried me home in her arms. They had no telephone or car, nor did we. Our family doctor, Dr. Aaron Pratt, came to our house, sterilized the tear in my thigh, sewed it up, and drew a picture on my leg with his iodine to cheer me up.

That may have been my last visit to the Schillingers. I think we moved soon after, but I know Johnny was the apple of his mother's eye and a young person of much promise who was killed early in World War II. I saw his mother on a bus a little while after we heard of his death, but her face was so full of grief, I didn't dare speak to her. I wish now that I had.

SURROUNDED BY FORDS

My father, John Lee Brooks, was born and raised in Camden, New Jersey. He ran away from home with his mother's help when he was 14 and had severed most of his ties to his family by the time I knew him. However, my mother, Genevieve Marie Ford, was surrounded by family. She had grown up in Woodbury, Connecticut, but by the time she was married, she and most of her immediate family had moved to the Hartford area. Mother's brother, George, 19 years older than she, was the first to leave rural western Connecticut for a bigger stage. He left Woodbury when Mother was still young to work for the Cudahy Meat Company in Bridgeport. Eventually he and two friends decided to start a grocery business in Hartford, and he was made manager of the Hartford Market, an elegant big store on Hartford's Main Street. It became the second largest grocery store in New England, second only to S.S. Pierce in Boston.

Uncle George had built an impressive three-story red brick house in Windsor close to our Stony Hill School on the corner of Windsor and Park Avenues, at Trolley Station 21. I assume that his obvious prosperity and position as oldest child were the magnets that pulled the rest of the family to the Hartford area too. Mother's oldest sister, Harriet, had died childless in 1912 after being "dragged by a horse," but by the time Mother was in her teens, Mabelle, 11 years older and mother's nearest sibling, had moved to Hartford, begun to work at the Travelers Insurance Company, and married a man named Joseph Redavats. The Auntie Mabelle I remember had a caustic tongue, which she used on Doug more often than on me, and she sang gloriously and was full of mischief. When I was about eight, she died, a widow in her mid-forties, after a hysterectomy, leaving one 22-year-old son. Our Redavats cousin, Harold, musical, attractive, and capable, already had a responsible job at the old Bond Hotel in Hartford, but he had become an alcoholic and was starting down that slippery slope to homelessness and a lonely death. The last time I saw him, I was about 20. He still had a jaunty air about him, but his teeth were rotting and he was incontinent. Then he dropped out of our lives forever.

Uncle George's estate included about 100 acres of land stretching to the west of his house along Park Avenue, some of which he was developing into new streets. He had a side lawn several acres wide, bordering on Windsor Avenue, and behind the house two barns, one for horses and a larger one for cows. There was also a two-story red brick house in Uncle George's back yard, facing Park Avenue. It was into that house my grandparents, Adelaide Blackman Ford and Franklin Russell Ford, moved to be near their children in their old age. I didn't know Grampa Ford for very long. He died when I was three, and I only remember getting hugs and kisses full of shaggy mustache when I climbed up onto the high bed where he lay for the last two years of his life after suffering a debilitating stroke. The only other piece of furniture in that room that I remember was a piano on which Mother and Auntie Mabelle often played while the rest of the family gathered around for some grand songfests.

Grandma Ford, however, was to play a more important part in my life. Since we lived only a mile away, we spent much time with the Ford family, Uncle George, Aunt Alice and their four children. Rachel, the youngest of our Ford cousins, was only three years older than Doug, and we three formed a friendship that has lasted all our days. We celebrated Thanksgiving, Christmas and New Years at their house, eating spectacular dinners cooked and served by Katie Neupert, their all-purpose helper. Her twelve layer mocha cakes and apple pies are family legends. At one of those dinners, about three years after my grandfather died, my grandmother's face suddenly looked all twisted. She too was having a stroke and our lives were in for a significant change.

After the initial danger was over and the damage assessed, it was decided that Grandma Ford would come to live with us Brookses. She was very alert and could talk with a quavery voice, but she was pretty feeble and needed a full-time nurse. Our house at Station 14 was too small, so Uncle George's horse barn was remodeled and moved about 250 yards west of the Fords' house on Park Avenue. Of course, the animals had long since been sold, the cows had made way for cars, and the horse barn was ready for recycling. A practical nurse named Myrtle was hired and our family, now numbering six, moved to Park Avenue, close to the Ford ménage at Trolley Station 21. Grandma Ford and Myrtle were an essential part of our family for the next six years. Grandma sat most of the day in a sunny corner of our den looking almost regal in spite of being partially paralyzed, her hair neatly fixed in a kind of bee hive effect. She always wore a dark velvet band around her neck, fastened with an elegant pin at her throat. She was usually cheerful, but she could express disapproval clearly and sternly at times – if she thought Doug was being mean to me or if we began to play cards or dance on Sunday. She backed our parents in ensuring that no liquor or cigarettes crossed our threshold. Dad on rare occasions wanted to smoke a pipe, but he had to go to the cellar to do so.

Myrtle turned out to be a definite plus. She planned exciting birthday parties for us and was a built-in baby sitter for mother, who was organist and choir director at the Windsor Methodist Church. With Myrtle at home, Mother could go off to direct her choirs or attend her Eastern Star meetings without worrying about us. Myrtle cared about us and was a fair disciplinarian – on the whole a very adequate surrogate parent. I do remember one time being very angry when she sent me to my room for some well-deserved punishment, so angry I quietly emptied everything out of my drawers into a heap on the floor. When Myrtle came to tell me I could come out and saw the mess, she calmly told me that I could join the rest of society when I had put everything back again. As I remember I was almost relieved to have to clean up the mess, and I never did that again.

Mims with Ford cousins Rachel and Ruth

Grandma Ford

Girl Scouts come in all sizes: Alice Haliday, Miriam, and Helen Skebliskus

Doug in first long pants with Dad

Mims on her first bicycle

STATION 21

Uncle George's barn made a very respectable house, and it was to be home to me until I married in 1940. I liked growing up in Windsor. There were only two other houses for quite a long stretch west of us on Park Avenue, the main road to Bloomfield, but more and more houses appeared on the two new streets both north and south of Park Avenue, and soon we had a good group of neighborhood friends who made our house a center. Television was still about 30 years in the future. We didn't spend hours staring at a screen, and there weren't any organized sports, at least until high school, so we made our own entertainment. We played outdoor games by the hour: hide-and-seek, red rover, one-o'-cat, and capture-the-flag. When it rained we played board or card games on our living room floor. Mother loved games and often played with us, and she played to win! As we got older, we ranged farther afield. I think I was given a bicycle when I was about eight. We rode to school, explored Windsor and even neighboring towns, and eventually, in our teens, we really traveled. I remember riding as far as the Congamong Lakes in Massachusetts for afternoon swims. We had a wind-up victrola and later a radio. Shortly after we moved to Park Avenue, Doug was given a crystal set, and we all marveled at the sound that came by way of a hunk of quartz through some earphones we took turns using. By the time we were teens, though, we had radio sounds that you could dance to, and we often did.

Beyond our fringe of houses were meadows and then quite extensive woods which Doug and I often explored. We each laid claim to our own special secret glade where we had picnics and sometimes even cooked marshmallows over carefully hidden fires. There was an ice pond where we learned to play hockey, and across some fields to the northwest was the Sage Park race track. Twice a year, on Memorial and Labor Day weekends, our quiet rural street was crowded with cars zooming past and people walking from the trolley station to get to the races. We used to climb over the fence when no one was looking to watch drivers sitting in their two-wheeled sulkies, maneuvering their high-stepping trotters around the track. As you can see, Doug and I lived vigorous outdoor lives that were seldom dull. To be sure, some of my energy went into running away from him, although he remembers it the other way around. I know that once he shot me in the leg with a BB gun when I was trying to steal his bicycle, and once after he had started going to Loomis and had learned to throw the javelin, he threw a homemade one at me that caught my blouse as I jumped back to avoid it. Yes, there was a lot of rivalry between us. Doug had a bad temper and didn't like to lose, but some of the hostility ebbed when he started school at Loomis and began to find girls in general intriguing. I sensed this when I was about twelve.

A lot of other things happened when I was twelve. It was 1930 and life became a good deal more complicated. The Great Depression struck hard at our family. Grandma Ford died, Myrtle left, and the long-simmering antagonism between my mother and father boiled over so I could no longer close my eyes to it. Most teenagers begin to look critically at their families and I was no exception. With typical adolescent melodrama, I began to imagine we were the most unhappy family in the world. Just who were those two people who had begotten us, and how could two such conflicting temperaments have hooked up together in the first place?

CHAPTER 2

MOTHER'S WOODBURY CONNECTIONS

I liked and admired almost all of Mother's family. They were mainly into food, music and religion. There must have also been a touch of romanticism in the mixture. Why else would a good Methodist child be named Genevieve Marie? Her father's parents, Sarah Saxton and Russell H. Ford, were farmers in Southbury, Connecticut, and had seven children, of whom our grandfather, Franklin, was the second child and the first son.

Here is a short autobiographical sketch Grandpa Ford wrote. It's undated, but it must have been written in 1883 when he was about 39 years old, ten years before Mother was born.

> *I worked at farming for my poor blind Father until I was 21 years of age; when my Father says to me you are of age go work for yourself; Well I started to seek my fortune with less than one dollar to my name; rather discouraging; I hired out on a farm for one year after which I came to Woodbury seventeen years ago and bought out a retail butchering business; gave my note for $450; Followed this business for nine years sold out and bought express (stage coach line from Watertown) to New Haven, have followed this business ever since. Was married to a Miss Blackman at 25 – brought up a family of three children two girls and one boy; and by honest toil and hard labor I have accumulated quite a fortune; and best of all no man can say but that I have always paid 100 cents to the dollar. I have in my possession today one large shop with good water power 50*

acres of land and three houses which are rented besides the nice house we now occupy . . . . There is no mortgage on any of my property besides I have a good deal of money in my jeans. Truly the Lord helps those that helps themselves.

I like this breezy, self-congratulatory assessment of his achievements. Here are some other things I know about him. He was the town's champion wrestler during his early years in Woodbury and couldn't resist a challenge even if it meant he'd be late delivering meat to his customers. He stopped wrestling abruptly and for good after he injured the back of a friendly opponent. He was elected to the Connecticut state legislature in 1884 for a one-year term as Woodbury's representative.

He liked good food – meat and potatoes for breakfast! When he and Grandma Ford retired to Windsor, he had fried cakes (a kind of raised doughnut) sent express by trolley once a week all the way from Watertown to Station 21! And he was unusually compassionate and humane. "He had a lovely disposition and was the kindest person I ever knew," one of my older Ford cousins told me more than seventy years after he died. He kept a special account at Canfield's General Store in Woodbury where he would send people to get decent clothes if they couldn't afford them otherwise. He sent tramps there too for new shoes if theirs were worn out. "Don't tell Addie," he urged Mr. Canfield, trying to protect himself from Grandma Ford's no-nonsense arguments for thrift. Even during the last two years of his life when he was bedridden, he kept some money under his pillow to give to people he had known as Sunday School superintendent if they were in financial trouble.

A big part of Grandpa Ford's life was his ardent and active evangelical Methodist religion. My main acquaintance with his brand of religion was at the Methodist camp grounds in Plainville, Connecticut, where we went several summers for a week's vacation. We stayed in Woodbury House, one of a row of cottages around the edge of a field where evening revival meetings were held in a large tent. I may have been seven or eight when we vacationed there, but I remember feeling even then that those emotional revivals were pretty exotic and not quite me. However, there were exciting events planned for us children and track meets where I shone, so I enjoyed myself. Here are some excerpts from Grandpa Ford's obituary printed in the April 1921 issue of *The Woodbury Reporter*:

> He [Frank R. Ford] was a devoted husband and a kind and indulgent father... As an efficient organizer and superintendent of Sunday Schools few men were his equal. He was in love with the children and for years conducted a union school in Hotchkissville which was beyond doubt the largest of any Sunday school in town. Later he organized the West Side school, and for a number of years before his death he was superintendent of the Windsor Sunday School. His cheerful, helpful life, his devotion to the many poor in Woodbury during all the years of his activities here will long linger as a...memory....

My Ford cousin also said that Grandpa empathized with anyone who seemed in trouble and was particularly concerned about the way Blacks were treated. It didn't seem strange to me that a Black family lived in one of Grandpa Ford's three houses next door to our old homestead. And of course his Sunday Schools were integrated. I didn't realize while I was growing up that this was an exception to the norm. Not until the 1960s did I discover that membership in the other churches in Windsor had been for Whites only. Only the willfully blind can doubt that race is the most explosive issue in American life and that the treatment of people of color by the white majority is the shame and scourge of our 300 years of history. Ford Cousin said that tears would come to Grandpa's eyes when anyone sang "Old Black Joe." I like to think this was not just mawkish sentimentality but that he was sensitive enough to recognize our American tragedy before many of his peers.

You've already met Grandma Ford in her later years, an invalid who kept her dignity and even her sense of humor. Miss Blackman, daughter of John E. Blackman and Harriet S. Nettleton, Grandpa's Addie, Mother's mother added some talents of her own to the Ford family genes. She was musical, a leader in church dramatics, women's clubs and debating societies, a capable manager of the Ford household, and probably a big factor in helping Frank to have "a good deal of money in (his) jeans." She taught her

Grandma Ford

The Ford Family in Woodbury. Back row: Harriet, Genevieve, George, and Mabelle. Sitting: Franklin Ford and Adelaide Blackman Ford

Grandpa Ford

Mother with Dandy

Mother's high school graduation picture

children to play the piano when they were still sitting in her lap, and two of them, Mabelle and Genevieve, became exceptional musicians. She taught elocution when it was more than just speech, and provided generously, maybe indulgently, for her family. Was it here that Uncle George, the only boy in the family, learned to expect something delectable and different for breakfast every morning? When I knew him, many years later, his adoring cook, Katie, was serving him kippers, pork chops and potatoes, omelets, mushrooms, waffles, biscuits or pastries – whatever she could dream up to please him for his favorite meal of the day. Mother must have learned from Grandma to be indulgent in her turn. I remember cakes half with nuts and chocolate frosting and half with raisins and vanilla frosting to cater to *her* family's whims.

Evidence of Grandma Ford's good management and perhaps strong will is the size of her family and the spacing of her children. Unlike Grandma's mother and her mother-in-law who each had seven over a short period of time, the Frank Fords had three children spaced over ten years. Then eleven years later there was Mother. She obviously was not planned and we are told that Grandma Ford was so embarrassed (because here was evidence that she and Grandpa were still making love after 22 years of marriage?) that when her pregnancy became obvious, she stayed in the house out of sight during the day and only emerged outdoors after dark. Fortunately, although Genevieve may have been a surprise and even an embarrassment, she was certainly loved and never for a minute showed the lack of confidence that might indicate an unwanted child.

THE BLACKMANS

Two of Grandma Ford's siblings died in childhood, a third when he was 28 and a fourth, Uncle Ed, went off to Oklahoma, married, but had no children. However the other three were very much a part of our family. Aunt Gus, two years older than Grandma, was pretty eccentric by the time I knew her. We children laughed at her behind her back because she always warmed her ice cream on the stove and wore a red wig. She was a widow with no children and lived for a while in the Ford's back-yard red brick house until Grandma had her stroke. Then she lived in an attic room on the third floor of Uncle George's big house until Grandma died in 1930. She was even more odd by that time, obsessively in love with Dr. Pratt, who had to watch his step when he was called in to take care of her. Eventually, Uncle George moved Aunt Gus to Windsor's town farm, sometimes called the poor farm, a kind of nursing home, I suppose, where she died a few years later.

UNCLE SAM

Probably the most interesting of Grandma Ford's family was her brother, Sam Blackman. When he was about 25 years old, he left Woodbury for Minneapolis. He was given a farewell party and a gold watch by his friends in the Methodist Church who must have sacrificed to give their departing member such a keepsake. He must have been a star in their firmament. Imagine their chagrin when he wrote back about six months later that he had met some Salvation Army folk, traded his gold watch for an Ingersoll, and given the money he made to his new enthusiasm. From that time on, Uncle Sam was a zealous Christian Soldier, helping to save this wicked world, holding God right in his heart – and hard to live with. There were no rings exchanged when he married Ida May Berquin from Peoria – too frivolous. Their daughter, Harriet, was Mother's favorite cousin. She married an Army lad, Donald McMillan, who became the United States Commander of the Salvation Army, and their son, Donald (Bud) McMillan Junior, was our contemporary and friend. He had his grandfather's zealotry, but it took a different form. He became an ardent Communist. He'd show his family how to save the world! He dropped out of Harvard to join the Merchant Marines during World War II to help deliver supplies to the Soviet Union, and after the war joined the Longshoremen's Union where he courted danger by being the last off the picket lines, holding out against sellouts. He became a bodyguard for Gus Hall, who was for many years Chairman of the Communist Party of America, and he refused to believe anything bad of the Soviets. I remember how devastated Bud McMillan was when Khruschev began to expose the crimes of Stalin. He, his beautiful wife, Polly, and their two interesting children brought a New York world into our living room when they spent occasional weekends with us. We would argue till early morning whenever they came, but we stayed friends. That cousin was the only Communist I ever really knew, and he broadened our understanding of a whole different universe.

UNCLE WILL

Mother's Uncle Will, the youngest Blackman, had also married, lost his wife, and had no children. When I knew him, his two remaining passions were the stock market and the Danish Olympic skater, Sonia Henie. He was still handsome even in his seventies and eighties, with piercing dark eyes under black bushy eyebrows. He dressed smartly, ogled almost all women he met in a non-threatening way, and was a great tease. Cousin Rachel tells about visiting him once with Mother at the Waldorf Café, where he was working. He hadn't seen her for some years, and when Mother told him who Rachel was, he said, "No! This isn't Rachel. I know Rachel. She doesn't look at all like this. No! Not Rachel." Rachel said later that he almost had her convinced for a while! Uncle George said with admiration that Uncle Will was the only person he'd ever encountered that he couldn't get the better of. Uncle Will spent a short time in a little room in Uncle George's attic after the stock market crash of 1929. At age 69, for the second time in his life, he'd lost all the money he owned. However, undaunted, he soon recovered, found a job as a night cashier in a diner on Main Street in Hartford, and moved into a miserable room in a dingy Hartford hotel near the railroad station. The single unshaded light bulb hanging over his bed made it sadder still, although he always seemed cheerful. He started to save again, invest again, and amass money once more. When he died at age 94 in 1954, he left $60,000 to Mother, his niece who had kept him in touch with our family and seen that he had care when he needed it. She spent some of that windfall, I'm glad to say, on a European trip for herself and Dad.

These then are the Blackmans and the Nettletons, Saxtons and Fords, Mother's Woodbury relatives. They were farmers and entrepreneurs. Some Nettletons were furniture makers, and I believe Grandpa made shears in his "shop with good water." (We forget how many small industries were scattered throughout New England in the 19th Century.) The old homestead where Mother was born and which I remember visiting as a little child, is still there – a substantial house with a spacious yard, handsome stone walls, and some grand trees. It was this house, this town and these relatives, important in their community, that Mother left when she, too, moved to Hartford, soon to be married to the Wesleyan student who came one Sunday to preach at the Woodbury Methodist Church.

CHAPTER 3

THE CITY MAN FROM NEW JERSEY

In painting a picture of the Brooks family, I need darker colors and fainter ones at that because I have no contacts with and few memories of Dad's relatives. Mother and Grandma Brooks didn't get along well, so although we had some visits from Dad's mother, they weren't numerous. Once when I was 7 or 8 years old, Dad took us children to Atlantic City to show us the church where he had once been a lay minister. On the way we stayed with his older brother, Uncle Will, and his wife Lydie. They lived in a comfortable row house in Wilmington, Delaware, but all I remember of them is that Uncle Will was a big man who snored so loudly the whole house shook. I don't know if Dad kept in touch with them or when they died. Dad's younger brother, Everett, visited us just once in Windsor and brought us both a boomerang. I got the impression that he was a sailor wandering the world, putting in at exotic South Sea ports, a black sheep and I think an alcoholic who died "a long way from home." I don't remember seeing or hearing about him again. Neither of these brothers had children that we knew about.

Dad's father, a tailor, drank heavily, especially when times were bad as they were in the 1890s. We know he sometimes beat Grandma Brooks because it was Dad's interference during one of those crises that catapulted him out of Camden. Grandma Brooks immediately persuaded Dad to leave for Wilmington, Delaware, where she had a cousin who owned a grocery store. Grandma was afraid Grandpa Brooks would kill Dad or that Dad would kill his father. Dad, at age 14, arrived in Wilmington with 25 cents in his pocket. Not knowing the address, he walked the streets of the city asking people if they knew the cousin or the store. Finally someone was able to give Dad directions and he stayed and worked with his newfound relatives for several years.

About all that we know about Dad's forebears comes from a letter written by his mother, Caroline Lee Brooks, and postmarked Camden, N.J., April 22, 1933. I'll quote:

> *My father, John Douglas Lee. Born in Liverpool, England, 1830... His mother, father, 2 sisters, 1 brother was all drowned when father was 9 years old so a guardian was appointed and he let a captain of a boat take Father away to sea as a cabin boy, and the Captain treated Father so bad when Father was 14 years old he ran away when the boat was in port in America. Your father was James William Brooks born 1855 in Green County, Ps. His father was killed three months before your father was born in a railroad accident.*

Grandma Brooks was born in Trenton, NJ. She tells about her children, listing the three boys who lived.

> *Then there were 2 baby girls and one baby boy, who died in their birth. One girl and the boy would be older than Will and the other girl was between Will and John. But thank the Dear Lord they are little angels in heaven and do not have to go through these trying times.*

She wrote about her sisters and reminds Dad that his cousins,

> *Alice and Will Benham was killed in an auto accident both at same time in Chicago, and left Mary Benham 7 years old the only child they had.*

Nothing breezy or self-congratulatory about *that* letter! And there wasn't much joie de vivre about Grandma. She had had 3 children by the time she was 20 (Grandpa Brooks was just two years older) and 5, only two of whom had lived, by the time she was 23. That plus an abusive husband would take the starch out of any of us. I remember Grandma Brooks when she was in her late 60s or 70s as serious, goodhearted, uneducated and vulnerable. She made a delicious cough medicine of onion juice, lemon and honey. Like her son, Will, she snored loudly too, and once when visiting us at Park Avenue she stumbled over our German shepherd and spilled boiling water on his back. He lost hair where he had been scalded, but that grew back. Grandma's ego was less easily healed.

The last time she came to visit us was one summer after Grandma Ford died. Myrtle was gone and Doug had been given a scholarship to a summer music camp, so there was space for Grandma Brooks to come for a rare visit. Late one night I woke up to hear my parents quarreling. There was always plenty of tension between them with nagging and sharp words, but not long quarrels with raised voices – at least so we could hear. But that night was different, and I realized that Dad was packing his bag, preparing to move out. Eventually I heard Mother go downstairs and out the front door, and I came out of my room crying. It was Grandma Brooks who showed up to comfort me. I asked her if Dad was going to leave, and she told me no, but I could see him sitting in the bedroom looking distraught with his suitcase open on a chair. I asked where Mother was, and Grandma told me she had gone out for a walk. At 1 o'clock in the morning? I was persuaded to go back to bed. Dad didn't leave, Mother eventually came in from her walk, and life went on almost as before.

Years later a Windsor friend's mother said, "Of course you know your mother had an affair with Mr. Holiday." Was that what the argument was all about? Had Dad finally put his foot down, objecting to the relationship Mother was developing with our neighbor with the beautiful baritone voice? Wasn't there a scene in our kitchen a little while later – Mr. Holiday mad at something, arguing with Mother? The performances those two with one or two others used to put on to entertain groups did stop at that time, I think. Perhaps there was a pact made between Mother and Dad that night. I believe Mother kept her part of any agreement, and Dad made a space over the kitchen into a rather nice office, den and bedroom for himself. The truce held.

I don't know when Grandma Brooks died although Doug remembers that he and both our parents went to her funeral. I don't know where I was or why I wasn't taken along. I don't know how she coped in her old age. I hope she was better cared for by Uncle Will than she was by us.

Grandma Brooks (born c. 1860?)

Dad's father (born 1855)

GROWING UP

My father, John, the middle of the three living children of the J. W. Brookses, grew up a member of a gang on the streets of Camden. Think what exciting stories he could have told us if we had shown more interest in him or if he had been less self-effacing. He didn't know how to embellish facts and would have been sensitive to "Oh, you've told us that before, Jack," so we don't have much to tell about him. But I do remember one story he told us because it was a turning point in his life, and I wish he had told about it more often. Once when he was about twelve years old, he and some of his gang were walking down a street in Camden when they saw a policeman coming toward them. Dad's friends disappeared, but Dad said they'd been doing nothing wrong so he refused to slink away as if they had. As he and the policeman were about to pass, the policeman put his hand on Dad's shoulder and said, "Why do you hang around with those guys? Why don't you make something of yourself? Why don't you go in to the library and start getting yourself a good education and become somebody?" Dad said he jerked his shoulder away and didn't reply, but several days later he walked past the library, looked up at the impressive carved doors, and finally got up courage enough to climb the big solid stone steps. He stood for a while in the magnificent foyer until a librarian came up to him and asked him what he wanted. He answered, "A book." The librarian, without a smile, took him over to a table and brought him either *Grimms'* or *Andersen's Fairy Tales*. He read for a while and then left, but he went back a few days later and soon he was hooked. I would like to be able to thank that policeman and that librarian for the encouragement they gave at just the right formative moment. I'd also like to know what Dad read in the next two years. I gather he began to get ideas, probably becoming fairly uppity at home. He and his father grew more hostile until that disastrous clash which compelled his mother to whisk him out of harm's way. Dad read a great deal all the rest of his life and ideas he came across continued to give him nourishment and pleasure.

Dad worked 14-hour days for several years in his cousin's grocery store, but sometime in his later teens he took different jobs so that he could prepare himself for the Methodist ministry. I think he had a janitorial job at one time and taught himself Latin and Greek while stoking fires. I know that somehow he became a Methodist lay preacher. By the time he was 20, still without a high school education, he was in Atlantic City ministering at the Methodist Church. When Dad took Doug and me on the trip I have mentioned, we saw Dad's picture on the wall along with all the other ministers who had served there over the years.

We learned more about his life when Doug married Betty Thatcher during the 1941 Christmas holidays. Betty and her family were Philadelphia Quakers and, for better or worse, the congregation was expected to participate in the ceremony whenever the spirit moved. After one of those long meditative silences which give everyone time to contemplate the enormity of the steps being taken, Dad rose and told about his experience with Quakers. While preaching in Atlantic City, he had met an older Quaker gentleman who urged him to go back to school and offered to send Dad $5 a week to help him through. Evidently that Atlantic City Quaker did just that for the next 8 years. In the fall of 1905, at age 24, Dad started formal education again at a prep school in Hackensack, New Jersey. He was ten years older than the other freshmen and at age 28 he went on to Wesleyan University in Middletown, Connecticut. He must have been an anomaly to his much younger and probably wealthier classmates. He told us about going home once for the weekend with his roommate whose father owned the Mohegan Hotel in New London. When he was offered a shrimp cocktail as an hors d'oeuvre at dinner, he told his friend, "No thanks. You know I don't drink." I thought that was funny, but I sensed that Mother felt uneasy. It certainly was gauche!

All during those eight years of formal education, Dad earned money as an itinerant preacher. On weekends he served small communities within walking distance as their minister, although he was not ordained, not even a probationer deacon, but merely a lay preacher. Some time during his years at Wesleyan, he preached at the Woodbury Methodist Church where Grandpa Ford had his Sunday School and Mother was organist. Jack and Genevieve fell in love. He was 10 years older than she, a serious college man with laudable integrity and very handsome. When Mother and a friend took their Camp Fire girls camping, Dad took his Boy Scout troop camping too – within walking distance, of course. Mother moved in with Auntie Mabelle and enrolled in the Hartford School of Religious Pedagogy, a division of the Hartford Seminary, "to learn how to be a minister's wife." She finished the 2 year course early in June, 1915, and they were married on June 30th, after Dad finished his senior year at Wesleyan.

I wish I could report that they lived happily ever after, but coming from such diverse backgrounds, I suppose the chances for that kind of harmony weren't great.

COUNTRY GENTRY AND THE CITY PROLE

I've hinted at some of the obvious personality differences in my parents: Dad, serious, contemplative, earnest, awkwardly affectionate; Mother, with her "million dollar smile," spontaneous, generous, exuberant, confident and capable, a take-charge person. My daughter, Kate, who was especially close to Mother, was talking about her the other day, remembering among other things how she always chewed Black Jack gum when she played the organ. "She was more frivolous than you," Kate told me, and the hint of criticism in her voice was of me not her grandmother. There was something else, though, besides personality that kept our parents apart, and that was class. Since our society doesn't like to admit we have classes in America, we didn't express this difference to ourselves at the time, but it was there. Dad had put himself through college and later taught evening classes in business English, but he had been born and bred in a poor section of a poor city by poor parents. His father was a hard-up tailor and his mother said "ain't."

Mother, on the other hand, was a favorite youngest child in a prosperous, middle-class, entrepreneurial family, prominent in their rural Western Connecticut town. I believe now that I sensed and absorbed their class antagonisms without realizing it, and in true oedipal fashion, I empathized with my father, the low man on our totem pole. It has occurred to me that my lifelong concern for society's victims may stem somewhat from watching the sparring between Mother and Dad during my teenage years. For a long time, my memories of Mother have been tainted by my resentment of her treatment of Dad – her unfair attacks, her sarcastic criticisms, her lack of respect for him. I remember how I winced when, after suffering insults in silence long past the time he should have fought back, he would suddenly erupt inappropriately at some insignificant remark, opening himself up again to Mother's ridicule.

Do you suppose I am exaggerating the extent of their conflict? They lived many more years together and I know Dad still loved Mother when she died. Besides, she did respect him sometimes – his ideas, at least. On one hilarious occasion, at a family gathering after we children had started our own families, we began to debate with our parents about religion. I suspect we had argued Mother into a corner when finally in frustration she turned to Dad and said, "You tell them what I think, Jack." Almost all the other memories I have of her are happy ones and this winter I've rediscovered how much she meant to me. So, Pax Vobiscum, Mother. I do love you.

DAD BECOMES A BUSINESSMAN

The honeymoon was evidently not a great success. Genevieve complained that Jack took along lots of books and papers to work on during that week of vacation. The man didn't know how to play! To be sure, Jack was preparing for the next step in his career. He was ordained a deacon of the Methodist Church, starting a probationary program that would lead to full ordination, and he was assigned to Saint Andrew's Methodist Church in New Haven. Doug was born in August of 1916 during Dad's two year stint there. Dad interrupted his probationary program to become social secretary of the Hartford YMCA for two years during World War I, and then he was assigned to a church in Windsor Locks. However, in 1923, when I was 5, he opted out of the probationary program entirely and his career as Methodist minister was over.

This was a drastic decision to make. Dad was abandoning the ministry he had devoted 25 arduous and enthusiastic years to, and as a result he went through a good deal of emotional turmoil. I don't know exactly why he took that action, but I do know some of the surrounding circumstances. Mother felt they couldn't live on the salary a probationary deacon was getting with two children to feed and clothe. I think the salary was $500 a year, a parsonage with heat provided, and donated clothes. Doug thinks there was a blowup with the bishop who turned down a request for Dad from a West Haven church where he would have been paid more. Doug also thinks the bishop's refusal had something to do with the work Dad did with the YMCA in the war years when the Y "served the needs of the fighting men," providing the kinds of services now provided by the USO. Was the bishop annoyed because Dad had interrupted his program? Did he have something against the Y? There was one other factor: Dad had been very sick with pleurisy in his junior year at Wesleyan, so sick he couldn't take final exams in two of his courses. He had finished his senior year but didn't have enough credits to graduate. One of the qualifications for final ordination as an elder, which

*John and Genevieve Brooks
as newlyweds*

Genevieve at the piano

The marital getaway car

would have made Dad a full-fledged Methodist minister, was a college degree. Did the bishop think Dad should make up those lost credits before being sent to the next assignment? When Dad felt strongly, you could hear it in his voice and see it in the tensing of his body. He used to say with his voice quivering, "Never start anything you aren't going to finish!" College? Career? Years later when I was going to be married, I opened those wounds by asking him if he could reinstate himself into the ministry to perform the wedding ceremony for us. (I obviously didn't understand the system.) "No," Dad burst out, his voice shaking with intensity. "I went back on my vows once. I couldn't possibly do that again!"

Fortunately for us, Dad got a job as personnel director of Sage-Allen Department Store in Hartford, and for the next 5 or 6 years he had a salary that was constant and big enough to support our family. He didn't give up the church when he gave up the ministry. He became superintendent of the Sunday School at the Windsor Methodist Church where Mother was organist. Perhaps it was lucky he didn't stay in the ministry, painful as the disassociation process was, because he eventually moved away from Methodism. Once when I was a teenager, he came home sputtering about some women in a Bible Class he was teaching who were insisting on a literal interpretation of the Bible, a belief that by that time Dad felt was ignorant. Later, in the 1940s, he and Mother joined the Hartford Unitarian Church where Mother was then organist and choir director. At the end of his life, he told me with some bemusement that he had traveled a long way in his beliefs, from being a fundamentalist as a young man to an agnostic in his old age.

I think Uncle George urged Dad to leave Sage-Allen to start a real estate agency with a neighbor for a partner. Dad made that move early in 1929. What timing! Later that year, the stock market crashed and the Great Depression set in. The struggling new agency never had much business and soon had none at all. It folded, leaving Dad with no job and, of course, no income. His career as a businessman was over too.

CHAPTER 4

THE GREAT DEPRESSION

There is nothing more corrosive of the spirit than an obsession with money, or the lack of it. Now, adding to the difficulty of personality clashes, there were everyday crises over nickels and dimes. On Monday Mother needed 25 cents to pay the insurance man who collected on a policy once a week. On Wednesday, at least in warm weather, she needed another quarter to buy a big chunk of ice to keep our icebox cold. In cold weather, food that could spoil was kept in the pantry with the window open a crack. Always money was needed for kerosene for the kitchen range or coal for our furnace or to pay the phone or electric or gas bill or the vegetable man who pushed his wagon down our street.

We certainly never went hungry, but we did change our lifestyle considerably. Before the crash, we had had several automobiles, first a ponderous Hudson and then a rattly Essex. Doug and I both learned to drive at that time, taking turns on the back roads returning home from church on Sundays. In 1929, I was a camper for a two-week session at Alice Merritt Girl Scout Camp. A year later, I was a camper again but I worked my way by washing dishes. Lifestyles changed, but opportunities were still there. In the '20s, Mother's zest for life had infected us too. It was she who arranged for music lessons – violin for Doug; piano for me, along with tap, acrobatic and "interpretive" dancing on Pratt Street in Hartford, where I went on that convenient trolley line.

When money became scarce, Mother still found a way for me to take both junior and senior life saving courses at the Hartford YMCA, a skill which would enhance job opportunities in the future. After Doug went to college in the fall of 1934, Mother took in boarders, usually a young man who needed room and board for a few months, but in 1935 for almost half a year, she took in a mother and her 7-year-old son so that I could spend a summer at a camp on Newfound Lake in New Hampshire as Junior Counselor. That seemed like a one-sided arrangement to me. To be sure, horseback riding lessons were thrown in to make the exchange more balanced. This meant a lot of work on Mother's part, and I'm happy to say that even at the time I was grateful.

Fortunately, Mother had prodigious energy and I don't remember a time when she was unwell. She was a good housekeeper and often, on top of a long day, she would start cleaning house after we had gone to bed. It was Mother who found ways to keep our house in good repair in spite of an empty bank account. When the outside of the house needed painting, Doug and I got brushes and paint, borrowed ladders, divided the house in half and went to it. The result was a little weird because one of us put on a thicker layer of yellow paint than the other, but at least the house looked more cared for than before. Mother also started a "tea house" in a lovely old brick house a block north of our street with an older friend who could put up the money. They served lunches, tea, and dinners. They didn't make much profit because Mother, who did the cooking, used expensive ingredients and was lavish with her servings. For several years we ate all our dinners at the tea house – good food and always ice cream for dessert. Too much! It still cloys to think about it. In addition, Mother was bringing in some money with her organ and choir work.

I too earned a respectable amount of money, quarter by quarter. I did a lot of babysitting and even got a steady job, taking a blind neighbor for an hour's walk every afternoon after school. Miss Knox had lost her sight as a child during a bout with Scarlet Fever. She was in her 40s when I knew her, always cheerful, and eager to hear about my life, living it vicariously, I suppose. She had keen hearing, knew all the birds by their songs, and often pointed out a thrush or warbler that I hadn't even noticed. The 25 cents I earned for each hour I walked Miss Knox added up. In the spring of 1933, I went to my first formal dance in a pink evening dress I had bought for $5.00. A friend and I had taken the trolley to Hartford, lunched at Kresge's 5 and 10 Cent Store, and paid for the dress I had found in a shop on Church

Street, all with my own money. I felt pretty good about myself. Doug got summer scholarships to the Eastern Music Camp in New Hampshire in 1932 and 1933, but he worked during other vacations for the Loomis School maintenance man. In 1934, before going to Yale, he helped the farmer at Loomis get the hay into the barn. He remembers being unbearably hot and choking with the dust.

In the meantime, Dad was struggling to make money too. At first he tried selling refrigerators, but that was a dismal failure. No one was buying that kind of big ticket item, but I think he would have made a lousy salesman in the best of times. He started a column in *The Hartford Courant,* reprinting news that had appeared in the paper 25, 50 and 100 years before, and he began to teach evening courses in business English several nights a week at Hillyer College, a job he held for the next 25 years. But none of this paid him very much. Finally, Uncle George gave him a job at the Hartford Market in the shipping department down in the basement of his store. The Market did a big business in packing and delivering orders that had been telephoned in from a wide geographical region. That kind of work was hard on a man approaching 50, but fortunately Dad was in pretty good physical shape. However, he would often come home so tired he had little energy left to take part in family affairs. The shipping crew was especially busy on the eve of holidays, and on those occasions Dad would get in late at night, ready to sleep through as much of the holiday as we would let him. I remember realizing one cold Christmas Eve that Dad had walked 5 miles from Hartford after working overtime to get out the Christmas orders. He had given all the money he had to Mother to spend for Christmas and didn't have enough left for car fare home.

I resented Uncle George at that time. To be sure, he had given Dad a job, but hadn't it been his idea for Dad to leave his secure Sage-Allen job to start his real estate agency when he did? Wasn't there a better, or at least an easier job he could find for Dad? Couldn't he at least have given Dad a ride home? I think now that Uncle George was having problems of his own. Aunt Alice, his wife, had died in 1926, leaving him with four children, the youngest, Rachel, only 12 years old, but I think he had begun to drink excessively before that. Once, Rachel got a peak into the large room over the garage. It was usually kept locked, but she found it open and

State Highway Veteran Retires

COMMISSIONER Newman Argraves, right, congratulates John Lee Brooks of West Hartford on latter's retirement as executive assistant, personnel, State Highway Department, effective Dec. 14. Mr. Brooks has been with state since 1937.—[Times Photo.

saw a tremendous pile of empty whiskey bottles. Uncle George's chauffeur, Selden Loveland, a lovely man whom we all called Love, was his confidant, and together they were fairly successful in keeping his family from finding out about his addiction. Earlier in his life he supposedly had often been the life of the party, and he surprised me by being amusing at occasional gatherings we had after family funerals. I've been told that when young he was a noted practical joker, which not everyone appreciated. But when I knew him he seemed heavy-handed and didactic. He used to say with a good deal of pomposity, "Without question! Without doubt!" Dad had to take whatever help he could get, of course, but he must have found Uncle George galling. "Being an underdog was not a good place to be around my father," said Rachel. Finally Dad got a break. He took and passed a state examination for the position of Personnel Director of the Connecticut Highway Department, and he started that job in January of 1938. At last the family had some security again, and he stayed in that job until he retired 20 some years later.

In spite of some struggles, our family survived the Great Depression almost unscathed. We never stood in a bread line or ate at a soup kitchen, as did so many. I can still see the face of a man wearing a thin overcoat with its meager collar turned up against the cold, who sat in the shelter of a projection on the G. Fox and Company building, selling apples. I was told that he had been an executive of some company before the depression. We never sank that low, thanks to help from family as well as our own initiative and lots of outside assistance with our education. Neither Doug nor I had to give up anything of consequence, and most importantly we were both able to work our way through college. Dad suffered the most, and I think his spirit, though not broken, was badly bent. As for me, I learned that it is no disgrace to be poor, nor is everyone who is unemployed lazy. I also learned at this time that political leaders can add to a feeling of despair or create an atmosphere of hope, but that is grist for another chapter.

CHAPTER 5

NAVIGATING THE TEENS

LOVE OF LEARNING

In the fall of 1931, at the depth of the Depression, I started freshman year at Chaffee, a small private day school, the girl's part of Loomis Institute, a half mile beyond Windsor Center. The boy's part, Loomis, was mainly a boarding school with some day students from the surrounding areas added to the mix. Because of the Loomis family's legacy, all day students from Windsor at both schools were given free tuition if they qualified for entrance. Doug had become one of those Loomis day boys in 1930. There had been a lawsuit some years earlier that forced the Institute to provide schooling for girls as well as boys as stipulated in the Loomis family's will, and Chaffee was the reluctant answer. It was treated as somewhat of a poor relation and was for day students only. There were about 50 girls in ninth through twelfth grades, and as a Windsorite I got tuition free and even a $50 scholarship for books and lunch. We took turns doing the chores, sweeping classrooms, serving lunch and cleaning up afterwards. In addition to Windsor students there were some from Windsor Locks, Enfield, and Suffield; and a group came by train from the Hartford area to Windsor Center, then went on foot along Palisado Avenue across the bridge over the Farmington River, past the beautiful old Congregational Church, and around the old green on the right to the two historic houses that were Chaffee. I walked or biked the 2 miles from Park Avenue, often joining the train contingent as I passed through Windsor.

Schooling had always been easy for me. I had learned to read well at the Stony Hill one-room school house and there, since we could hear and see the teaching that went on in all the classes, I paid enough attention to finish four years in three, going on to 4th grade a year early. I was a poor speller but otherwise didn't have much trouble during my early schooling, and I used to read every chance I got – in the bathtub, doing dishes, almost anywhere. I even read while riding my bicycle until I once crashed into a ditch. Since I liked school and Doug was already at Loomis, I wasn't surprised to find I was accepted for the Chaffee class of 1935. The fact that both Doug and I went to the available private schools undoubtedly reflects our parents' ambition for us both.

My social life continued to be uppermost in my mind, Chaffee or no Chaffee. The neighborhood gang still gathered together often, now doing a lot of good dancing and even holding hands and smooching. Fortunately we were all pretty unsophisticated, and although sometimes I thought I was in love with D.J. and the next month with Irv, we were careful to keep things relatively cool. On Saturdays we played basketball, boys' rules, at the Loomis gym or watched Loomis football games, especially after Doug made the team. I had lots of time for all this because I didn't take as much work home with me as the other girls did. Why on earth were they doing so much homework? Well, you don't think I was going to get away with this for long do you? The axe fell in June of 1933, at the end of my Sophomore year. I picked up my report card and found I had flunked every subject except Algebra II. Surely I must have been warned that I was not going to pass. I shouldn't have been shocked but I was. Mrs. Cloud, the head of the school, had probably already talked to Mother before I got home because she wasn't as surprised as I expected her to be when I showed her that ruinous report. She let me recover a bit and then told me I had three choices: drop out of Chaffee and go to Windsor High School, take a 6-week summer course and hope to pass well enough to go back to Chaffee as a junior, or repeat sophomore year. Mother didn't try to tip the scales one way or another. The choice was mine.

It didn't take me long to decide to repeat the year, even though that meant taking Julius Caesar in Miss Ahearn's Latin class again. The other two choices didn't appeal to me at all. What? Sit in a stuffy class room for six weeks of summer vacation? I couldn't do that! And Windsor High didn't have a very good reputation at the time. Besides, leaving Chaffee altogether would have been a greater failure than taking another shot at sophomore year. So I went back to Chaffee in the fall to repeat tenth grade, and like the Great Fire of London, this catastrophe was a blessing in disguise. As far as I know, I am the only girl who took, or was given the chance to take, five years to go through Chaffee. Loomis boys were routinely allowed to repeat a year if they "needed time to mature," but not Chaffee girls. Until the two schools merged in 1969, the policy had always been and continued to be that a Chaffee girl who failed was dropped from the school.

Fifty years after we graduated, five of us from our class of fourteen got in touch with Mrs. Cloud, whose tenure as headmistress had coincided with the five years I was there. She and her husband had moved to Boston in 1936, she to take a job at the *Atlantic Monthly* magazine and he for a job with the Atlantic Monthly Press, where he became my husband Oliver's editor for his first children's book, *The Enormous Egg*. We had continued to exchange Christmas cards and knew that Mr. Cloud had died and that Mrs. Cloud was living alone in Wilburham, Massachusetts. We took her to lunch and found her wonderfully sharp, cocking her head like a little bird just as we remembered. She asked us penetrating questions and answered ours as we inquired into the mysteries of our Chaffee years. I had long realized that the decision to let me stay at Chaffee had had tremendous consequences for me. If I had dropped out in June of 1933, I would not have gone to Squam for the summer of 1934 with my schoolmates, Clare and Ann Butterworth, and would not have met their cousin, my future husband, known to us all as "Bud." I probably wouldn't have gone to college because few girls did in those days. It took a lot of encouragement and an assumption that college was a realistic goal for us girls even to think in that direction. I certainly wouldn't have gone to Connecticut College where by chance I majored in German and got a scholarship to study at Heidelberg University in the summer of 1938, giving me a first hand look at Hitler's Third Reich, the most disastrous development of the 20th Century. Nor would I have known Ella Tambussi, one of my new classmates in the Class of 1936, who 40 years later became Governor Grasso and appointed me commissioner on the Public Utilities Control Authority, the most interesting job I ever had.

At our luncheon, I told Mrs. Cloud how grateful I was for that second chance and asked how it had happened. She told me that none of the other faculty members wanted to make an exception to their policy for me. She alone had made the decision that set the stage for all that followed. She said she knew I was bright enough to do the work and felt they had failed me because they hadn't made learning exciting enough to entice me to do it. *They* had failed *me*! Well, she was a great educator.

I don't remember more than a momentary feeling of disgrace at repeating 10th Grade. I was the same chronological age as my new peers. My best friend in my Windsor gang was now my classmate. I tried to reform my studying habits, turning off the radio when I studied, and taking special pains to remember what homework we were given so I could really do it. It took a lot of effort to get out of bad habits, and of course I still loved to play, but gradually I got myself in hand. I took Geometry with my previous classmates and did well in the last math course Chaffee offered at that time. This meant I took no courses in the subject I most excelled in for the last two years of my high school years. But girls wouldn't really need much math, would they? I passed the rest of my courses the second time around. I still had trouble with Julius Caesar (who cares about those camps and military marches?) and not until my senior year did I do well enough to make the honor roll, but at least in June of 1934 I was promoted to the junior class and looked forward to a summer in New Hampshire with the Corwin Butterworth family whose two daughters, Clare and Ann, were both my friends.

LEARNING TO LOVE

I don't think there are words to describe the glories of that summer. I had first seen Squam Lake in the fall of 1933 when I went with the Corwin Butterworths to a cabin on Squaw Cove, a body of water that was itself as large as a small lake reached by the main lake through several other coves and narrows. Uncle Corwin and Bud had built the one-room cabin the previous year. They had also built some bunk houses and a privy because there was no running water or electricity. The whole complex they called The Squabbles, with Clare and Ann in mind, I suppose. At one point during that weekend, I found myself in a kayak, paddling out into the main lake alone. There seemed to be no one else in the world that bright October day, and the sun on the reds and yellows of the maples and birches, the huge clear lake surrounded by friezes of mountains, and the solitude made me catch my breath, glad glad glad to be alive. I have been to Squam many times since, at different seasons and under different, occasionally even sad circumstances, but each time my heart beats faster. It is there I most feel the immensity and grandeur of the universe. I didn't know then that I would be spending the whole of the next summer and many subsequent summers in that Eden.

During the winter of my second sophomore year, I had often taken the bus to Hartford (progress had made the trolley obsolete) and then transferred at the Isle of Safety to a West Hartford bus to spend a Saturday with Clare and Ann and their parents, Uncle Corwin and Aunt Elizabeth, at their house on Sunset Farm. At that time, this was a rural community of 15 houses being developed by Paul Butterworth, Uncle Corwin's older brother and next door neighbor. We played in the nearby reservoir, tobogganed on the two big hills on the Farm, and played hockey with neighbors of all ages on the pond behind Ann and Clare's house. Uncle Corwin skated with us and taught us some dirty tricks. So that was where Clare had gotten her fighting spirit! They took me canoeing down the Farmington River, too. On one such trip, during a school vacation, Clare and Ann's shy cousin, Bud, went with us. We stopped for a picnic lunch and he went out of sight behind a bush for a few minutes and came back with a flower – a delicate touch, I thought. That June, Doug and I were invited to a supper party at Paul Butterworth's house. We ate a buffet dinner in their huge living room and we were even offered wine! Doug says he was about to take some when he heard me say, "We Brookses don't drink!" After dinner someone put on records and we danced. Here, I could shine, but I noticed that the only boy who didn't ask me to dance was that same cousin, Bud. There was a challenge

During that winter Aunt Elizabeth had pneumonia, and although she had recovered by summer she still felt weak and needed family cooperation with household chores to get through the long summer vacation. They apparently despaired of getting that kind of cooperation from Clare and Ann, who were so jealous of each other they squabbled over everything. Clare was constantly competitive. She and I were captains of opposing school teams, the Greyhounds and the Pelicans, and sometimes when a game was close, Clare would hit me under my chin with her left arm as we centers jumped for the starting ball. Of course everyone was watching the ball and didn't see what else was happening! I learned to be on my guard. Much later, when our first child was born, she stopped by for a visit, took one look at Mike and said, "I bet I love my cat more than you do your baby." You can imagine how that style of aggression affected her younger and more brilliant sister, whose defensiveness sometimes became a whine. I often heard a family story about an early Christmas when Ann gave Clare a present with a card on it saying, "To Clare from Dear Ann." I think she couldn't bring herself to say it the other way around. Their jealousy intensified in later years. They both fell in love with the same man – Clare won – and when they were in their '50s a California court ordered them not to speak to each other! But back in our Chaffee days, I got along with them both. Clare tried to dominate so openly, almost naively, that I found her funny. Ann had a wry, self-deprecating sense of humor and was more open to friendship.

I evidently served as a buffer when we were together, and that June Uncle Corwin asked me to go to Squam with them for the summer. Since I would have worked at various jobs if I had stayed home, he offered to pay me a sum that would approximate my lost income. My job would be to help and to get Clare and Ann to help with the housework, making meals, doing dishes, etc. That is how I found myself living in a small made-over boat house in the corner of Rattlesnake Cove on Squam Lake that long and carefree summer. We three girls slept on a porch with a tin roof that made a loud roar when it rained. We were the Tin Roof Dwellers, and I was called Secunda by Uncle Corwin, making me feel very much a part of the family. As in Connecticut, the brothers Uncle Corwin and Uncle Paul kept their families close for the summer. Paul's sons, Bud, then 19 and a college sophomore, and Harrison, a few months younger than I, and sometimes their sister, Wise Old Dinny, 22 years old, had taken over The Squabbles, a mile down the dirt road, and the two households merged during the day for meals and fun and frolic.

Our days were full of long swims, picnics, mountain climbing, and canoe trips. Doug came up for a visit sometime in August, bringing his violin so he could practice every day. Such ambition seemed odd to the Butterworths and the Butterworths seemed odd to Doug. Or at least Clare

SPIRITS OF SQUAM

THE GOAT-HOUSE + BOAST

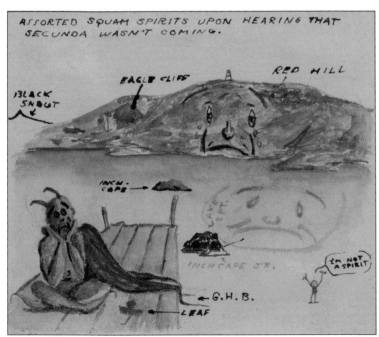

Bud's artwork wooing his Secunda

Secunda herself

did. When he first got there, we were going canoeing and Doug, trying to be chivalrous, offered to take the bow Clare was carrying during a portage. She swung her hips and Doug went flying into the bushes. I was surprised that he stayed long enough to become friends with Bud. In the course of the summer we canoed down the Saco River in Maine, climbed the Squam Range, Lafayette and the Presidentials, and spent a night in the Summit House on top of Moosilaukee, a mountain owned by Dartmouth College, where Bud and some of his friends who visited Squam that summer were students.

Of course all those older college men provided some of the summer's excitement and a few paid me some attention, but I soon realized Bud was the one I liked best. I guess he was not handsome at that age, though I think he became so, but he had impressive broad shoulders and a marvelously slim waist and hips. I liked watching him paddling canoes and got much satisfaction keeping up with him as we ran down mountains together. Besides, he was very funny with an offbeat sense of humor and was wonderfully clever. Evenings in the Boathouse we played games like Squiggles, a drawing game, or maybe Sonnets. Someone would write down the last word of each of the 14 lines with the appropriate rhyme scheme, and then we would make a sonnet to fit them. Bud was the best artist and one of the best poets. The only sonnet I remember, though, was one of Uncle Corwin's that started, "The loon's wild cry is still –."

We read a lot and talked about ideas, and this too was a revelation to me. Aunt Elizabeth did most to encourage these intellectual pastimes, and she was an important part of the glamor of that summer. She had an intriguing European accent, part German because she had spent most of her childhood on her father's estate in Pomerania. Her father, Henning von Arnim, was a count from a distinguished Prussian family. Her accent was part English too. Her English mother, called "Little Granny" by the family, was a celebrated author whose first book, *Elizabeth and Her German Garden*, published in 1898, was an instant best seller. It described the family's life in Germany, and Aunt Elizabeth and her sisters played major roles in the book. Another of Little Granny's best sellers, *Enchanted April*, was made into a movie in the 1990s. After Count von Arnim's death, she married Bertram Russell's older brother in 1916, and became Lady Russell.

Aunt Elizabeth had been tutored as a child in Germany by Hugh Walpole, E.M. Forster and other talented young Englishmen. (In those days, part of an upper class Englishman's eduaction involved some experience on the continent.) She studied at Cambridge before coming to the United States, where she met Bud's Uncle Corwin. Four years later I lived for a while at the von Hirschberg's, the household of Aunt Elizabeth's sister Trixie, where I became acquainted with more of that remarkable family under very different circumstances. But I am getting ahead of myself. During that Squam summer of 1934, you can see I was not only reveling in Nature's Paradise but also in a hot bed of "Culture," where I was less at home. Fortunately, Aunt Elizabeth didn't expect as much of me as she did of her own children, my friends Clare and Ann, so I could sit back, observe, and wonder at a new world opening up before me.

Before the summer was over, Bud and I were feeling close, holding hands of an evening and taking every opportunity to be together. Toward the end of August, Aunt Elizabeth took me aside and told me Uncle Paul wouldn't like me to encourage any closer relationship with his son. I was taken aback for a while. To be sure, I was paid help that summer. Was she implying that I was not good enough for Bud? Some years later Clare was told she couldn't marry Johnny Hardham, a friend of Bud's working *his* way through college. Was Aunt Elizabeth in both cases showing some cultural snobbery? Well, I confess I wasn't worried about her admonitions for very long. I thought if Uncle Paul didn't like us to be holding hands, he could talk to his son himself! So I returned home and to school in the fall, and found my Windsor boyfriends looking very young. I was in love with a college man.

CHAPTER 6

THERE'S A NEW WORLD TO BE WON

Would the rest of my life be an anticlimax to that summer of 1934? Getting back to school was a bit humdrum at first, but I was beginning to find some of the work we were doing pretty exciting, especially history, civics and English. Not all the education we got at Chaffee was very good. Some of the teachers were barely adequate, but I was learning that I had to do homework in the courses they taught as well as in those taught by teachers I liked better. And, of course, the more I understood in any course the more I found interesting. The civics we were taught was a textbook version of how our political system works and later, when I became involved in politics, I found the reality very different, but we were taught most of all about our responsibilities as citizens in a democracy. Remember, this was only 15 years after women were given the vote, and some of our teachers, all women – particularly those who were active members of The League of Women Voters – took their new status as voters seriously. They tried to get us interested in political and social issues, and under their guidance I got my first understanding of how laws are made. Our history class was taken to the State Legislature in Hartford to hear our representatives debate the Child Labor Law. Connecticut was joining other states in setting 16 as the age at which young people could be hired except for farming and household chores. Till then young children had been exploited in factory jobs and often worked long hours and in terrible conditions. The age of mandatory schooling was also being raised to 16. Many of the legislators were farmers from small towns, and we heard them say in opposition, "What was good

CHAFFEE BUDDIES

Audrey Bengston & Mims

Our Team, the Pelicans

Clara Louise Riggs, Franny Hoke, Audrey Mahl, Mims, Anne Taylor

enough for me is good enough for my children." There weren't any women in the legislature yet to answer that, but the law passed anyway, maybe because jobs were so scarce in those depression years that eliminating competition from children would increase the chances of jobs for adult men.

Mrs. Cloud taught us Senior English, and during the luncheon we had with her she told me how pleased she was when she heard me urge my friends to read *War and Peace* in the winter of 1936. I remember living that book for days, imagining myself Natasha growing up in that romantic 19th Century Russian society. I think it was then that I began to dream of traveling on the Trans-Siberian Railway, a goal I reached 35 years later. With the help of Mrs. Cloud's insights, we experienced Iago's treachery and the agonizing jealousy of Othello and, because of her, I became absorbed in Joseph Conrad, exploring the moral deficiencies of Lord Jim. Because of her enthusiasms and depth of understanding, we lived the lives we read about, broadening our perceptions of emotions and people before we met them in real life, becoming aware of motives and feelings we would probably never experience ourselves. Does television adequately replace literature in enabling us to understand people who differ from us? Are today's students still learning to empathize with others who grow up in circumstances unlike theirs? Tolerance and appreciation of "the grand pageantry of life" is learned mainly from family attitudes, I suppose, but books can widen one's view too. It was happening to me.

At the last minute, in June of my senior year, I decided to take what were then called College Entrance Exams. Not everyone in our class of 14 went on to further education. Families were still tightening their belts to cope with the continuing Depression. Certainly my family couldn't pay any college expenses for me, but neither did they pressure me to help support them. Doug had been given a big scholarship to go to Yale, where he was finishing his second year. He worked at jobs both at Yale during the school year and in summers as a life guard at a fancy resort, earning enough to pay his college costs. If I wanted to do the same, I was encouraged to try. I passed the exams and decided to go to Connecticut College for Women in New London, which was within easy reach, and I thought there was a possibility I could find a way to pay for it. I wasn't given a scholarship before I went, but I was told there might be one available for me later in the year. I was assigned to the co-op dormitory, though. Nineteen girls lived in that dorm, planning their menus, getting their meals, doing the housework, and saving a good portion of their board. Also there were jobs I could apply for. This didn't add up to enough to get me through even the first semester, but I took the chance. Something was bound to show up. It always had.

COLLEGE YEARS

I didn't go to college to find a man. Connecticut College for Women was on an isolated hilltop in New London, far from any men's college except the Coast Guard Academy. Some of my classmates felt that was a pretty big exception. We weren't allowed to have cars on campus, assuming that we had one, until the last semester of our senior year. But I was used to having no car and to long distance courting. The closeness Bud and I felt during the summer of 1934 turned out to be THE REAL THING, not just a momentary summer romantic fling. For you who want to keep a good relationship going, I recommend Bud's methods, especially if you have some writing or artistic talents. During the last three of his college years, he wrote me a slew of letters and included an amusing drawing in almost every one. He described his days in a way that made me feel I was living them too. What strikes me now when I reread those letters is his exuberant love of life. He wrote less frequently during his senior year and rarely when he started teaching at Kent School in the fall of 1937, but by then I was hooked. We kept in touch during vacations too, of course. In the summer of 1936, Bud worked as part of the crew at the Inn on top of Mooselaukee and was also painting murals of climbing types in the deep window recesses of the dining room at that mountaintop hotel. I believe I climbed that mountain nine times that summer. We spent time together at Squam and at Sunset Farm and at several Dartmouth Winter Carnivals too, and I for one was pretty well committed. Perhaps this made it easier to focus on other matters. I know it provided me a helpful stability on many occasions during those four college years.

My first problem at college was to find enough funds to get through the first week. During orientation, I discovered I needed $50 immediately as a down payment for tuition, and I didn't have it. Was my college career going to end before it began? Someone suggested I see the bursar about my problem, and she promptly opened her drawer and counted out two beautiful twenties and a ten. I did get a scholarship later in the year. The Newcomb family in New London gave me $400 and did the same for each of the years I was there. I got a job working 14 hours a week at the main desk of the library. I was paid by the college, which was then reimbursed by the federal government through the National Youth Administration. I don't forget that the NYA and other New Deal programs gave a boost to many of us during the Depression, much as the G.I. Bill gave hope for a better life to returning soldiers after the Second World War. The only trouble with the library job was that two nights a week I worked from 6:00 p.m. till the library closed at 9:30. This meant I had to leave our dorm before dinner both nights, and I missed the conviviality and good discussions that went on at the end of each day. At the co-op dorm, we were all in the same boat financially, and most of us were serious about ideas, arguing about government and bringing up new insights we had about religion or psychology or history. I had a good deal of fun but studied hard too. After all, I had once flunked a year at school, and I didn't know whether I was going to measure up at college. You can imagine my surprise when I found I had tied for second place in the freshman class at the end of the first semester. Hooray! What would my old Chaffee teachers say about that!

During the summer of 1937, I waitressed at an inn in Old Lyme, Connecticut. Boxwood Manor was not like those Cape Cod resort hotels I had heard about where college kids worked and enjoyed some prestige. My Connecticut College friend, Lee, and I were treated no differently than the professional waitresses we worked with, and I have empathized with every waitress I've seen since. The first meal I served was on a June weekend to two couples returning from the Yale-Harvard boat race. They were two brothers, the older one with his wife and the other with his girlfriend. I heard them talking about the race, and asked who had won. "Yale," said the younger – "Are you sorry?" I answered, "No. My brother is a senior at Yale. He lives in Saybrook College." "Oh, do you suppose he knows...?" and he began to list a few names. At this, the married brother broke in with a voice full of scorn: "Don't bandy your friends' names about with a mere waitress!"

C C DAYS

a) Mims and Lee, Mosier porch

b) Lee, Mims and Brickie

c) The Class of 1941

Members of Mosier House Co-op, CT College

Then there was the dentist from Springfield who stared at my somewhat generous breasts and leered, "You must have a lover!" Perhaps the pits was the plump, middle aged school teacher I waited on for a month. As it came time for her to leave, she said she was too poor to tip me. but she knew I would like this slim book of her poetry and if I had a letter from a boyfriend, she would read his handwriting for me. She said she was good at that. Since I wasn't getting anything else for waiting on her, I showed her one of Bud's letters. She studied it a short time and said, "I advise you *not* to marry that man. He would be impossible to live with." If that isn't enough to give graphology a bad name! There were some sweet guests there too, of course, and I decided that people were at their best or at their worst at meals. I learned a lot that summer. For all our long hours and hard work we were paid $5 a week plus tips. I ended up in September with $150, which made it possible for me to continue college into my sophomore year.

Since Connecticut College was comparatively small and intimate, a good many of us were given responsibilities for running it, not just through student government and clubs but on advisory committees where we became well acquainted with faculty members. I soon found myself choosing courses on the basis of those who taught them rather than subject matter. That must have been why I majored in German. I am not particularly adept at languages. In fact I took German my freshman year, starting an altogether new language to fulfill a requirement for graduation because my high school French was so poor. I took more German courses my second year and decided on a German major because the professors were so impressive, the literature so enlightening, and the events happening in Germany so absorbing. Since there weren't many of us who majored in that subject, it seemed natural for Miss Hafkesbrink, the head of the department, to stop me in the hall one day in the winter of 1938 to offer me a scholarship for the summer session at the University of Heidelberg. I hesitated only long enough to think about how to finance such an adventure. The scholarship included room and breakfast for the six weeks of the summer session, and I was offered a round trip ticket on the Hamburg/American Steamship Line. The Bursar's Office told me the Groton Grange wanted to lend a College student $50 for further education and if I would join the Grange, I could qualify. Could I live on $50 for three months in Germany? I thought so. My answer to Miss Hafkesbrink was "Yes. Yes, of course."

CHAPTER 7

THE THIRD REICH: OBSERVING HISTORY

A little past midnight in the early morning of June 11, 1938, I watched from the deck of the *St. Louis*, one of the smaller ships of the Hamburg-American Line, as Mother, Dad, my brother Doug, several family friends and the lights of New York City grew smaller and smaller and then disappeared. I made my way down to my third-class cabin to meet my roommate and get my things stowed away in preparation for the 12-day trip to Germany. All the other passengers were bustling about too, finding the way to their rooms, unpacking, and some of them rather furtively passing something to the stewards, who seemed very available and eager to help. What were those round balls of various dimensions being quickly tucked away out of sight? I found from my German roommate, who had just completed her master's degree at New York Teachers College and was returning to a teaching job in the Third Reich, that they were rolls of tinfoil collected in the U.S. from candy and cigarette wrappers. Hitler had asked all Germans traveling abroad to bring back as much of this material as they could to aid his rearmament program!

Although the real adventures of the summer were still ahead, those days at sea were lively enough. In addition to the excitement of exploring an ocean liner and the joy and awe of being afloat for days on the immensity of the broad Atlantic, I had a taste in that shipboard community of a truly Germanic society. The food was plentiful and hearty and German, the crew was German, and most of my fellow passengers were German too. Some were returning from relatively short vacations, but others had emigrated to America some years before, had experienced hard times during the

Depression, had lost hope for a better life in their adopted country, and were returning to their fatherland where they were sure they would find good jobs or at least good old-age, illness and unemployment pensions. I heard my first *Heil Hitler* as sailors and officers greeted each other with their right arms raised in the Nazi salute. No more *Guten Tag* except mine for the next three months. This could have been serious. Later in the summer I once answered *Guten Tag* to a policeman as he passed me on his motorcycle, giving me a *Heil Hitler* and a salute. He wheeled around and came back to talk. He soon satisfied himself that I was not a rebellious German but an ignorant American, so he smiled and went on his way. Only in some rural parts of Catholic Bavaria was I greeted with *Grüss Gott* by some older women, but I didn't know if that was a habit that couldn't be broken or an act of defiance.

There were some other American students going to the summer session in Stuttgart, and we made friends with the officers who occasionally invited us to tea in the second mate's quarters. It was there I sensed tension in the air when we heard on an English language radio station that Joe Louis, the representative of an "inferior race," had knocked out the Aryan champion, Max Schmeling. It was there, too, that one of the American students began a political discussion, saying favorable things about Hitler and Nazi Germany. The second mate stopped him quickly by saying, "We won't talk any further about this please. As Hitler says, "Come and see for yourselves. Visit us, but don't believe in propaganda." That's pretty ambiguous, I thought. Whose propaganda? I liked those officers very much and often wondered if my ability to judge people failed me at that time. Were they the decent people they seemed to be, or were they convinced Nazis conniving with Hitler to dominate the world, ruthlessly scapegoating Jews and other vulnerable minorities?

As it turns out, I know the answer to that question because the *St. Louis* and its Captain Schroeder played an important role the following year in the saga of Jewish persecution, so important that there is a section devoted to it in the Holocaust Museum in Washington. Eleven months after I knew those officers, in May of 1939, the *St. Louis* left for Cuba with 930 Jewish passengers trying to escape the humiliations and ostracism, the concentration camps and the gas chambers that were their inevitable lot in Germany if they stayed. The story of that trip is heart-rending. Seven hundred and thirty four of the passengers had fulfilled U.S. immigration requirements and had quota numbers that would have permitted them to enter the U.S. in three months to three years when their numbers came up. They were planning to wait in Cuba until then, and they all had the proper official landing certificates to do so, but Cuba's president invalidated those certificates by decree before the ship reached Havana. Only 28 passengers were allowed to disembark and the *Saint Louis* was eventually ordered out of Cuban waters. Captain Schroeder then tried to get the United States to provide temporary haven, at least to those who had valid immigration papers. To our shame we refused them entry here too. Finally the ship sailed back to Europe with those despairing people still on board. Some lucky few finally made it to England and the rest were taken in by France, Belgium and the Netherlands, but they were not safe for long. In the fall of that year Germany bombed Warsaw and all of Europe went to war. Most of the people who were on that ill-fated trip ended up in concentration camps when Germany occupied Western Europe and imposed Nazi policies against Jews there too. Captain Schroeder resigned from service when he finally reached Germany. Several books written about this "Voyage of the Damned" show him and some of his crew as caring people actually distraught about the fate of their passengers. But of course in 1938 I had only unanswered questions about any of the friends I was making.

I regret that airplanes have made passenger ships obsolete because a long sea voyage can make you understand how far you are from home. Those 12 days made me realize too how far apart our cultures were. I got accustomed to a different language, enough to show me that my two years of German would be highly inadequate to my needs when I reached port and was on my own. I felt safe on board the *Saint Louis*, but I began to sense the uncertainties I would face when I bade farewell to my all-too-transient shipboard friends in Hamburg.

a) Off to New York and the "S.S. St. Louis"   b) left: Mims with Second Mate
c) Mims and fellow students with Fourth Officer   d) Shuffleboarding en route

EXPECT THE UNEXPECTED

My German cabin mate shepherded me through customs in Hamburg, helped me buy a ticket to Heidelberg at the train station, and got me on the right train going in the right direction. I was certainly glad she was there because my German failed this very first test. Hamburg was a sudden nightmare. The first thing I noticed was that everyone was wearing a uniform – even young boys and girls – all ages being in a high state of excitement, on the move. The train I took south was crowded with young policemen returning to their posts from a sportsfest. One of the nicer ones sat next to me for much of the day, describing the passing scene. I was able to catch a word now and then and could at least say *Danke* and *Auf Wiedersehen* as he helped me change trains in Frankfurt. On that second train, a young woman who spoke English told me about a women's hostelry, something like our YWCA, near the station in Heidelberg where I could spend the night and get myself organized. The next day I could introduce myself to the Weisses, my future host family, leave my trunk with them, and then take off for 10 days of exploring the Rhine River area until the university summer session began and the Weisses would be expecting me. I took her advice and spent my first night in a women's dormitory in that very foreign country. Several of us there spent the evening up on the roof watching some astonishing festivities. I had arrived at the beginning of a week-long celebration when students from around the country, all wearing beautiful uniforms, gathered "to make plans for the coming year," and the sight was spectacular. Down below along the streets beside the Neckar River, thousands of students carrying torches marched briskly to the music of German bands. And above us, part way up the mountain side, the ruins of the old castle suddenly burst into flames as bonfires were lit in every turret and courtyard and in every gaping window. About midnight, fireworks erupted into the sky on both sides of us, from the bridges across the Neckar and from the castle above. It was magnificent. After that, I crawled into my assigned bed in a large dormitory room and fell asleep. It had been a long, exhausting, exhilarating day. I knew that tomorrow and for many tomorrows I could expect the unexpected – and I knew that I would be experiencing it alone.

That was the beginning of months full of kaleidoscopic impressions and emotions. I kept a diary, and here are a few excerpts from the first week:

June 23 – I met my future landlady and left my trunk there. She's extremely jolly . . . . I'm terrifically happy.

June 24 – I felt on the top of the world this morning, so I climbed around the ruined castle and then on up to the top of the mountain behind . . . . This trip is like a movie . . . geese paddling around a peasant Frau, herds of sheep, cobble-stoned, narrow, high-walled streets, ivy and flowers, church towers and woodsy mountains! This morning I came upon a market place in full swing. One woman was selling fish, live ones in water-filled wooden buckets. I watched her throw a tremendous squirming eel onto the cobbles and then cut off its head. When her knife grew dull, she used a cobble as sharpener. I bought my lunch there for 30 pfennigs (7 cents) . . . . [Later that evening] I'm in my first Jugendherberge [youth hostel] in Dilsberg. I walked about 10 miles to this small, walled hilltop Dorf . . . . I've taken pictures of some of the peasants driving cows hitched to queer wagons . . . . It's only about 4 cents to stay here overnight and the meals are also amazingly cheap. What a view of the Neckar Valley!

June 26 [In Mannheim Youth Hostel] – Every German man is almost too friendly. If I had a bike I could get rid of them, but on foot it is impossible . . . . I don't feel as happy now as I should, but with some sleep and some time away from the city I'll feel better; June 28 [In Lorch Youth Hostel] – Yesterday a funny painter helped me find a second hand bike. It cost 18 marks, but I think I can sell it again for almost as much . . . . today I found a good spot to see the Mause Tower and the Rheinstein . . . but I contracted a most awful case of homesickness and had to leave before anyone saw me . . . . if I feel like that often, the U.S. will see me sooner than it expects.

July 2 [Back in Heidelberg Youth Hostel] – I had time to go further along the Rhine, but I had too many longings for letters from home. I turned back . . . and continued on to

Zwingenberg where I found 65 Hitlermädchen . . . and helped them peel potatoes for supper . . . . In the morning I found that I was getting supper and breakfast free for the potato peeling! I wandered down to the village and passed the village smithy hard at work at his forge . . . . In the town I bought some marmalade from a woman who thought America was in Austria . . . . It began to rain just on the outskirts of Heidelberg, my first bad weather. I limped into the YH and walked to the Weisses for mail. Heard from Bud and felt better . . . . Nothing from Mums, though. I hope Monday'll be another story."

HEIDELBERG SUMMER SESSION

As you can see, every day was full of excitement and feelings of exhilaration, vulnerability, anticipation and loneliness. I sometimes had trouble believing I was not dreaming and sometimes I wondered how I had ever dared risk such an adventure. This may sound melodramatic to today's young people who do so much traveling to more exotic places than Germany, but in the 1930s it was rare for women my age to travel by themselves. Besides, I don't think I had ever before been alone for more than a few hours at a time. Almost always there had been family members, nearby neighbors, or friends within hailing distance. And I had rarely been out of New England before that summer. Two years earlier, I had travelled to New York City for the first time in my life and that is only 2 hours away from Hartford. To be sure, I was accustomed to making many of my own decisions, but I was always within a short bus ride or a quick telephone call to Mother or Dad if I needed reassurance, or within easy access of a friend's good advice. Now suddenly I was about 3000 miles away from anyone I knew. Any trip back home would take days at sea. No chance for a quick flight home – there were no planes to take me. And there were no available telephones to use either.

I have never been homesick before or since, but I certainly was that summer. But the lump in my throat left sometimes. It helped when classes at the university started and I had more structure to my life, a family to stay with, and a schedule to follow. I liked the women in the Weiss family, especially Frau Weiss. She was from peasant stock and I got to know her best. She liked to walk in the mountains with me, and I helped her with her housework, especially when she had one of her frequent migraine headaches. The two of us attended Sunday services at her Lutheran Church several times, and she taught me how to cook *Schinkennudeln* and *Heidelbeerkuchen*. Her 18-year-old daughter, Ella, helped me make a *dirndl* and took me to her gymnastics group where I got acquainted with some of the friends who went with her to a huge Hitler rally in Breslau at the end of July. Herr Weiss was a janitor at the university and a member of the Nazi party. I didn't get to know him much, but he seemed boorish to me; and Fritz, the 15-year-old son, who trained his own group of younger uniformed *Hitlerjugend* in military maneuvers under my window, was also unapproachable. But I was treated well, ate good breakfasts, and felt comfortable and safe.

I did a lot of traveling on weekends, exploring other parts of Germany and staying at different youth hostels where I often met merry company and usually felt secure. One problem was that I didn't have adequate clues about men in that foreign culture. I learned to be cautious. I never did discover when it was safe to go walking with a soldier. Should you be friendly to that group of men that are passing? And if you're not will they be angry at you for being "stuck up"? Yes, I had some anxiety there, but not so much that it kept me house-bound. However, whatever the cause, I lost my nerve by the end of July and went to a travel agency in Heidelberg to swap my September 9th ticket for an earlier one. Not a chance! I tried seven different ships but every bunk was taken, undoubtedly by people who needed to leave Germany more desperately than I. My only recourse was to continue with the plans I had made for the rest of the summer and hold tight to the ticket I fortunately already had.

There are some advantages to traveling alone. There is nothing like it to sharpen your awareness of people and situations. There's no one to distract you with their needs or attentions. Also, I was forced to learn German because I seldom was with anyone who spoke English. I soon managed street conversations with some confidence, but the lectures in the university were usually too difficult for my complete understanding. I did record a rather detailed lecture on the social aims of the Third Reich. This is from the July 29th entry in my diary:

Most of the lectures are very worthwhile listening to – packed full of propaganda . . . . Everything encourages a back to the land, simplicity movement. The German "folk" is glorified – the folk art and songs and dances. Such a movement is part of the effort to make the people realize that they are bound together – are one in tradition, feeling, and needs. The Gesellschaft of Hitlerjugend and all the uniforms, the jolly songs they sing are all for this one main purpose. Hitlerjugend all have maps of the 19th Century and must learn where so-and-so wood is, the old streets of Berlin, this-and-that famous castle. K.d.F. [Kraft durch Freude, Strength through Joy, was a workers movement that provided workers with cheap tickets to various cultural events and arranged outings to Germanic historical spots.] Groups going around the country are really getting to know their fatherland as a whole.

Here was Germany's Romantic movement, a unifying of the country with myths and propaganda for what purpose? Of course, part of such a process employs "enemies," people who are outside so that the rest can feel in, and that was obvious too. I saw *Juden sind verboten* signs posted at city boundaries, and some shop windows were smeared with chalk and had *Juden* scrawled across them, but a much more terrible campaign to destroy all Jews began a few months after I left. Another story I heard that exemplified this scapegoating was told to me by an American businessman who lived with his wife in an affluent suburb of Heidelberg. I had a letter of introduction to them from a Windsor family friend and they invited me to their home several times that summer. Dr. Allen told about a prominent Jewish doctor friend, a professor at Frankfurt University, who had saved many German children suffering from malnutrition during World War I by feeding them greens and exposing them to the sun. In spite of this service to his country, when Hitler declared all Jews anathema, especially those in the universities and the rest of the education system, the Frankfurt professor's colleagues stopped talking to him, he dropped out of the university and disappeared. I found that a horrendous story of cowardice. How could the government have taken such action if *everybody* had refused to cooperate with it? I tucked that away for future consideration.

Heidelberg University was rumored to be a Nazi stronghold, and what I understood of the lectures bore that out. One professor dwelt on German history and claimed that Germany had not lost World War I militarily but had been stabbed in the back by the press and liberal civilian defeatists back home. Another lectured about genetics, explaining why German Aryan blood was so superior to that of other "races." One of our courses described German economics but I was unable to follow that at all, although it might have been more informative than any of the others, which were so predictably slanted. The Lutheran church sermons I heard with Frau Weiss were helping the Nazis in their way too. One pastor spoke about how small our little earthly worries are in comparison with the tremendous Universe of God. We should forget them and be concerned with joining the heavenly kingdom. Don't get involved! I met students from many different countries at the university – Latvians, Lithuanians, Finns. Danes, Swedes, Swiss, Japanese, a few French, English and Americans. No Russians, though. Once I brought Vanda, a dainty Polish student, back to my room to eat a lunch we had bought in the market. She asked to use the bathroom and while she was there, Frau Weiss, looking very distressed, whispered to me that all Poles are *dreckig* – all Poles are filthy! – and would I please not bring her into their house again. That was an ominous note. When biases like that came up in our conversations, I would suggest there were good and bad people in any group, and she would murmur an unconvincing assent.

There was more entertainment than just the university for us that summer. The people of Heidelberg proudly hosted a drama festival held in the ruins of their castle, important enough for Goebbels himself to preside over the opening ceremonies. That led to another surprise. Ella, knowing from her father what Goebbels' route would be, took me into the street to watch him go by. As luck would have it, his car was held up by a passing train right in front of where we were standing. An S.A. guard who had been flirting with Ella thought he would do us a kindness by making way for us to shake hands with the Propaganda Minister of the Third Reich. Goebbels had cold eyes, my diary says, and a narrow, impassive face a bit like a weasel's. I didn't dare write home that I had been that close to one of the most fanatical and notorious members of the Nazi dictatorship.

However, I enjoyed the festival. Herr Weiss got Ella and me some inexpensive *Kraft durch Freude* tickets through his workers council, and we went to two of the plays being offered that season, both of them by Goethe. *Faust*, which I had read in a sophomore German course, was the first, and we watched, open mouthed, sitting out in the open courtyard, stars overhead, with the castle walls and doorways for props. Then two nights later, we walked up the hill again to the castle and watched *Götz von Berlichingen*. This was perhaps even more awesome for me. The action of the play took place in the very villages and mountains I had been wandering through, and there were real horses pounding over the castle yard!

As if that weren't enough excitement for one night, we walked home with a boy who wore a Breslau pin, so he and Ella had something in common. He turned out to be a German Czech, and I wrote in my diary (note the German sentence structure), "Such bitterness against the present arrangement I have never before heard. He reads mostly German newspapers but . . . Czech papers too and he told what lies the Czechs have printed. I imagine Goebbels has done here another prize bit of propaganda, but there's no doubt that this proud *Sudetendeutscher* who so fervently *Heiled Hitler* was heart and soul for an *Anschluss* (for joining with Germany), and he said that there were 6 thousand of them at the Breslau Fest." None of us knew at the time that Czechoslovakia would be swallowed up by Germany in a very few months. By the end of November, the Sudeten territory had become a part of Germany and the rest of Czechoslovakia an undefended satellite of the Third Reich.

TWO ON THE ROAD

A few days later, after packing a bit and saying goodbye to friends, Ella and I set off together on our bikes. She seemed eager to travel with me through the Schwarzwald and Bavaria for several weeks, staying at youth hostels as I had done so often on my weekend roamings. That arrangement didn't last long. We parted, still good friends, five days later after spending two nights at Frau Weiss's cousins' farm at Pfullendorf in the Black Forest. Although very poor, the family there took us in and sheltered us through a rainy day. We all ate together – Mama, Papa, two daughters, hired hands – from a central bowl of stew, passing big loaves of bread from one arm pit to another as we each cut ourselves a hunk. The older of the two daughters had become a farm laborer herself, working in the fields and barn, as strong and subdued as the men. The much younger one was lively, graceful, and petted, obviously with the expectation of a different future. The independent-minded father took us with him into town where we joined his friends at a local pub for a glass of schnapps. I got the impression these peasants gathered together almost daily to exchange news and discuss politics, and for the first and only time that summer I heard Germans openly and fearlessly criticize their government – to be sure only for its agricultural policy.

The next day Ella, homesick herself, took the train back to Heidelberg and I headed south to the *Bodensee* and then east through Bavaria. I had a letter of introduction from Aunt Elizabeth Butterworth to her sister, Trixie, who lived in Murnau, south of Munich, with her husband, Baron von Hirschberg, a German general. I hoped I would be as hospitably treated by Clare and Ann's aunt and uncle as we had been by Ella's peasant cousins.

ON THE ROAD ALONE

There were five more days of biking from youth hostel to youth hostel before I knocked on Aunt Trixie's door. Along the way, I toured the factory in Friedrichshafen where the Graf Zeppelins were made. These were huge rigid airships, shaped like sausages, propelled by several motors and held aloft by hydrogen gas. They had been used up to that time as weather observers and in warfare during World War I for raids on England and were being developed in the '30s into strategic weapons. One of the largest, the Hindenburg, had crossed the Atlantic in 1937 with 97 people aboard. Many of us had seen newsreels of the big lumbering airship as it approached the Lakehurst, New Jersey, airport and then exploded and became engulfed in flames as the highly flammable hydrogen caught on fire. No wonder the tour guide looked at me with hostility because my government had refused to sell the Germans helium that would have been a safe substitute for the hydrogen gas. And no wonder my government was refusing to sell the helium that would have made that new zeppelin we were looking at, already almost three quarters built, a safer military weapon. I believe the airship I saw was never finished, and by World War II, only a year in the future, zeppelins were considered obsolete.

In Immenstadt I saw another facet of Nazi Germany. I reached the youth hostel there about 1:00 P.M. and sprang up onto an alpine trail for an afternoon climb. I soon realized I was being followed and looked around to see a young blond German who was also staying at the Immenstadt youth hostel. He didn't look too dangerous, so we climbed together and I discovered he was an enthusiastic pilot in Hitler's newly organized air force, on Rest and Recreation after spending half a year bombing for Franco's fascist forces in the Spanish Civil War. I knew Hitler was aiding Franco against the legitimate, freely elected government of Spain and incidentally giving training to his untested pilots, but it took me awhile to grasp that the man walking beside me had enjoyed killing men, women and children while staying relatively safe himself (the Spanish Government Forces had no antiaircraft weapons), and that he was preparing himself for future killings of Poles, French, Belgians, English. Is "murderer" too harsh a word for him? He was licensed, to be sure, because he wore a uniform and thus represented his country, but was a murderer nonetheless. On the way down the mountain, we came to a roadside shrine and my pilot companion did some random damage to it as we passed. "In our country," I told him, "we think everyone should have the right to worship in whatever way they please." "Here," he said, "we're going to have only one religion, a state religion." I think he meant worshipping the state.

And then biking on through miles and miles of Bavarian Alps, passing hillside huts, cows wearing their brassy bells, alpine meadows, mad King Ludwig's astonishing castle, a Rococo cathedral, the *Staffelsee,* and finally to Murnau and the von Hirschbergs. When at last I introduced myself to Aunt Trixie, her first words were, "When did you last have a bath?" Did I look that bedraggled? At least we were discussing my personal habits in English!

a) Dilsberg   b) Frau Weiss   c) Frau, Herr, and Ella Weiss   d) Heidelberg Market   e) Neueschwanstel, Bavaria   f) Heidelberg Castle

MURNAU INTERLUDE AND HOME

I didn't know whether I would be offered lunch and then sent on my way or if my friendship with their nieces Clare and Ann would be worthy of a longer stay. The Murnau house seemed pretty full and busy, but still I was invited to stop over for several nights – maybe because ten or twelve young Nazi army officers had been invited for a buffet dinner the very evening I arrived and one more girl was welcomed. So I took a bath, borrowed an evening dress from absent Billy (Sybilla), the older of the two von Hirschberg daughters, who evidently was about my age and size, and spent an evening so outlandishly different from the rest of the summer I felt almost disoriented. Elegant food, spectacular uniforms, young German officers, some good dancing – I would have to wait till the next day to figure out what kind of a household this Murnau establishment was.

Much to my relief, Aunt Trixie kept extending her hospitality until, after ten days, I had to sell my trusty bike and scuttle back to Heidelberg by train in time to prepare myself for going home. I had opportunity enough to get acquainted with an entirely different class of people and to marvel at many contrasts – between the Schwarzwald peasants and the Bavarian nobility, between my wandering student summer and the previous one of hard work as a waitress, and between the luxury of those ten days and probably the rest of my life. I wrote in my diary, "Augusta does our washing and ironing, Maria cleans our shoes every day, beds and rooms are tidied while our backs are turned, and all meals are cooked by jolly Racine and served by the other two. Can you imagine such an idle state!" But nobility or no, the von Hirschbergs took in boarders, just like mother! That was why the house was so full. Three young English women and a younger French girl were paying guests for the summer. Pam, handsome, sophisticated, somewhat detached, amusingly ironic – Lady Pamela was the oldest of the three. Libby, like Pam engaged to be married, was more open and friendlier. Ann, the youngest of the three, talked only about men, clothes, dances, gossip, sex, and above all being presented to the Queen. The two older ones had been through all that and so could advise her, but I, an ardent democrat, felt quite scornful of such foolishness and wrote of Ann's "fluff of peroxide blond hair and baby face packed with eye-blacking and ruby-red lipstick." Sylvia, the French girl, was extremely shy and retiring (convent educated?) so I didn't really get to know her. I had a good time with Billy's younger sister, Spatzi, because we did quite a lot of work together, weeding the strawberry patch and the vegetable garden. We even had a glorious mud fight one wonderful rainy day.

The von Hirschberg household spent a good many of the ten days I was there going to tea, having cookouts, climbing in the nearby Alps, swimming and playing tennis with another household not far away where friends of the von Hirschbergs had six or seven young British men also boarding with them for the summer. The conversation there was about Cambridge and Oxford, traveling to India, brothers and fathers in Cairo and scattered around the British empire. When one of the young men who was talking about his friends at Cambridge asked me what I thought about men who wore rouge and lipstick, I had to admit I had never heard of such a thing. Frankly, I found most of the Castle Riedon crowd effete and not very attractive except for one Scotsman who was more reserved and reminded me of Bud.

As for the von Hirschbergs, Aunt Trixie was so hospitable and nice to me, I still feel grateful. Spatzi was a remarkable eleven-year-old, fun and clever and so independent she had not joined the *Hitlermädchen* as girls her age were expected to do. I wondered if that would complicate her parents' future, which seemed complicated enough as it was. Although I didn't get much of a chance to talk with gruff Uncle Tony, I discovered he had recently retired from the army. In his early sixties? That must have sent an unwelcomed message to the Nazi government.

Those of us passing through the Murnau household that summer, enjoying their hospitality, didn't guess how anxious our host family was. They were obviously good at covering up. My later insights come from a biography of Elizabeth von Arnim, Lady Russell, written by Clare and Ann's mother in 1968, containing many family letters written during those dangerous years. I could tell war worries over the Czechoslovakian situation were rising throughout Europe in the latter part of August and throughout September. Much of the world was holding its breath while Hitler sounded more and more belligerent leading up to the Nuremberg Rally which started September 6th, the day before I left Germany. William Shirer in

The Rise and Fall of the Third Reich writes, "It is difficult to recall the dark and almost unbearable tension that gripped the capitals of Europe as the Nuremberg Party Rally . . . approached its climax on September 12." What I didn't know was that the von Hirschbergs were in such despair with the anticipation of war they even obtained the means to end all their lives if the worst they could imagine should happen. On September 30th, just a month after I left Murnau and a day after it was clear there would be no war over Czechoslovakia, at least that fall, Clare and Ann's Little Granny wrote Aunt Elizabeth about her other daughter:

> *My poor little Trix . . . . She wrote the other day and asked me to send her narcotics – which I promptly did – enough she said to put them all to sleep. Now she wont need it, but only, probably, for a bit, so I'm exhorting her to keep it as her dearest treasure, for I have no more . . . .*

In January of 1939, Little Granny wrote again to Aunt Elizabeth:

> *[Trix's] letters to me. . . . lately have been nothing but wild and hollow expressions of happiness. Frightened obviously . . . . Since the Jew baiting, I've not seen her [the reference here is to Kristallnacht, the government instigated and organized pogrom in November of 1938, when Synagogues, Jewish homes and shops were set on fire, and the systematic genocide of Jews was launched] . . . . If I succeeded [in taking in a Jewish refugee] the Nazis who have spies everywhere would probably clap Trix into a concentration camp because her mother pities the Jews . . . . She told me she never dared say she was sorry for them, even before the pogroms. I think hell is loose . . . .*

In March, after the takeover of Czechoslovakia, Little Granny wrote:

> *What do you think of Hitler's latest? Barefaced conquest this time with no excuse of minorities anywhere in it. He is a wonderful recruiting agent for us in England . . . . I have a*

feeling he will now go downward . . . . The German nation simply groans under his horrid yoke. I was appalled by what he has done to the Jews . . . . Never has there been gangsterism on such a scale . . . .

And in April of 1939, Billy von Hirschberg, who was studying to be an actress that winter in Berlin, wrote to her grandmother:

> *Darling little Granny I can't go on living in Germany. I hate it, oh I hate it, everything, the people, the government . . . could you adopt me and give me an English name? . . . . I would be a servant or everything only to get out of here . . . . You can't think how awful they all are, those Nazis . . . . suppressing everything, marching, marching, marching soldiers. Marching on in their Prussian way over culture and civilization . . . . Oh darling and what shall I do here in a war among those awful patriots in a country I hate? . . . . I am going to try to have this letter sent by [diplomatic] bag, because otherwise it wouldn't get out . . . .*

As I said goodbye to my Murnau friends, I had little inkling of the anguish the von Hirschbergs were feeling. They all did manage to live through the devastation of the Third Reich. Billy married an Englishman in the summer of 1939 and escaped to England just before the war began. Spatzi stayed on in Germany and married an Australian diplomat after the war. Aunt Trixie was finally arrested "for anti-German activities" and sent to prison for the last six months of the Nazi regime. Uncle Tony visited her there every day until he fell into a bomb crater which made him have "trouble with his going." Little Granny, who had been living in France, took herself into exile in the United States where she was lonely but nearer her daughter, Aunt Elizabeth Butterworth, and where she died in February of 1941. She had one final literary triumph, early in 1940, when her last book, *Mr. Skeffington*, was published in London. Job Skeffington, a Jew, appears in person only at the end of the book. He had been living in Vienna and when he shows up in London, although still relatively young, he is blind and shrunken and penniless, terrified by unexpected noises, physically and psychologically destroyed by the Nazis. At least Little Granny knew and cared a good deal about what was going on, and she tried to use her talent and influence to tell about it. What happened to the others I met I don't know. I would particularly like to know about Libby Hornung who went with me to Munich when I left. We spent the day together, looked through several museums, shopped, ate lunch, and said a "one-eye-wet, one-eye-dry" goodbye. I was sad because I knew that I would never see her again, but elated at the thought that I would soon be packing and on my way to Bremerhaven and home.

I spent one night in the Munich Youth Hostel, alone and on the road again, regaining my previous state of heightened awareness that I had suspended during those secure and frolicsome ten days in Murnau. My diary says of that youth hostel stay, "Had a bit of a talk about Jews with the manager of the Y.H. Had to go to bed before it turned into an argument." Oho! Fear makes cowards of us all! I caught the train to Heidelberg, and found 16 letters waiting for me – and Frau Weiss in tears. She had been listening on the radio to Hitler's increasing belligerency, and she too saw disaster coming. So her approval of Hitler didn't extend to approval of war! I was grateful for the warm welcome the Weisses gave me as I slipped back into the same place I had had in their household before, but the rumors of war and the letters from home combined to make me jubilant that I would soon write *der Schluss* to my German summer.

I signed out with the Heidelberg police and said goodbye to all my familiar haunts and to the friends I had made in the market. I had one more dinner with the Allens, and they too were gloomy. Mr. Allen said war was inevitable "not this fall, because it's hard to campaign in the winter, but probably next spring." At the station Frau Weiss and Ella saw me off to Bremen on the evening of September 7th. A motley bunch of us sat up stiffly all night in a third class compartment, desperately trying to find a place to rest our heads so we could at least catch a cat nap, and arrived too tired to realize we were happy. We finally boarded one of Germany's fastest transatlantic ships, the *Europa*, and sailed by way of England toward America, where we landed five days later. That wasn't time enough to make many friends but time enough to think over all I had seen and done for the past three months.

What *had* those three months meant to me? I learned something about myself. I found I enjoyed my own company, that being alone wasn't all that dreadful. I also learned I could survive unhappiness, especially if I knew it wouldn't last forever. In fact I found life could be pretty exciting and interesting even when I was desperately lonely. But what else? The most disturbing things I saw that summer were the signs that war was being planned by the Nazis, using every insidious method guile could devise – by sowing hatred against Jews and Poles and other vulnerable groups, by pounding Aryan and folk lore myths into the German people from an early age, instilling in them a willingness to sacrifice for the glory of the fatherland and giving them a belief they were superior to and worth more than everyone else in the world, and most of all by immobilizing any opposition through fear. It was not a pretty picture and, I thought, not the kind of regime I would ever consent to live under. Most of all I wondered how such a state of affairs ever came about and if it could happen in America. I quickly reassured myself that I needn't worry about that. All our myths are so different, so alien to dictatorship that we would always be saved from such a catastrophe. The *Bill of Rights*, the ideals of tolerance, the concept of a government of laws, our entrenched democracy itself would save us. Our wide participation, I thought, in so many organizations was also a plus – the PTAs, the League of Women Voters, the Chambers of Commerce, to name just a few, would give us such diverse loyalties we would not allow ourselves to be divided against each other. However, on the wild chance of any such attempt to create the kind of society I was sailing away from, I realized we would need to speak out immediately, support whoever was being scapegoated and defend all points of view, whether we liked them or not. Well, having answered any worries I had about my own country to my immense relief, I watched from the deck, in the dusk of September 14th, as we sailed slowly into New York Harbor and saw that great lady, the Statue of Liberty, emerge through the mist. My heart leaped up with as much excitement as any immigrant's. I had made it home.

I, the undersigned, Secretary of State of the United States of America, hereby request all whom it may concern to permit safely and freely to pass, and in case of need to give all lawful aid and protection to

MIRIAM FORD BROOKS

a citizen of the United States.

The bearer is accompanied by his
Wife, X X X
Minor children, X X X
X X X
X X X

Given under my hand and the seal of the Department of State at Washington.
APR. 18TH 1938

Cordell Hull

2

Ausgereist
- 9. SEP. 1938
Grenzübergangsstelle
Breme-

Sichtvermerk
für M. F. Brooks
(Name des Inhabers)
zur ein-maligen Einreise in das Reichsgebiet über
jede amtlich zugelassene deutsche Grenzübergangsstelle
die Grenzübergangsstelle(n)

Deutsches Generalkonsulat
(Unterschrift)

Hamburg, Hafen.
eingereist am
22. JUNI 1938

22. Jun 1938

Photograph of bearer

CHAPTER 8

BACK TO A FAMILIAR WORLD

It had been a more eventful summer at home than I knew, absorbed as I was in my own adventures. Doug had graduated from Yale in June when I was already on the high seas, so I had missed that chance to tell him I was proud of him and his triumphs. He was a man of many talents – a musician who played the violin and sang well enough to solo in various church choirs. He excelled in sports. At Loomis he had thrown the javelin 18 feet farther than any other Loomis boy had thrown it before, a record not broken for seven years. He came within 10 inches of the Yale record and his academic work, especially in math and science, was superior. He later became a highly respected meteorologist and oceanographer, advising Presidents and congressmen as executive secretary of the Washington-based National Advisory Committee on Oceans and Atmosphere (NACOA). By the time I got home, he had already left for his first job, teaching at Hill School in Pottstown, Pennsylvania, so we wouldn't be seeing each other until Thanksgiving.

Dad had more spring to his step than I remembered. His new job at the Connecticut Highway Department was restoring his self-confidence. Mother's news was more worrisome. A week after I had sailed in June, she'd had a hysterectomy. She kept this from me before I left so that I wouldn't give up the opportunity "to see the world," and she didn't write me about it so I wouldn't worry about her while I was away. That was brave, I thought, because she must have had plenty of worries herself, remembering the fatal consequences of her sister's similar operation. Fortunately, by September she seemed well recovered and had resumed her very active life.

There was much news from Bud's family too. Several weeks before I got home that September, Bud's father, Uncle Paul, married a young widow, Libby Elmer, who had two daughters, Jean and Lucy, 11 and 10 years old. I already knew them as neighbors on Sunset Farm, but now we would have a new kind of relationship. Bud had also started his second year of teaching at Kent School in the Housatonic Valley, and because I had to return immediately to Connecticut College to be Junior Advisor to the incoming Freshmen, we didn't see each other until a later weekend – not until after the worst hurricane of the century came crashing through. The winds and rains struck two days after I reached New London, blowing down trees, moving houses off their foundations, and thrusting boats of all sizes onto the shore, causing the whole water front of the city to go up in flames. This was a reminder that Nature as well as mankind was capable of demonic fury, and I was glad I was not still on the ocean bobbing around on those terrifyingly destructive waves.

When Bud finally came to see me, he acted preoccupied until he told me that during the summer he had taken his old girl friend, Mary Eddy, out canoeing and had kissed her. So that was what was troubling him! Well, I was too happy to see him to be bothered by his confession, particularly since, once his mind was eased, he was as loving as before.

Years later Miss Hafkesbrink told me she hadn't found me very interesting until I returned from Germany. I wasn't sure I deserved that backhanded compliment. I was a little older, of course, but didn't realize I had changed in any perceptual way. I think she was referring to changes in my thinking, what she would have called my *weltanschauung*, but I am afraid it has taken a whole life time of experience to reach any significant depth of understanding of the big issues we talked about during those prewar Depression years. I had entered college with the typical American outlook on life – a Panglossian optimism, the belief that people are basically good and rational, that free play of all historical forces would automatically bring about progress and justice. I believed logic and the Scientific Method would convince people of The Truth. I believed TRUTH could be found! Milton's *Areopagitica*, that wonderful essay against censorship, said most eloquently what I believed: "And though all the winds of doctrine were let loose to play upon the earth, so Truth be in the field, we do injuriously . . . to misdoubt her strength. Let her and Falsehood grapple; who knew Truth put to the worse, in a free and open encounter? . . .For who knows not that Truth is strong, next to the Almighty? . . . Give her but room, and do not bind her when she sleeps . . ." "Isn't that magnificent? Yes, sir! That's what we were fighting for," I remember hearing myself say. Once enlightened, people would do the right thing. Reason would prevail. That is what made democracy work. I accepted the idea that people voted according to their own self-interest, but I believed all those self-interests would balance each other out and the result would be good.

Somewhere along the line, even before I left home, I began to realize this thinking was too simple. Oddly, I heard it in my ear first. Those Methodist hymns! "Jesus loves me this I know for the Bible tells me so," to mention one of many, was the hardest to bear. It wasn't just the words, it was the melody and the harmony as well. I got so I couldn't sing the melody, so I sang the alto part, then that was too cloying, so I sang tenor, and eventually I couldn't handle it at all. My German summer perhaps did carry my thinking fast-forward somewhat, forcing me to question my assumptions earlier than I might have. Certainly, by that time the courses that seemed most interesting to me were the courses that asked the most difficult questions, and I found I cared about the answers.

There were two new subject matters introduced into the curriculum in the '20s and '30s – psychology and anthropology. The former, as it was taught to me in those early years, was bloodless, mainly made up of biographies and sound bites of theories. Penis envy, for instance, didn't strike a chord in my psyche, although I could see that a penis is "a mighty handy thing on a picnic." Freud and Jung would have to wait for a later time. But Margaret Mead's studies of primitive peoples, especially her *Coming of Age in Samoa*, shook us. So relations between men and women could be different from those we are used to? Is one society better than another? If so, how do you tell? If not, are there no absolutes?

We didn't talk about feminism in those days, although we decried women's ignorance about sex and their (our) bodies. I made up for my own shortcomings in that area during my freshman year by reading all the books on reserve for the courses delicately called Marriage and The Family while I was at my library job. Havilock Ellis was an eye-opener! Were these signs of the sexual revolution which would engulf the next generation? Whatever the case, we didn't appreciate the overwhelming strength of patriarchal views that pervade our society and guarantee that sexual liberation will not necessarily liberate women. We should have listened more intently to Virginia Woolf. I read her *A Room of One's Own* in college because one of our professors raved about it, but I wasn't much interested. Forty-five years later, I read it again and *then* it meant something – so much so that I read it straight through three times.

We should have taken to heart what Thorstein Veblen was telling us in his *Theory of the Leisure Class* – that "The earliest form of ownership is an ownership of the women by the able bodied men of the community . . . this extends itself to include the products of their industry," and "There is in all barbarian communities a profound sense of the disparity between man's and woman's work," and "These upper class occupations [men's work] may be roughly comprised under government, warfare, religious observances, and sports." He also wrote, "Whatever has to do with the everyday work of getting a livelihood, is the exclusive occupation of the inferior class . . . which includes . . . women." I understood Veblen's description of "conspicuous consumption" and the part upperclass women play as trophies and vicarious consumers, enhancing the reputations of their men. I would never put myself in that position, I promised myself. But we didn't imagine that the idea of women as property and of certain employments being the exclusive prerogatives of men and others being exclusively women's were still so deeply ingrained in 20th Century America. In the '30s, we felt we were already liberated. We had the vote, didn't we? All we needed now was education and we were getting that!

But women's issues were sideshows in a sense. Even more somber questions had to do with the nature of Mankind and Truth? What if human nature is predominantly made up of greed, hatred, prejudice, pride and envy? Of desire for power? What happens when fear gets the upper hand, or insecurities and envy at inequalities of wealth turn people to despair and violence? Our deepest concerns had to do with the persistent Depression and the burgeoning of totalitarian regimes and ideas. We questioned whether our capitalist economy, with its rewards for the accumulation of wealth and unregulated competition and its punishment of those who failed could survive in an advanced 20th Century industrialized country, or if the stresses between the haves and the have-nots were too great for revolution or Fascism to be contained.

Of course, college life for me wasn't just courses and ideas, but sometimes the problems we discussed followed us even when we thought we were playing. For instance, in my senior year a fortuitous sprained ankle took me away from basketball into modern dance, an art form I continued to enjoy for several more decades. We chose as our final project the choreographing of a dance to Archibald Macleish's *The Fall of the City*. In it the citizen chorus says:

> *Masterless men!*
> *Masterless men must take a master!*
> *Order must master us!*
> *Freedom's for fools:*
> *Force is the certainty!*
> *Freedom has eaten our strength and corrupted our virtues!*
> *Men must be ruled!*
> *Fools must be mastered!*
> *Rigor and fast*
> *Will restore our dignity!*
> *Chains will be liberty!*

Were men too frightened to cherish freedom – and too hungry and poor to find democracy meaningful? This all may sound pretty intense, but at the time it just seemed exciting and challenging – and I suppose academic, although I should have known better after my German summer. In February of 1940, however, in my senior year, I got sent to Washington into the Real World for a five day Youth Congress, and all of the questions we were asking ourselves came together. We weren't dealing with esoteric theories, I discovered. There were stronger forces in the air, even in our own country, than I had thought.

a) Miriam as President of Inter-Club Council at CT College   b) President Blunt, CT College   c) Hannah Hafkesbrink, Professor of German; Rosemary Park, Assistant Professor of German   d) "Rhythm and Movement in the Twentieth Century Mood" featuring Mims (which one?) and friends

CHAPTER 9

ONE MORE ACADEMIC ADVENTURE

Several of us had heard about the American Youth Congress and the Washington gathering while attending a conference at Yale. The AYC was an offshoot of the World Youth Congress which had met twice, once in Switzerland in 1936 and again in 1938 at Vassar College. We knew Eleanor Roosevelt attended some of the Vassar events and had become a defender of the American organization and an enthusiastic sponsor of a long weekend in February, an event in Washington sometimes called "a citizens' institute" and sometimes "a monster lobby for jobs, peace, civil liberties, education and health" for young people.

Four of us went to our college president, Miss Blunt, and said we thought Connecticut College should be represented too. She pulled out $50 from some secret source and told us to report to the college community when we got back. We got in touch with the local Youth Congress organizer, who found us seats on a bus leaving New London Thursday afternoon. For the long 8-hour trip, we four pale faces sat rather primly, I expect, in the midst of a group of young Black people in boisterous high spirits traveling south. They greeted old friends with enthusiasm and visited up and down the aisle, getting to know each other while we sat subdued, restrained, stiffly perhaps – exhibiting our puritan inheritance? We were treated with what seemed to me to be a wary politeness – certainly not hostility. After all, we were heading for the same demonstration, presumably caring about the same problems.

We stopped at several bus depots along the way and for the first time I saw "COLORED ONLY" and "WHITES ONLY" signs on rest rooms and drinking fountains. Somewhere in Delaware or Maryland we stopped to eat at what I would have labeled a "road house," not a spot my family would have picked, but I suddenly realized that the places we would have picked were not open to "Colored." We were in "Jim Crow" country where Blacks had to sit in the back of the bus and in the balcony at movies, and go to highly inadequate schools that were "separate but equal."

Before we left the restaurant, someone put some money into the juke box and our bus companions began to dance. What exuberance! Sophisticated syncopated rhythms! I wanted to join in but didn't dare. I was conspicuous enough as it was, and my Ginger Rogers' style, smooth, pretty, and self-contained, wouldn't suit.

Once in 6th or 7th grade, the word got around that a classmate, one of a handful of Blacks who attended Windsor elementary schools, would show us a special dance at recess. In one corner of the playground, we made a circle around a boy I had seen up to then as a rather bright but silent loner and watched him for about five minutes do what he called "cutting a pigeon wing." I think we were seeing a forerunner of "break dancing." And once, as teenagers, some of us drove over the Massachusetts border to Riverside Park and sneaked over the fence near the death-defying roller coaster to hear Cab Calloway. But in reality a whole vital part of American culture had been essentially shut out of my life. No one I knew mentioned the Harlem Renaissance, Langston Hughes, W.E.B.Du Bois. Not only the South, but my life was segregated too. There were no black faces at Chaffee and none at Connecticut College, and until then I hadn't even noticed.

When we reached Washington, we found our inexpensive "whites only" hotel and even before unpacking, some of us walked out into the misty moonlight to the Mall, past the Washington Monument to the Jefferson and Lincoln Memorials. We read the inscriptions: "We hold these truths to be self-evident, that all men are created equal..." and "We...Resolve... that this nation, under God, shall have a new birth of freedom – and that government of the people, for the people, and by the people shall not perish from the earth." Great words! A little tarnished at that moment for me as I found myself reading them through the eyes of my new friends from the bus. Not for another 25 years would those phrases, which we had taken for granted for two centuries, at least for white men, have much meaning for them. We walked back to our hotel and went to bed wondering where in that segregated city they had found a place to stay.

About five thousand young people poured into Washington that week, and it looked like a big crowd to me. Of course, compared to the anti-Vietnam War demonstrations of the 1960s and '70s that were at least 100 times larger, the AYC gathering was a Sunday school picnic. Yet we were enough to frighten some legislators. A New York Times headline read: "YOUTH ADVANCING ON CAPITAL MEETS GENERAL ATTACK – MRS. ROOSEVELT'S DEFENSE OF CONGRESS IS ASSAILED – TUNNEY AND OTHERS RENEW COMMUNIST FRONT CHARGES." At various times in our country's history, people have lost faith in an open society, the very foundation of democracy, and the forces of repression have gained the upper hand. This was one of those times. In the 1930s, Congress had set up the House Un-American Activities Committee (HUAC) to investigate "subversion" in all areas of American life. As in previous periods when civil liberties had come under attack, it was foreign ideas (anarchism, socialism, communism, and the like) and foreigners (immigrant laborers and labor organizers in particular) that were being investigated and punished. These attacks on "suspicious" groups and ideas gathered momentum all through the 1940s and reached a climax with Senator Joseph McCarthy in the next decade, but that is another story. By February of 1940, HUAC had already heard testimony accusing labor unions, especially the CIO with its president John L. Lewis, many university professors, the whole New Deal, and even the Boy Scouts and the Campfire Girls of being communists.

Some members of the Youth Congress had already been called to testify before the HUAC, which issued a report saying that the vast majority of the Congress had no connection with communism or fascism, but that the communist element "has at times exerted an influence . . . out of all proportion to its size." This meant to some people that the AYC was made up of "fellow travelers." It was tainted, made up of wrong people thinking wrong ideas and advocating wrong solutions to society's ills.

It seemed ominous that although it was Fascism under Hitler and Mussolini propelling us toward war, it was Communism that was considered the greater heresy, the foreign ideology. Both were equally inimical to democracy but Communism is the greater threat to capitalism, and I guess there's the rub. This was the beginning of a worry I still have. Will we ever reach a point when democracy seems inadequate to deal with crises? If we do, it seems to me that Fascism would too easily win out.

Despite the turmoil and suspicions expressed so loudly in our capital, Mrs. Roosevelt showed only serene cordiality. Like a local League of Women Voters' president hosting delegates attending a regional meeting, she had persuaded her friends to open their homes to those who couldn't find lodging. The Roosevelts themselves took 20 young demonstrators into the White House for the week and other delegates lived with families of the Secretary of State, the Speaker of the House, and the Secretaries of War and Navy. In contrast, how tightly guarded the White House and today's Presidents now are! In spite of growing attacks on ideas, we were living in innocent times.

President Roosevelt was nearing the end of his second term and contemplating running for an unprecedented third. His New Deal policies had inspired and given hope to those who were losing their farms and homes and life savings and jobs. During the 30s, these policies established regulations of banks, set up the SEC (Securities Exchange Commission) to control Wall Street, devised antitrust legislation, and even enhanced the power of labor, trying to guarantee the right of workers to organize without fear of reprisals. The New Deal is more than I can describe here (this was the beginning of Social Security and job-creation and training too); but to sum up, it was an attempt to empower the have-nots to balance the previously unbridled power of the haves, and the haves have never forgiven Roosevelt for this "assault." Some say FDR saved capitalism and democracy by mitigating the suffering and giving hope; others say the New Deal led to the welfare state, the decline of morals, illegitimate births, chilblains and anything else that is bad. This argument is still hot half a century later.

The opening session of the AYC would occur on the evening of February 9th, so we had a whole day to explore the city. In the afternoon, I watched the movie version of John Steinbeck's Pulitzer Prize-winning novel, *Grapes of Wrath*, showing the migration of the "Okies," forced off their farms by drought, dust storms and banks that owned the mortgages they couldn't pay. That put us in the mood for the coming meetings, but didn't really prepare me for the excitement to come. Over two thousand of us crowded into the Department of Labor Auditorium. A small band of German Bundists, American Ukrainians, Armenian Youth of America, and other groups indicated their affiliations, but mainly we were a milling, unidentified crowd of young people looking expectant. We didn't have to wait long for fireworks to begin. In the middle of the introductory speech by the National Chair of the AYC, a young man jumped up and cried, "I rise to a point of order!" The moderator banged on the table and roared, "Out of Order." Others shouted "Sit down" and "Shut up" and one of his friends shouted, "Let him speak!" After a short wrestling match, one person was escorted out by the sergeant at arms and soon several others left and the program went on. The interruption was made by a dissident group that had been protesting "Communist influence" in the AYC since the 1938 meeting. All weekend that group, sponsored by Gene Tunney (what was he doing there?) and others tried to present resolutions to condemn the Soviet Union for invading Finland and to expel the Young Communist League and other "communist front" groups. They were told Monday would be the time for resolutions, but by that time the dissidents, which included Archie Roosevelt, a distant cousin of Mrs. Roosevelt, had announced a rival organization dedicated to anti-communism and had invited any dissatisfied groups in the AYC to join them. "Was that interrupter really a relative of yours?" a newsman asked Mrs. Roosevelt at one of her daily press conferences. "Yes, I know Archie," she said.

When Attorney General Robert Jackson finally got to speak that Friday night, he made a surprise announcement to roars of approval. Earlier, the AYC Chair had denounced the Dies committee for trying to punish people for their "un-American" politics but hadn't looked into the Ku Klux Klan, whose activities in denying Afro-Americans their constitutional rights were really "un-American." Attorney General Jackson told us that during the past week his department had posted agents in South Carolina gathering evidence of KKK terrorist activities and, in another infamous case of injustice to labor, had "dismissed 100 indictments against WPA workers in Minnesota." He also commented on the furious opposition to the AYC: "To some people such an assembly of young people is a symbol of dark and nightmarish plottings against government…[but] no honest man can expect a free and hopeful youth" to accept a status quo in which "involuntary unemployment foreclosed opportunities for independence and dependent old age and so many injustices play so large and disastrous a part." He praised the achievements of President Roosevelt for enacting the minimum wage law to protect women and stated that the President had won for the nation the ability to "govern the powerful and protect the weak."

The next day we paraded to the White House carrying signs against war and for jobs, led there by a girl on a white horse. We piled onto the East Lawn and waited a long time for the President to appear. I found myself standing beside a young Black woman, a share cropper who lived with her own and several other families in a barn somewhere in Oklahoma. She told me about the difficulties getting medical treatment when it was needed and not having enough shoes for all the children to go to school, and often having too little to eat. Just when the President began to speak from the South Portico, it began to pour, and my new friend and I huddled under a shared newspaper. By that time we were so well acquainted we exchanged addresses and actually wrote each other several times that spring.

The President condemned the Soviet Union for its dictatorship and the invasion of Finland and defended giving loans to help that country. He denied this would drag us into a war with the USSR. "That's silly." He said anyone had the right to advocate governmental changes as long as they conform to the processes for change laid down in the Constitution. He urged us to be patient. "Don't expect utopia over night. The employment of youth is hitched to Old Age Pensions." That was a novel idea. Evidently there were only a certain number of jobs available, and youth would have to wait until the old retired. This was one of a piece with the Child Labor Law and the Eight Hour Day – providing jobs by sharing the available work. Roosevelt's speech was long and as usual persuasive and eloquent with a little scolding mixed in: "Don't pass resolutions on things you don't know anything about." But the President was mainly encouraging and sympathetic to the aims of us listeners.

John L. Lewis, President of the United Mine Workers and of the CIO, spoke that afternoon. He had been added to the program late in the day and was in the middle of a fight over merging with the AF of L, differently organized and less militant and less inclusive than the CIO. Lewis was astonishing to look at, with black bushy eyebrows and a demagogue's

YOUTH ADVANCING ON CAPITAL MEETS GENERAL ATTACK

Mrs. Roosevelt's Defense of Congress Is Assailed by Keefe in House

BOLTING GROUP OPENS FIRE

unney and Others Renew ommunist Front Charges— Lewis Added to Program

---

Proposal to Exclude Foes of Democracy Ruled Out—Anti-War Note Sent Abroad

By FRANK S. ADAMS
Special to THE NEW YORK TIMES.

WASHINGTON, Feb. 12—After ruling out of order a resolution by a Socialist delegate which would have barred all supporters of totalitarian governments from the American Youth Congress, the National Assembly of the Youth Congress adopted today a broad program with the avowed aims of keeping this country out of war, getting jobs and governmental aid for young people and safeguarding civil liberties.

LABOR LINK MAPPED BY YOUTH CONGRESS

Officials Arrive at Formula for Cooperation With the Non-partisan League

RED FACTOR IS ASSAILED

Creal in House Says Events Show There Are Communists in the Organization

---

FIRST LADY BALKS AT ADVISING YOUTH TO UPHOLD FINLAND

Congress Should Not Vote to Condemn Russia Unless It Believes in This, She Says

BUT SHE BACKS THE FINNS

LEWIS PROPOSES 'A LABOR PEACE PLAN'

C. I. O. CHIEF'S OFFER

Asks Two Groups Meet March 15 in Same Hall at Washington

R A VOTE ON REUNION

es Suggestion in Speech Youth Session—'Submit to A.F.L.,' Says Green

Soviet Trade With U. S. Swells, Especially Since War in Finland

December Purchases Here More Than Fourth of Year's Total—Machinery to Make Planes Is the Principal Item

YOUTH TOLD STAND

4,000 Fall Silent as President Chides Them on Pro-Red Resolves.

PERIL OF U. S. WAR 'SILLY'

Lewis Later Replies on This Point in Speech Declaring Statesmen 'Accountable'

of Delegates From 62 National ps Has Won Powerful Support And Stirred Bitter Attacks

Attorney General Robert H. Jackson, who addressed the Congress last night.

Wired Photo—Times Wide World

Mrs. Roosevelt asked the presiding chairman, Jack McMichael, whether there were any more questions. He replied that there were many more but that they were repetitive. Then Mrs. Roosevelt thanked her young audience for the patience and courtesy with which they had listened to her.

"I am very, very fond of many of your leaders," she told them. "I would like to know you all personally, and I hope you will go home to your own communities and continue your interest in government problems."

Mrs. Roosevelt received an ovation from the audience as she departed.

Youth Congress

Standing in a drizzling rain on the south lawn of the White House in Washington, 3,000 members of the American Youth Congress yesterday listened to the President of the United States. They heard—as did a nationwide radio audience—a defense by Mr. Roosevelt of the economic effects of the New Deal at home, as well as his major statement of government policy toward the Soviet-Finnish war. They also heard some advice directed particularly at themselves: (1) a suggestion that all of them change to dry clothes after the meeting; (2) a warning to those among them who "call yourselves Communists" to "confine your advocacy of changes in law to the methods prescribed by the Constitution of the United States"; (3) admonition not to adopt resolutions like the

voice. He encouraged us to defy the President and to pass any resolution we wished. "Who had a better right to protest getting into war than you who will be the cannon fodder?" he asked rhetorically. When he finished, the crowd shouted its approval and someone grabbed my arm and said, "He's going to be our next President!"

On the third and closing day of the Congress, Mrs. Roosevelt was the main speaker. She repeated her position on the invasion of Finland but agreed that the Spanish Loyalist Government too should have been helped against Franco. She claimed her husband was trying to keep the U.S. out of war. In her press conferences she defended the decision of the AYC not to oust the Young Communist League from its membership. "A Youth Conference must stand for the same tolerance . . . that we as a nation have stood for under the Bill of Rights." (The Communist Party was not outlawed until 1950 when it was declared an "agent of a foreign power.") Many members of the conference spoke that afternoon, describing a wide range of civil liberties violations. *The New York Times* reported that a large number of Negro youth told of racial discrimination and "others in the long array of speakers were white girls [sic] and young men." The Administrative Secretary of the AYC warned that this was "fast turning into an age of persecution." She assailed the Dies Committee for conducting a "vigilante campaign, calling unreliable witnesses, slandering both individuals and organizations, ruining many people's lives." She declared that many of our elders hadn't learned from history but youth had learned "that the opening gun in the war on civil liberties has [always] begun by outlawing the Communists, suppressing their literature and meetings. The next step has been the suppression of all groups suspected of communism and this includes the entire trade union movement." She claimed, "We in the American Youth Congress have always maintained that there is no halfway mark for civil liberties in a democracy." And on that note the first and last American Youth Congress, the citizens institute, the "monster lobby," came to an end.

But not for me. In the course of the weekend, a young labor union delegate who came from the New London area offered me a ride home in the big limousine he and some friends had rented. However, they were part of the AYC General Assembly that would meet all day Monday, and also they had been invited to tea at the White House with Mrs. Roosevelt. Would

I mind waiting around during the day and then going with them to the White House? MIND! Tea with MRS. ROOSEVELT! Of course I leapt at the chance.

My three friends and I from Connecticut College joined many of the AYC Assembly delegates at the White House after their all-day session, drank tea poured by Mrs. Roosevelt herself, and listened to the others chatting about the past few days of the Congress. I myself was awed almost into silence by the experience. I did most of the listening, too, on the way home, taking a turn in the early hours of the morning at the wheel of that big car, although I didn't have a license, while the other passengers discussed politics, various U.S. Congressmen, and pertinent bills being debated that winter. I was impressed with their knowledge of current events, which was much greater than mine, and with their intelligence and concerns. I was delivered back to my ivory tower with a higher opinion of trade unionists than I had left with five days before.

We did report to our sponsor, President Blunt, whose character suited her name. She greeted us with enthusiasm and said she had read in the paper that the AYC had booed the President but "I didn't believe a word of it. Now tell me all about it!" We had to admit that there were a few boos but that most of us had shown proper respect. We also spoke in chapel to the whole student body (chapel was compulsory then), warning of a coming revolution, and we felt satisfied that we and the issues we talked about were taken seriously.

Soon after that, I went home to Windsor to register to vote. My parents asked if I intended to register with a party too, and I said yes, I was going to sign up as a Democrat. Mother burst into tears (she wasn't the weeping kind either) and cried,"What will my friends think!" Dad persuaded me to wait for the fall to declare my affiliation because I'd be living in another town by that time and people in Windsor wouldn't know. Of course, such subterfuge didn't work and Mother was right about her friends. About forty years later, I went with Bud to the Windsor Annual Shad Derby beauty contest. One of his former students had inveigled him into being a judge. As this was my home town, I looked around to see if there was anyone there I knew. Yes, there was – Mr. Ransom, the uncle of my childhood best friend, chairman of the Republican town committee for so many years he was called "Mr.

Republican." He must have been 90 years old by that Shad Derby night, and I imagined his memory would be pretty weak; but I went up to him anyway, introduced myself, and explained that I was Genevieve Brooks' daughter. "Oh yes," he barked. "You're the Democrat!" then turned his back on me and tottered away.

That spring I evidently sent a little money, one dollar, I think, to my sharecropper friend because I have a letter she wrote thanking me for helping just when their food was running out. They "took the money and bought a 50 cent sack of meal and 50 cents worth of lard." In June, Bud and I decided to send her a more substantial amount in lieu of buying me an engagement ring. Shades of Mother's Uncle Sam! Would I too be "hard to live with"? Fortunately, I didn't connect my impulses with his Salvation Army fervor and I had no qualms.

I graduated in June as a Phi Beta Kappa but not with honors. My thesis had been scandalously bad, I discovered some years later when I found it in the attic. I wanted to show how Romanticism formed a base for Fascism, and I still think that would be a good subject to explore, but I went at it with little discipline. *Romanticism in the World* was its title, and I guess I don't need to say any more. In spite of that touch of failure, I was very happy. I had made lots of lasting friends, my world had expanded in many ways, and in a few weeks I would get married. A whole new stage of life was opening up. I was ready for the Real World full time.

wilderness area with several river systems, lakes and forests full of wildlife. There we met our three guides, Jacque, Pierre and Louis, packed our gear into three canoes, and took off. We shot rapids, crept up on several moose, helped our guides, who did most of the work, to paddle the canoes and make camp at the various campsites, caught many fish, told each other stories, and gloried in ten adventurous days. The one somber note of that carefree time came in the middle of our expedition when we got word by means of a radio that Germany had invaded Poland, and that England and France had declared war. We emerged from the wilds to a Canada also at war, since it was a part of the British Commonwealth, but although somewhat subdued by the news, I was happy and healthy, in harmony with my companions, ready to tackle my final year at college.

ONLY ONE HITCH

Well, as I was saying, I was very much in love, so much so that once, when I saw Bud's car tootling up the drive on Connecticut College's campus, I thought I was going to faint. Would that have been called "swooning" in another age? Wait a minute! I was not the swooning type! Surely it wasn't because of an irrational fixation that I was going to marry him! There were sound rational reasons too, weren't there? Of course. He was fun to be with, very witty but never malicious. He was good with children, throwing Easter egg hunts for the neighborhood kids, for instance. He was steady and strong and clever and kind. Did I worry because my parents' marriage was not very happy? Never! I was sure we could do better than that. So we had a simple ceremony on the lawn behind Bud's house at Sunset Farm where I still live. On June 30, 1940, Mother and Dad's 25th wedding anniversary, Dad walked me out of the French doors of the living room to where Bud and Reverend Dorchester, our Windsor Methodist minister, were waiting. Mother played our family's old renovated melodeon, a grand wheezy early pump organ. Nursey, who took care of some neighborhood children, baked the cake, and with relatives and friends looking on, Bud fished out of his pocket the gold wedding ring he had ordered from the Sears Roebuck catalogue, and we were pronounced man and wife.

a) Graduation with Doug & Bud   b) Graduation with family
c) Relaxing before the wedding with Bud

a) Uncle Dutchy —"Have you got the ring?" b) Father and bride come down the aisle c) Mother of the bride on melodean d) Ann and Clare with Mims e) Uncle Paul, Libby, the bride and her parents e) Bride and groom

PART II

FAMILY MATTERS

CHAPTER 11

SAPS AT SEA

The morning after we were married, Bud's brother, Harry, drove us to Troy, New York, with Uncle Corwin's old green canoe tied to the top of the car. We put into the Hudson River, waved goodbye, and started on a five-week, 700-mile honeymoon, up the Hudson, through Lake Champlain, down the Richelieu River into the Saint Lawrence, and eventually down the Saint John River in New Brunswick to Westfield near the Bay of Fundy. As we paddled off, just the two of us, I suddenly panicked. Would I have enough ideas to last for such a long time alone together? After a few strokes, I realized I could just be quiet until there was something I wanted to say. The panic subsided and for the next fifty years I never had that worry again.

For six days we were part of the active river traffic plying the Hudson that summer of 1940. We mixed with all sizes of motor boats, fuel barges, a dredge or two, and most impressively, huge freighters carrying pulp wood from Canada to Mechanicville where "the world's largest paper mill" made paper for *The New York Times, The Harold Tribune* and other U.S. newspapers and magazines. We made slow time, averaging about twelve miles a day, paddling upstream and often waiting at the locks for a more important boat than ours to make it worthwhile for the Champlain canal men to "lock us up."

There were ten locks along the stretch from Waterfliet to Whitehall, bypassing rapids and falls, and we paired with whatever came along – sometimes an elegant yacht, its passengers looking over their cocktails at us with mild curiosity, and sometimes a freighter so big I expected to be crushed between lock and freighter before the incoming water rose high enough for the upper gates to open, allowing us to escape into wider water. Once in the long boring waterway leading into Lake Champlain, a family in a motorboat threw us a line and towed us for over an hour to Port Henry, changing our mileage average considerably.

We kept a log of our trip, taking turns in its writing, and it reminds me that we easily found places to pitch our tent, sometimes in a field, on a small island, or in a pasture. We encountered poison ivy, mosquitoes, showers, and one night a herd of inquisitive calves. I remember we had to guard our breakfast from those calves, and like Horatio, hold the horde at bay while we packed up our camp stove, pans and dishes, tent, and sleeping gear, stowed them all back into the canoe, and made our retreat, shoving off triumphantly, all equipment accounted for and no man lost. In Schylerville, the third night out, at an island campground, we found an abandoned Marine map that gave us exact details of the waterways we would be using for the next several weeks. Great luck! We also bought supplies in town and went to the movies. The kooky Laurel and Hardy that we saw, *Saps at Sea*, gave us the title for our log, outranking Bud's suggestion of *Travels with a Donkey*.

We spent another six days paddling north on Lake Champlain, heading for a farm above East Alburg on the Vermont-Canadian border where we planned to visit a Swiss family named Beck. We made a little better mileage without a river current, about seventeen miles a day. Milk shakes and cookies seemed to loom large whenever we bought supplies along the way. The weather was important, too. On July 8th, I find in my handwriting, "Muggy. Paddled sluggishly. M driving B remorselessly to small, buggy, shadeless island." Sounds grim! But by the end of that day we had paddled to the mainland and decided we deserved a fancy dinner, so we moved on to

Basin Harbor, an elegant resort, where we were hospitably invited to sit in the kitchen, the proper place for not very clean, casually dressed canoeists. Many years later, we were delighted to enter Basin Harbor's front door to attend a conference for New England utility regulators, ending with a banquet at which I sat at the head table next to the speaker, Vermont governor Snelling.

We had a few more days dealing with the vagaries of Champlain's weather. On July 9th, for example, we "went on during shower to Schyler Island. Last four miles riding before howling gale." On July 11th, "Continued to Blockhouse Pt.... made worst tent of trip – hurt B's camper's vanity. Brisk north wind gave us a billowy night." On the 10th we found shelter from the wind at a public campground outside of Plattsburgh, where we heard some of the most enduring quotes of the trip. A large family had established itself on a big campsite for the duration of the summer. We heard "Pop" come back from work at the end of the day, and we listened to his booming voice bring order out of his children's high-pitched chaos: "Pretty soon I'll come out there to make a fire that IS a fire." And later, when the hubbub was rising again: "You kids leave that popcorn alone. I'll do all the popping around here!"

The Swiss family Beck showed us other parenting possibilities. Our log says we made slow progress against a strong headwind on the 12th and (in Bud's handwriting) "Mims about to throw in the sponge when we hove in sight of the Becks who waved from the porch." Herr and Frau Beck and their two sons, Skip and Peter, greeted us with great enthusiasm, although we had never met them before. Skip had been Harry's roommate at Dartmouth and when his family heard the route of our canoe trip would take us more or less in their direction, they urged us to visit them. Herr Beck thought it would be "amoosin'" to entertain a canoeing honeymoon couple for a few days. We had agreed, judging rightly we would be ready for a change of pace by that time, even though East Alberg was a day or two out of our way. What did a few days matter on a trip that had no deadlines and not even a set destination?

We brought the Becks a melon, a Cuban Queen which we had bought in North Hero, big appetites and a week's laundry. They offered us much farm excitement: a colt born our first night there; a tame crow; and huge, delicious meals. We helped Skip get in the hay, and Frau Beck taught us a courting song, *"Deine Beine, meine Beine, unt' den Tisch."* On the afternoon of the 14th, we said goodbye and shoved off, never to see the elder Becks again. However, the next summer Skip Beck shared living quarters with my brother and us in Cambridge, where we were all going to Harvard Summer School, and the year after that, he was drafted into the army and, in early action, was killed.

We were relieved to be quit of the big lake's buffeting winds we struggled with until we reached Rouse's Point and went through customs into Canada. It was harder to find available tent sites on the Richelieu River that flows north out of Champlain and down from the heights to Sorel and the Saint Lawrence. Fortunately, the French-speaking farmers whose farms fronted on the river were very hospitable. Unfortunately, our French was none too good. Once when an older couple indicated with nods and smiles that we could pitch our tent in their front yard, we couldn't find adequate brush cover. I finally decided I must ask for bathroom facilities and explained to the woman of the house that I'd like to "*laver les mains.*" She brought me some soap and warm water in a basin. Months later we asked a Kent School French teacher what we should have said. Some years after that, in the Tuilleries, I remembered his answer, but judging from the wild laughter of the kiosk lady we were talking to, "*Ou est le chalet de nécessité?*" didn't cut it either.

CANOEING ON THE FARMINGTON: OPEN WATER

O.B.

The Richelieu carried us down to the St. Lawrence by way of the Chambly Basin. There we went through a series of small, cozy locks with wooden gates that were manually cranked open by man, woman, or child – whoever was at home in the little canal houses decorated with window boxes of bright red geraniums and blue lobelia. We could see very quickly that the Saint Lawrence was too big for us. We passed Sorel, which seemed all industry, "rusty D.T.s and grain elevators," thinking we could find an overnight cabin on its other side. "Instead – wound through maze of marsh into Lac St. Peter." a body of water with no solid ground on its shores that we could find. "Paddled on through darkness and flouzy grass for 20 odd more miles. Heard whistles, saw lights, encouraged. Soon arrived in channel. Large boats crossing, lights blinking, waves dashing, shoals shoaling. Quickly sought haven on sand bar. Tied up to bunch of grass and slept in canoe." Did the tide reach that far up river? We weren't sure. It was well past midnight and we had covered about 35 miles that day.

We woke to find Trois Rivières only six miles away across the St. Lawrence. There we whiled away some time, saw a movie, *Doctor Takes a Wife,* then got ourselves and the canoe on the 1:15 A.M. night boat to Quebec. "Taxied up hill to Governor's Garden Hotel. Homey place $3.00 a day. Sallied forth and bought B a jacket, shirt, 'n tie, M a skirt 'n blouse…HOT SHOWER…" and settled in for a week of civilized living.

QUEBEC, THE HONEST CITY

In Quebec, we saw for the first time that Canada was at war, and as we knew, had been since the previous September as part of the British Commonwealth. Early in June, the British had evacuated their beaten troops from Dunkirk and in July were watching Germans making invasion preparations and collecting ships to cross the Channel. In the middle of June, France had surrendered and was now an occupied country, so both of Canada's mother countries were in perilous condition. We were aware of this, and I was upset when I found myself asking for *"Ein Glas Milch, bitte"* when I meant to speak French. Would they think we were German spies?

Most of the time, however, we were typical oblivious tourists doing touristy things. We rented bikes, went to movies (*Blondi Brings up Baby* and

Moulin dans le Soliel). We took an excursion bus to Montmorancy Falls and to the shrine of Sainte Anne de Beaupré. It was at Ste. Anne's that we picked up another quote that became part of our household lingo. As we left the desultory blessing of the "souvenirs ceremony," one of the black-robed monks attached himself to me, asking where I went to school, what I was studying, etc. Bud wrote "Brother guide became enamoured of 'Meeriamm' and fairly drooled." Where was Bud when I needed him? I looked around to see and the monk asked, "Who's that?" When I answered, "My husband," the monk looked startled, veered away suddenly, wagged an admonitory finger at me and said, "Watch out for Plahto," – and I've been looking out for Plahto ever since.

At the end of the week, we packed our gear, collected our canoe, and boarded a ship going down the St. Lawrence to Riviere du Loup, where we intended to get ourselves overland to Edmunston and the Saint John River. Every trip has its low point, I guess, and this was ours. About 20 miles out of Quebec, we discovered we had left all except $5 of our money in our money belts hanging over the bedpost in our room at the Governor's Garden Hotel. There were no credit cards in those days, so we carried a good deal of money in the form of $100 bills on our persons, safe not only from thieves but also from a river disaster – enough, we thought, to cover the whole trip. We had grown careless in the city. At the first available port, we telegraphed back to the hotel, asking them to send the money, minus postage, to general delivery, and then we waited. Well, believe it or not, two days later, belts and money minus postage arrived intact and the crisis was over!

THE LAST LAP

Hearts light again, we arranged for the Lewisconata Railroad to add another freight car to carry our canoe and us on the next morning's run to Edmunston. The Saint John was much wilder than the waterways we had been traveling and the people of New Brunswick seemed wilder too. We had to dodge log booms and "intermittent rocks," and there were even some exciting rapids to shoot. At Great Falls, we "found a sleeping trucker to transport us down to lower flats" into some "swift current. We ticked off many miles

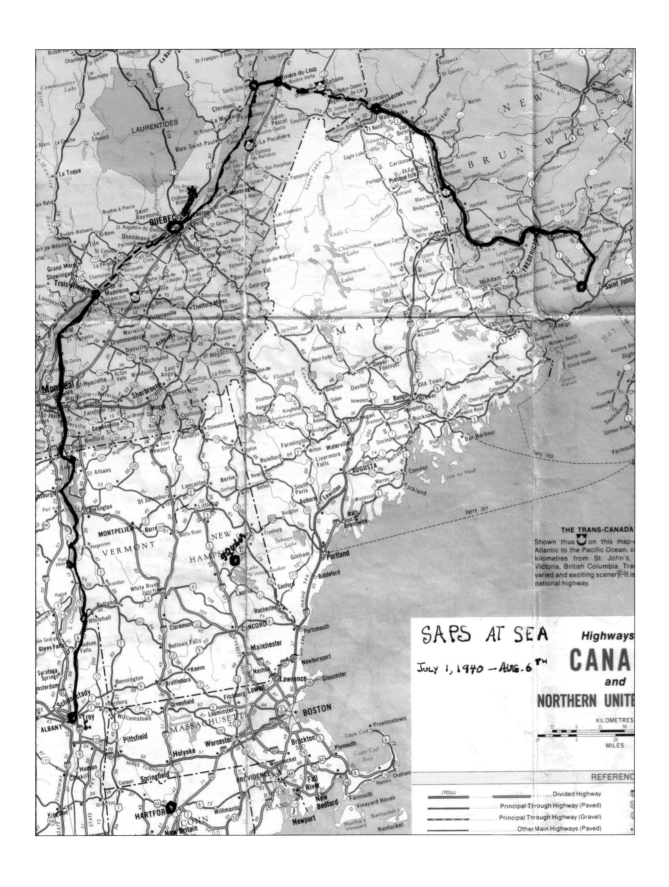

SAPS AT SEA

JULY 1, 1940 — AUG. 6TH

over Rapid des Femmes and other ripples. Made camp in perfect spot." We averaged about 30 miles a day on the Saint John unless the weather was bad. One morning we "woke to dubious day. Tent boisterous. Waited for further developments.... Tent finally blown completely off moorings so we started. Rain not far behind." And on August 1st, "Day consisted of dodging showers and eating cookies." That day we also "babied canoe over Meductin Rapids without trouble. Ended day with burst of sun, sky clearing and blessed calm – and cookies." At Andover we "found a whiskey-loving store keeper, an old time rider of log river rafts. Sold us some bees honey that 'eats good.'"And once we met two *courriers de bois*, speed demons, propelling themselves swiftly with short strong strokes. They obviously knew the country well, traveled at night, were not fishing, and spoke of their traveling as their job. Who were their employers and what were the messages they were carrying?

A common sight on the swift St. John River was the ingenious homemade ferry – a raft attached at both ends to an overhead cable and running on river power. The river end of the raft could be tilted by adjusting the two ropes. If made to head upstream at an angle, the raft would be pushed across to the other side by the strong current. Clever and inexpensive too. There were fish nets with little bells and once "a huge salmon leaped and fell back into the river like a boulder."

We took in a big summer fair in Fredericton and Bud won a tie clasp – for guessing his girlfriend's weight? Or hitting the gong in a test of strength? We were developing some pretty good muscles by that time. We also got a telegram in Fredericton's post office from Bud's father, setting August 6th as meeting time in Westfield, less than ten miles from the Reversing Falls and the Bay of Fundy and within easy reach for us. We still struggled with headwinds and significant tides, but on August 5th we "made Westfield, located R.R. station and good beach camp site just behind it. Set up good tent. Had canned steak and mushrooms and peas. No mosquitoes."

Bud's folks arrived at noon the next day: Uncle Paul, his wife Libby, and her 11-year-old daughter, Lucy. We arranged to send Uncle Corwin's canoe home by freight and packed our gear and ourselves into U.P.'s car, headed for Squam and a few weeks of debriefing and preparing for the next phase of married life. It had been a sweet five weeks. I don't remember any arguments or questions of who was boss or gender assignment of jobs. We took turns paddling stern and writing the log, and we worked together getting meals and putting up the tent. Neither of us panicked when we lost our money or the weather was rough. The purpose of a honeymoon, I suppose, is to create the intimacy and shared experiences that will carry you through early adjustments and the inevitable bumps of married life. It was an auspicious beginning.

```
Twenty-two years ago today
We started out(in an unusual way)
On an unknown river to unknown parts
And we didn't have much in the way
                              of charts
We followed wherever the river wended
On a little trip that never ended
taking turns at steering and towing
With vague ideas of where we were going
Even enjoying the wet and the hot
(It all depends on the partner you've got)
And playing together a funny tune
That if it never ends it will be too soon
Paddling in various kinds of weather
O thank  you for letting  us go together!
```

O.B.

CHAPTER 12

KENT

In September of 1940, we traveled over the Litchfield hills to the little town of Kent in Bud's old brown Chevrolet coupe, rumble seat packed with things I would need as the wife of a Kent School master. Bud had been a student there for his four high school years, and returned to teach when he graduated from college in 1937. Whenever school was in session, we lived at Kent for the first eight years of our marriage.

The town is on the east and the school on the west side of the Housatonic River where it is joined by the Macedonia Brook, flowing down a long, narrow valley from the west. Mount Algo and, a little further north, Skiff Mountain crowd the river at Kent, and it was at the foot of those mountains that Father Sill, a member of the Episcopal Order of the Holy Cross, started a boys' school in 1906. A number of boys' preparatory schools were started around that time, each with a distinctive identity molded by the strong and sometimes eccentric personality of its headmaster. Kent was probably the most rugged of them, a self-help school where the boys did most of the chores from those on the school farm to dormitory supervision. If rules were infringed, the miscreant was given hours of community service to perform, the community being the school, since contact with the town was strictly limited.

Father Sill's school was unique in another way. A persuasive idealist, he instituted a sliding scale of tuition payments based on ability to pay. Theoretically no one but "the old man" and the involved parent knew who was given a scholarship or who had been persuaded to pay more than the cost of his son's education. Setting a good example and molding a boy's character were Father Sill's aims.

But along with the emphasis on character there was a thinly disguised anti-intellectualism and, although many of the students went on to good colleges when they graduated from Kent, that seemed almost incidental and no great

Kent School chapel, under Mount Algo

achievement during the Depression years of the '30s. Five of the faculty, teachers of history, math, and English, had not even finished college. Father Sill recruited Bud in his senior year at Dartmouth to teach – well, he wasn't sure what would be needed, perhaps Latin, German, or English. He'd let Bud know when school started in September. In Father Sill's mind, any good man could teach anything. Bud had taken no German at Dartmouth. He'd had some Latin, but he majored in English. No matter. Bud joined the Latin Department right out of college and didn't get a chance to teach English until several years after I arrived.

Sometimes we found these Kent attitudes funny. One year someone thought it would be good to teach a little about Art. Bud had had an Art History course at college? The course was his! Once an engineering classmate of Bud's came back to a reunion, singing the praises of the head of the English Department. He'd been taught English Literature so well he hadn't had to read another book! But much of the time the prevailing attitude toward teaching was discouraging. A newly hired teacher with the elegant name of Smith Palmer Bovie joined the Latin Department the first year I was there. He later became head of the Classics Department at Rutgers, so Latin and Greek really were his specialties. He and Bud decided to make their courses more meaningful by adding some Roman history and culture to Caesar and Ovid. They worked hard on a detailed program and one night went off to present it at a department meeting. They were weak with laughter when they returned. The proposal had been turned down. One colleague said he liked to start on page one of Caesar and go right on through, and it was important that other classes were on the same page at the same time. Another argued that boys need discipline. Every other course they took had been made significant or amusing or exciting in some way. Latin was the only course left that was unspoiled. The whole value of Latin would be lost if it were made interesting! Bovie and Bud collapsed when they reached our apartment, but I thought I heard a catch of rue in their laughter.

The English Department wasn't much better. Bud was finally given some courses in that department, but he had to teach them the way the department head wanted them taught and that meant a big dose of grammar taught from a book that all other English departments in the country had given up as outmoded.

This sounds more dismal than it really was. Bud enjoyed teaching and I know he was good at it. He also liked coaching third and fourth formers, the beginners, in football which he never took seriously, and in crew. He had been on the famous Kent schoolboy crew that won the Thames Challenge Cup at the Henley Regatta in England in 1933, perhaps another reason Father Sill, an avid oarsman himself, had hired him. Eventually Bud outgrew the school where he had spent many of his formative years as a teenager and the eleven years of his first job. But, except for the last year or two when his frustration grew so large it began to affect his teaching and his peace of mind, Kent was a happy and productive part of his life

Father Sill, OHC
Founder of Kent School

AND WHERE DID I FIT IN?

Kent changed my life too. I was surprised to see Bud grow more and more nervous the closer we got to our new home that September day in 1940. Finally he blurted out, "You'll want to get a job. Why don't you volunteer at the library?" The library! I had visited Bud and the school the previous spring and had caught a glimpse of it. I thought it was hardly worthy of the name. One pitifully small section held a jumble of cast-off novels and non-fiction donated by various parents, and there was a larger area of huge tomes on church history and the lives of the saints and similar topics guaranteed to turn most schoolboys off religion – and perhaps reading – for good. What on earth could I do in a place like that? Besides, I had worked three years in Connecticut College's library and now wanted to work with people. "Don't worry about me," I reassured Bud, hurt that he lacked confidence in me. "I've never yet had trouble finding something I enjoyed doing." Famous last words! I should have appreciated his concern and his understanding of the situation he was getting me into.

Kent was a sweet little town in the '40s, a bit shabby as it was emerging from the Depression. The resident population was about 1200 with households scattered widely throughout the hills and valleys. The Center consisted of H. H. Taylor and Son's lumber yard and Casey's general store, where I would buy groceries and any thing else we needed. Across the street was a beautiful red railroad station needing paint, a small stone library, and a post office. There was a drugstore run by old Doc Barnham when I first moved to Kent, but neither he nor the store lasted much longer. There was a garage, an elementary school on a side street, and a town hall with a room large enough to hold town meetings. On the main street there were some stately old houses, relics of the town's early iron industry, badly in need of repair, and a church, a dark stone Episcopal one. That was about it!

We crossed the river and turned left onto the River Road that passed through the school grounds. At the school, on a rise to our right, was an impressive grey stone Norman chapel with a cloister in the rear leading to a tall bell tower. It cast a shadow over the other buildings clustered mainly on the opposite side of the road, and it reminded everybody that Kent was a high Episcopal school. I didn't think I would be involved in the school's religion, however. If Bud, with his Quaker background, could stand living and teaching there, I, who would have few school obligations, could stand living there too.

Our apartment was over the dining hall. It had three small rooms, a living room and narrow kitchen to the right of the entrance hall, and to the left, a bedroom just big enough for our double bed and two small chests of drawers. The bathroom was long and narrow and had a quaint claw-footed tub. Not palatial digs, but the living room faced northwest up the Macedonia Valley, a grand view. By winter, we discovered some drawbacks other than the size of our apartment. We were in the shadow of Mount Algo, rising steeply on our southwest, blotting out the winter sun about one o'clock in the afternoon, and the prevailing winter wind funneled down the valley straight toward that window with the splendid view. *Perilously cold*, wrote a Kent graduate of his year in the dining room dormitory. We lived there two winters, but that first September it wasn't the apartment that bothered me. Where was everybody? Where could I find a friend?

SETTLING IN

Boys' prep schools are havens for shy bachelors. Many of the older masters had eventually gotten up courage to propose to the nurse of the moment, but the older wives seemed seldom to emerge from their houses. Luckily, there were two friendly younger wives with families, and after about three weeks one of them suggested I start a nursery/kindergarten school since there was none in town. I jumped at the idea and soon had a class of five. The next year there were ten. I ordered a kindergarten instruction kit from the Calvert School in Baltimore, excellent imaginative material intended for missionary families and others in remote areas. It was made for us.

Since most of the children came from town, I made some new acquaintances and heard what was going on across the bridge. I joined the Kent Girls Basketball team, captained by Dirty Gertie Kerr, a great tough team that played boys' rules against other town teams. We even played the big city of Torrington. Later I joined the Kent League of Women Voters and the Visiting Nurses Association. And Kent School was beginning to change. Father Sill, who plainly didn't like women, had a stroke shortly before I arrived, and Father Chalmers, another member of the Order of the Holy Cross, had taken over as headmaster. Within a few years, there were a good many more newlyweds and young faculty families. We started our family too and I found friends.

To return to June of my first year, we said goodbye to Bovie and two other young Kent teachers who decided to enlist in the army to get their two years of mandatory service over with. The previous September, at President Roosevelt's urging, Congress had passed the first peace-time draft in United States history. We had become good friends with Bovie's fiancée and so were delighted when they were married during Bovie's first home leave. We counted the months till the fall of 1943 when they would return and we could resume our close friendship. How could we have been so hopeful!

*Bud, Mims and Doug,
on the road.*

CHAPTER 13

ON THE ROAD

Bud, Doug, and I had one more stimulating and carefree summer together, first at Harvard Summer School. There in Max Lerner's course we felt the tension between the isolationists lauding Col. Lindberg and his admiration of the German airforce, which looked to many of us like approval of Hitler's Germany, and those who supported President Roosevelt's Lend Lease program, sending arms to Britain on credit. It was in that class too that some of the audience expressed outrage when Lerner called J. Edgar Hoover, the powerful, irresponsible FBI chief, the nation's "cop." That was much too irreverent for them.

In August, the three of us flew from New York to Wyoming, where we met up with Bud's family, explored Yellowstone Park, climbed in the Tetons and visited some friends who owned a ranch near Jackson Hole. Our Connecticut friend, Retty Scott, while a student in Europe, had met and married Austrian Fritz Mueller. They bought the Jackson Hole ranch and Fritz, with a heavy accent and rather poor command of English, seemed to be in trouble with some roughnecks in town. He was an enemy outsider! He complained of harassment to the sheriff, who looked sympathetic and suggested that next Saturday night he go into town and "shoot it out." Ah, the wild west!

The three of us drove home in Uncle Paul's top-down touring car, camping, drinking milk shakes with a friendly Indian in Gallup, exploring Mesa Verde, Taos, and Santa Fe, glorying in our increasingly disheveled looks. Once at a gas station in Tennessee we were asked if we were with the rodeo in town! We were living Kerouac's *On the Road*, but for us it couldn't last. We got home and cleaned up, the men shaved off mustache and beard, Doug took off for his new job at Hotchkiss School, about forty minutes up the Housatonic Valley from Kent, and I announced to Bud it was time to have a child. He gave me the impression he was surprised to learn marriage might mean children too. Fortunately, he soon recovered and I made an appointment with a recommended obstetrician to get acquainted before I was pregnant, as the books I was reading said I should. Dr. Holt's reaction, when I told him my visit was just preliminary, showed me *he* hadn't read those books. He showed me out with a look of disgust and told me to come back when I really needed him.

We were reminded of an earlier doctor's visit before we were married that was more sobering. Again, following book recommendations, I went to my Windsor family doctor for advice about contraceptions. I was shocked when he said with emotion, "Why should I help you when that would risk my practice and might even mean going to jail? What are you going to do to change the law?" Eventually, after making his point, he relented, but he was angry because advice, sale, or use of contraceptives was still illegal in Connecticut. The previous year, police had arrested two doctors and a nurse for giving out birth control information and devices in a Waterbury clinic, a violation of an 1879 Connecticut law whose chief sponsor, by the way, was Bridgeport Representative Phinias T. Barnum. Not until 1965 did the Supreme Court make a decision in Griswold vs. Connecticut which knocked down the old Comstock Law banning contraceptives, declaring the law unconstitutionally invaded the privacy of married people. I like to think my old doctor is resting easy in his grave now that contraceptives are legally prescribed and bought even in Connecticut.

Picnic on an empty western highway, 1941

CHAPTER 14

CHANGES AT KENT

THE "GOOD" WAR

On a crisp bright Sunday, December 7th, 1941, Bud and I spent the day climbing Mount Greylock near Lakeville with Doug and some friends. On the way down the mountain, Doug and I had a chance to exchange some exciting personal news. I had just discovered I was pregnant and he was about to ask Betty Thatcher, a Philadelphian Quaker teaching at Westtown School in Pennsylvania, to marry him. It was a warm sibling moment, and the glow lasted as we made ourselves hot chocolate in his Hotchkiss School apartment and turned on his radio to listen to the Sunday afternoon New York Philharmonic Orchestra concert. That was the afternoon when nearly everybody's life was changed. We were just beginning to warm up when the concert was interrupted for the announcement that the Japanese had bombed Pearl Harbor.

Three weeks later, Doug and Betty were married, and in March they left Hotchkiss for M.I.T. Doug joined an Army Air Corps program from which he emerged a 2nd Lieutenant with a masters degree in Meteorology. He then went to flight school, became a pilot and joined the Air Weather Service. He had orders to go to the Pacific when the war was suddenly over. By that time, Doug and Betty had two children and had become accustomed (as if you ever could) to a dizzying peripatetic life style that, it seemed to us, made for an almost impossible family situation.

Bud's brother, Harrison, declared himself a conscientious objector to the war and spent several years in a camp for C.O.s in Durango, Colorado, where his new wife, unused to rough living, set up housekeeping and gave birth to their first child in a primitive nearby cabin. Our friend Bovie, like many others, had his two-year enlistment extended "for the duration." A few months before fighting stopped in Europe, Bovie's wife sent him a "Dear John" letter. She had met a prince from Baghdad while doing graduate work in landscape architecture and wanted to marry him. "You're a good man but he's a great one," Bovie reported the letter said, when he made a short visit to Kent after the war. His hair had turned completely white and he was nervously chain-smoking, dismayingly changed in those four years.

Our lives were much less affected by the war than those of our friends and relations. Not until the spring of 1944, shortly before I gave birth to our second child, did Bud get a notice from his draft board to report for a physical exam in preparation for induction into the army. He had registered as a partial conscientious objector, willing to be a medic and to drive an ambulance, but like a long line of Quaker Butterworths, would not carry arms. His father had taken the same position during the First World War. One family story told of an Ohio ancestor who lost his flock of Marino sheep for refusing to pay his taxes during the Mexican War of 1840.

Bud came back from New Haven with a 4F from the army examiners, rejected, they wrote, because he was unstable. Unstable! I never knew anyone more solid emotionally than he! Was that just an arbitrary excuse because they wanted only younger men? Bud was a hoary 29. Did they think he would do more good for his country by continuing to teach? Did they think labeling him emotionally weak would cause him future trouble and serve him right for being a CO? Whatever the reasons, I was grateful for what this meant for our personal future. Unlike many others at that time, we were able to create a family, eventually consisting of four children, under very normal circumstances.

On the home front, Bud joined the plane-spotters at Kent, learning to distinguish different profiles of planes and spending many cold mornings before classes listening for German bombers, ready to give the warning that New York and military targets were about to be attacked. Our neighbors were sure Kent was key to the defense of the country and that the enemy, who would inevitably fly through our valley, was on the way. Actually not even many American planes passed through. There was the occasional false alarm. Once Kent Smith, who taught math, took umbrage when someone stuck his head into a faculty meeting shouting "Kent is yellow."

Bud also worked summers as a volunteer orderly at Hartford Hospital, and we experienced the shortages everyone else did. We swapped ration cards with friends who drank coffee and, for local transportation, we bought a little Cushman scooter made for delivery men, to save gas. And in the first months of the war, we planned and watched over the construction of a minimum house about ten minutes up the river road, adjacent to a Kent School farm field for calving cows and their new-borns. In the fall, we would move in with a new baby.

Our Kent house, up the River Road, at the foot of Skiff Mountain – 1942

GIVING LIFE

Early morning on the Fourth of July, 1942, with a huge misty orange moon rising, we drove in our old Chevy coupe to the hospital where, some hours later, Michael was born. The "natural child birth" movement had not yet been heard of, so Bud was banished, told to go home and get some breakfast. This was women's work – or maybe doctors'. I was put to sleep and woke to find we had a baby boy. Michael and I stayed in the hospital ten days, as did most maternity cases in those days. At least my obstetrician was avant garde enough to get me out of bed almost immediately so I didn't become weak from bed rest, as did the other mothers I saw around me. While we were "recovering," nurses gave us lessons and practice in dressing and bathing babies, and making up a formula. I had decided to nurse Mike although given little encouragement to do so. In those days, wanting to nurse one's baby was a whim to be indulged, not considered a rational decision. With a formula in a bottle you know what your child is getting and how much. It can be measured. Nevertheless, I persisted and the ten-day hospital stay gave me confidence I was producing an adequate amount of milk to keep Mike alive and growing.

I suppose in the 1940s new mothers and their babies were unnecessarily coddled and some of the practices surrounding births needed to be changed, but at least then everyone acknowledged something important was happening. By the 1990s new mothers were being hustled out of the hospital within twenty-four hours of giving birth. Fathers may have more part in the process, but I sense the novelty of including men in the action is fading. Today this most significant and miraculous event seems to be treated by all but the immediate participants as a business, denigrated by insurance companies, doctors, and hospitals alike. I find this a bad sign because I believe the treatment of children in all their stages gives an important clue to the health of a society, and by that measure we are slipping.

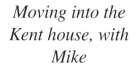

Moving into the Kent house, with Mike

AND THEN THERE WERE MORE

Bud had only a vague understanding of male and female roles. Uncle Paul had been mother and father to his children after their mother died when Bud was three. Bud knew how to cook, mend his clothes, and did his share of child-raising. Yet even with that support I felt a heavy weight of responsibility. Child rearing became my career for the next decade. I read Dr. Spock, took Red Cross courses in nutrition and First Aid, and copied my best friend's child rearing methods because she was so good at it. Benny and Mary Louisa Mattoon arrived at Kent with a two-year-old daughter and a baby boy about Michael's age just when we needed them. Mary Louisa and I did things together almost every afternoon, discussing children, talking about world affairs, gossiping, picnicking. She was a great model and a close friend, still making my memories of Kent rosy.

I realize how rare it is for modern mothers to have the kind of time and opportunities we had to concentrate on bringing up children. There may have been more physical work involved. There were no pampers or diaper services and no laundromats. I didn't have a washing machine until the war was over when Dan, our number three, was born. Even then there was no drier, just a wringer – two rollers that you fed the clothes through to squeeze out water. That was an improvement over bare hands, but the laundry still had to be hung out in all kinds of weather. I can see those diapers, hanging on the clothesline in winter, frozen stiff as boards but drying nevertheless. However, being on hand to observe and to be a part of a child's development was worth the effort.

MICHAEL

Mike was a great first child, interested is everything, and the teachers in us reveled. We read to him, showed him how things worked, encouraged his wonderful curiosity. So of course he was precocious, talking and reading early. He became a dinosaur maven at 4, correcting us when we mistook a Stegosaurus for a Triceratops, crying at Disney's *Fantasia* when the whole species met its end. On to Astronomy at 5, and beating us at chess not long after we taught him how to play. He was intrigued with numbers. "I was sitting on top of the slide (in a local playground) just thinking about 6 and 7 when..."

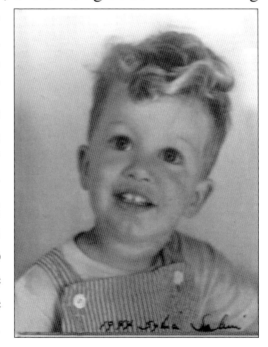

Mike seldom lied, but once when he was very young we caught him licking jam out of a jar. "My tongue bones got tired," he explained, winning the lifetime prize for outlandish alibis. He spent hours building with blocks, playing with a wooden train set, and making puzzles. In fact he was so much fun, we felt we could easily manage another. In May, before Mike was two, we had another son and named him Timothy.

TIMOTHY

Tim was mischievous, had red curly hair and a big appetite. He grew very quickly and too soon was crowding Mike's rightful place of first born. It was hard for our friends to tell which was the older. We had good advice from a pediatrician named Parker Dooley, whom Bud had known earlier when he was Kent School's doctor while Bud was a student. In the intervening years, Dr. Dooley had started a course for new fathers, encouraged Dr. Spock to write his first book, and become head of pediatrics at the University of Chicago. He fortuitously returned to the town of Kent when we were looking for a pediatrician. We cherished his advice. He urged us to give Mike the

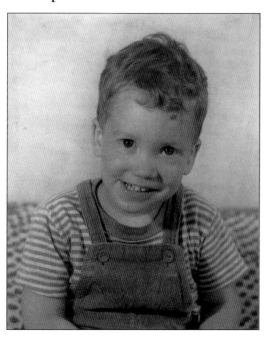

privileges of the older child, staying up a little later, for instance, doing things that Tim too would be allowed to do when he was older. A simple and effective suggestion!

Sometimes we needed more than a savvy pediatrician. At age one, Tim had a traumatic two-week hospital experience because of an inguinal hernia, the first of seven our children would eventually have to have fixed. Our West Hartford doctor advised us not to visit him during that time, as he would cry too much and harm the incision. Can you believe we did as the doctor suggested? His grandmothers did visit him, but that wasn't enough. Tim eventually got over the fear of being abandoned and regained his jolly nature, but it took a good deal of hugging.

Tim early showed unusual social awareness. For instance, when Dan, our third, was born, we needed an addition to our little red Kent house, but before the new construction was finished, we put Dan to bed in a small moveable crib in our bedroom until the two older boys were asleep. Then we'd wheel Dan into the kitchen and hope he would stay asleep through the early rising of his brothers so we could get some more rest. Mike and Tim, ages 4 and 2, were good at entertaining themselves, but Mike never learned to whisper and one morning I heard Tim say, "Shush Mike, or Mims'll come out wowing like a lion!"

When anyone really needed help, Tim came to the rescue. He still does. Also Tim was unusually eager to make things, and I tried to dream up projects to keep him busy. After finishing something, he'd come running with "What'll I do now. Mims?" After a while, I wasn't fast enough for him, and it was a great relief for us both when he discovered he could find things to make on his own. He is still doing that, too.

DAN

The 3rd time around, giving birth to Dan in May, 1946, and caring for him was easy enough, and he was to have been our last. By then I could nurse him while keeping an eye on the neighborhood: "Put down that stick, Billy. You'll poke someone's eye out." "Get away from that wall, children. You'll fall into the driveway." I could get dinner, cradling Dan in one arm while stirring the pot with the other.

Dan became the gregarious one. As soon as he was able to wander, he ran with a pack of neighborhood kids. From an early age he was a great entertainer. He would come into a room, pretend to stumble and land sprawling at our feet, or fall down the stairs so convincingly we would all come running. He was the one who experimented most and the one I worried most about. Some of his friends were not very savory: one from high school was a user and dispenser of drugs who died young; and, toward the end of his first year at Dartmouth, Dan brought his friends Sex and Rocky home for a wild Easter weekend, to mention just a few worrisome memories. He miraculously survived, bloomed late academically, graduated from Dartmouth, as did his two older brothers, and found a way to entertain a larger world. Now in his fifties, he puts on shows with his beautiful hand-made marionettes at the Newport Music Festival and Providence First Night, for example, and at the International Children's Festival in Hong Kong. He has

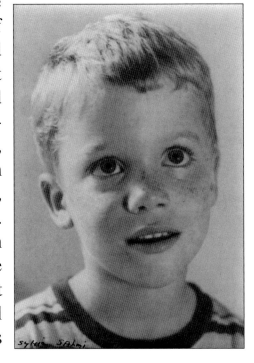

taught puppetry in Alaskan Eskimo villages and at numerous local schools. He is interested in many things, knows a lot about them – history, music, art – and is warmly affectionate with family and friends. Fun to be with.

THE END OF A CHAPTER

The summer before Dan was born, the devastating Second World War ended. Germany surrendered in May of 1945, and the war in the Pacific was obviously coming to an end, so instead of volunteering again as a hospital orderly that summer, Bud went back to Middlebury in Vermont to work on his masters degree in English. For years we had been following the news of raging battles, observers of a cosmic play whose outcome would impact us all: the London bombings, defeat of Rommel the Desert Fox, street-by-street fighting in Stalingrad, the siege of Leningrad, evacuation of the Philippines, retaking of Guam and Iwo Jima, and in August of that year, the dropping of a new kind of bomb on Hiroshima and Nagasaki. Daily shots of adrenaline. Then it was over.

Shizui Nishijima, a young Japanese American who was living with

Mike & Tim at Kent

the Paul Butterworths, was with me when we heard on the radio that Japan, the country of her ancestors, had capitulated. Early in the war, Shizui with her California family had been placed in a detention camp in the Tulari Valley where she had contracted Valley Fever. She needed a more healthful place to live and, through the efforts of a Quaker from the West Hartford Meeting, she joined four other teenagers in the P. Butterworth redwood house about 200 feet up a hill from our Sunset Farm home. There were Jean and Lucy, of course, and Molly and Joey Burns, English twins who had been sent to the U.S. to escape the German bombings – a lively household. Shizui, a few years older than the others, was a great addition. She was an American citizen, and her brother was fighting with the U.S. forces in Germany, but no matter. Her father, who had shown no evidence of disloyalty to his adopted country,

*Mike & Tim in
the Cushman,
Dan, Tim & Mike
on a fence*

lost everything the family couldn't take with them when they were suddenly evacuated from their home. This unjust disaster for the California Japanese was our gain. Shizui has been a caring and loyal friend, visiting at least once a year and rallying around whenever there has been a family crisis.

When the war ended, Shizui returned to California and the English twins to Oxford. Soldiers were coming back. Rationing and plane-spotting at Kent stopped. We could all concentrate on our everyday lives, and Bud's everyday life began to lose its appeal. Perhaps resuming his study of English at Breadloaf fed his frustration with his Kent classes. Perhaps the general lack of an outlet for his creativity discouraged him. Whatever the reasons, Bud wanted out. In June of 1948, we moved to West Hartford, not just for the summer but to stay.

I would miss Kent and friends. I'd miss the walks in the nearby mountains and the deer wandering past our house. I'd been putting down roots in Kent. In the winter of 1948, I'd begun to be politically active. The League of Women Voters pointed out that voting wasn't enough. To be a full citizen you should participate in a party where the really important decisions are made, so when we saw a notice of a Kent Democratic Committee Meeting, Bud and I and two other couples showed up. To our surprise, we outnumbered the regulars. Cap Harrington, the local chairman, and four of his cronies looked shocked and delayed the meeting till they could corral another friend. They then at least matched our voting power. The business afoot that evening was the election of a delegate to

*Shizui Dobashi and
Lucy Townshend*

~123~

the 1948 Democratic State Convention to be held in August in Hartford, and I ended up the alternate representing Kent. So that's how the system worked!

Also, after eight years at Kent, I knew who was having an affair with whom, who drank too much, how those in our little school community thought. A neighbor reported that Bud's department head showed up after going to the polls one election day looking dejected. He hadn't been able to vote all Republican but, he brightened, he'd voted all Anglo-Saxon. I would even miss conflicts with the school clergy. One year, Father Chalmers invited faculty wives to bring their children to a series of afternoon instruction sessions, and I took five-year-old Mike – once. Father Chalmers had a candle and a rose. He pointed out that the candle's purpose is to give us light and when it no longer does, we throw it away. He showed us the rose and said its purpose is to give us beauty, and after it wilts, we throw it away. He then jumped to humans and said our purpose is to love Jesus and if we don't, our lives are thrown away. Wait a minute! What about our Jewish friends, all those Muslims, people who have never heard of Jesus? I found myself explaining all this to Michael! How to confuse a five-year-old!

Yes, I would miss all that, and I wasn't eager to live full time at Sunset Farm. It seemed so ingrown: in-laws about 200 feet away, other relatives close by, and all presided over by a bunch of women who didn't have much to do but gossip. But it was obvious Bud needed a new start and I could do my job anywhere. So we said goodbye to the rural Housatonic Valley and our friends there and prepared to live in a very homogeneous suburban community.

MAUGHAM AND TOLSTOY

Bud went off to Breadloaf, Middlebury College's summer school, in June of 1948, to finish his masters degree, and I found I was pregnant. Any birth is a traumatic event, even under the best of circumstances. The first in the family is probably the most earthshaking. Michael's Fourth of July advent, for example, so sobered Bud I was afraid he was losing his joi de vivre. When Tim was born, Bud seemed unusually interested in the carefree young things living up the hill at his father's house. I must have looked matronly in comparison. We both took Dan's birth in stride. Number three evidently was just an expected part of life. But what would happen with unplanned number four?

~124~

I told Bud the news when he came home for a weekend visit and, in a series of letters during the next month, he described in his wonderfully articulate way, exactly what his reaction was:

Letter #1: *I was rather dazed by your startling news at first… Really it would be extremely selfish of me to be bitter about our newest venture…. It might even turn out to be that girl you were so sure of. So we can devote next year to creative effort. I will try to have a book while you have a baby.*

Letter #2: *By the end of the book, [Maugham] has adopted the philosophy that the meaning of life is not ideals, love, happiness, etc., but rather to be born, marry, have children, and die. Evidently it was possible to achieve some happiness in the process, but it wasn't part of the meaning. It is rather exciting at times to surrender yourself to the life force, and to realize that you are part of a continuing existence. I think I surrender to that more reluctantly than you do…. It is rather as if you had been sent to stud, and then sent back to the brood pen, and the sire is not expected to know or care what goes on after…. Our other babies were the result of conscious intent, and I was extremely aware of having begotten them; this time I can't seem to feel that way.*

Letter #3: *There's a full fat yellow moon just bulging up above the gap in the mountains. . . . I can't help the sensation of having been tricked out of something. But I must stop dwelling on this… I have been more and more sure since reading Tolstoy that what I need is more contact with the ground. Some livestock this fall will help but I would like to see us with a bit of pasture and arable land that we could get into….*

Kate was born the following spring, a girl child Bud felt particularly close to and for whom he provided a good deal of mothering. She was our last.

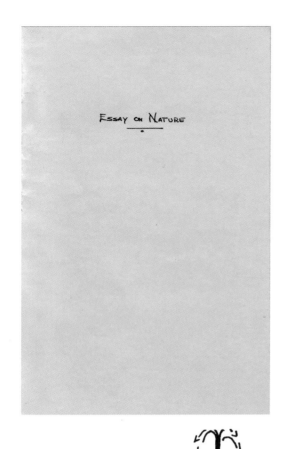

Essay on Nature

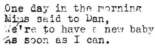

One day in the morning
Mims said to Dan,
We're to have a new baby
As soon as I can.

Dan told his brothers,
And they said, we know;
Dan told it to Bud,
And he said just, oh.

After it comes
Who will it be ?
Tim said to Dan,
Just wait and see.

Where will it come from ?
Dan asked him;
From Mims's stomach
Of course, said Tim.

But how did it get there ?
Tim only blinked.
Michael said NATURE---
That's what I think.

How did Nature get it
And put it inside ?
Nature just made it,
Michael replied.

Made it of oatmeal
Or whatever you like.
Nature is strong,
And clever, said Mike.

And what is this Nature ?
Dan said it was green.
Tim thought it a person,
And Mike a machine.

Volcanoes and earthquakes,
Said Mike, or an onion.
John Henry , cried Dan,
And Tim roared, Paul Bunyan!

It builds and it smashes,
Mike said with a whoop,
And Tim pounded cookies
And pears in his soup.

Mike cried, you're splashing!
And Tim said, of course.
Dan squealed, John Henry
On my Trojan Horse !

Mims cried, Enough!
And Bud growled, Oh stop.
Spare the remains
Of your poor mom and pop.

We'll answer your questions
One after the other.
Every life that begins
Has a father and mother.

The life that is started
Takes something from each,
And grinds them together
Like sands on a beach.

So all are a mixture,
No two are alike.---
It's good to be different,
More lively, said Mike.---

So the life that we have
Came to us from two others,
And theirs came to them
From their fathers and mothers.

And so on think backwards
For millions of years,
Past cavemen and monkeys
And huge megatheres,

And mammals and fish
To life's very start,
And each of us lived
In that first beating heart.

And how did life travel
From that time to this ?
'Twas the strangest of journeys,
On the spark of a kiss.

The children were nightclothed
And lured into bed.
Too late for more questions,
No more can be said.

At last they were folded
like the petals of flowers.
But Nature grinds on
Regardless of hours.

O.B.

CHAPTER 15

STARTING AFRESH

81 Sunset Farm Road, West Hartford, with additions

In the fall of 1948, we had a hen house with about six laying chickens. They came through the mail from Sears Roebucks as day-old chicks. And we built a sheep shed that housed five or six sheep. We had the chickens for maybe five years but our Dorset sheep for ten. Mike and Tim happily collected the eggs but not so happily helped clean the coop. Everybody liked the sheep, particularly at lambing season. We had so few we could make pets of them, even bringing them into the house to warm them if they arrived on cold winter days.

Six-year-old Mike started first grade at Sedgwick School with 700

other children from kindergarten through eighth grade, and he was overwhelmed. He got measles, mumps, and chickenpox that winter and brought them home to Tim and Dan. Bud erected a little one-room building behind our house which he heated with a potbellied wood stove and there he wrote his first book on his Royal typewriter, in spite of all the interruptions from animals and family. It was a novel about Kent School on the Adam and Eve and Tree of Knowledge themes, and it was rejected. He had sent it to Mr. Cloud, a friend of ours at the Atlantic Monthly Press, who sent it back with a gentle note saying, "Now that you've got your Kent School frustrations out of your system, write something else. Send the next book to us. We'd like to be the first to see it." That was encouraging, but Bud didn't feel confident enough to sit at his typewriter another winter. He took a job at Junior School, a private school in West Hartford Center, teaching third and fourth graders about Mike's age for two years. He identified with them and their interests and during Christmas vacation he wrote *The Enormous Egg*. The Atlantic Monthly Press accepted it at once, and it has become a children's classic, still in print, translated into a number of languages including Hebrew, Chinese and Japanese.

Sculptors Mike, Tim, & Dan

Bud also began to correct English papers for Laura Johnson, the remarkable president of Hartford College for Women. His corrections were evidently so satisfactory that Miss Johnson hired him to teach the courses she had been teaching. Bud had found his future. He wrote several other very good children's books, but he poured his heart into teaching Hartford College students for the next forty years and became a mainstay for Miss Johnson and the college.

KATE

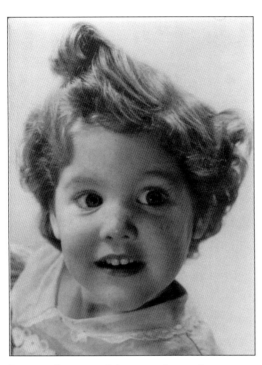

Our fourth child did turn out to be Kate, that girl Bud said I was hoping for, and she evoked some unusual reactions in all of us. When I first brought her home from the hospital, Mike heard her cry and rushed downstairs. He took a look at sibling number three and said with obvious disappointment, "Oh, I thought it was a lamb." However, a few years later he signaled his putting away of childish things and his love for Kate by ceremoniously presenting her with his two most precious possessions, a favorite small wooden pig and his security blanket, both somewhat the worse for wear. Tim quickly became her protector, especially from Dan, who teased her or ignored her unless there was no one else to play with. That sibling rivalry substantially subsided when Kate turned sixteen.

Kate, like Tim, surprised us by being a very curly redhead, making two out of four, with no other redheads in either of our families. Bud observed that I had at least been loyal in my way. She was a "going concern," as an older friend described her. When she was three, I funneled some of her energy into a home play group. Three mornings a week, five other three-year-olds, children of good friends, came to our house for several hours of "school." The mothers took turns spending the mornings with us, so I had adult company and also had the privilege of leaving Kate with one of the other families in between times if I so wished.

During her freshman year at college, Kate came home one weekend and told me she knew I loved her but hadn't found her as interesting

Kate's Doll House,
built by Bud

as the boys. Besides I hadn't paid enough attention to her as she was growing up – too many committee meetings, too many causes. (She doesn't remember this conversation.) I admit I found the boys easier to bring up as adolescents than she was. They liked to *do* things while she and her friend, Carol, seemed to hang around waiting for

something (boys) to show up. A long time later I discovered those two had made up an intricate language and elaborate religion for themselves while they were "waiting." Now I find her wise, strong, perceptive about herself and others, good company, and, as icing on the cake, uncommonly beautiful.

As for committees and causes, she may have had a legitimate complaint. I became active in the West Hartford League of Women Voters and once spoke at the state legislature against the law forbidding the sale of yellow margarine in Connecticut. "Mrs. Oleoworth Speaks For Margarine." That didn't take up much of my time, but when Joe McCarthy came along with his fake list of 205, 81, 57, or "a lot" of communists in the State Department, I saw him as a demagogue, destroying lives through irresponsible accusations and violating our country's most precious First Amendment principles. It was time to take a stand, as I had vowed after my summer in Hitler's Germany. The League, too, saw McCarthy a menace to our political and social fabric, and by the fall of 1953, I had become chair for the West Hartford League's national item on Civil Liberties. I organized and gave speeches, and our home conversations must have revolved around the McCarthy phenomenon, not our children's problems, for the next two years.

The full roster, 1951

You have gone through thick and thin
Held in thrall by Yang and Yin;
Under Celtic Mistletoe
You have borne my connubial woe.

The family tree has grown, of course,
Bowed beneath the grim Life Force;
Various conjugal pursuits
Have yielded all these sundry fruits.

With so much produce on the vine,
Dare I be your Valentine?

O.B.

CHAPTER 16

SPEAKING REASON TO THE WHIRLWIND

It wasn't until we visited my brother and his family in Arlington, Virginia, several months after McCarthy began his tirades, that I got a clear understanding of what was happening. At that time, Doug was working in an operation evaluation group for the Navy. The Brookses invited their next-door neighbor in for dinner, and sometime during the evening we began to talk about McCarthy. "The only communist I know," I started to say, "is our cousin, Bud McM…" when my brother interrupted. "I haven't been in touch with him for years," he said with what sounded a lot like panic. I began to express surprise and dismay when the neighbor, an up-and-coming State Department employee, broke in. "Mims, you don't understand. We can't know a communist cousin and keep our jobs. We can't be in contact with anyone who even sounds like a fellow traveler or we're vulnerable. Our careers can be ruined."

I told them I thought they were out of touch with people outside the beltway. They were too close to the action of a small group of fanatics and didn't realize that the people in the rest of the country were steadier and wouldn't support McCarthy's bullying for long. "Go home and ask the people you meet what they think of McCarthy," the neighbor challenged me. "Find out how much support he has." I did and was shocked to find our Washington friend's concerns were only too valid. So McCarthy did ruin a few reputations and denied the accused due process, so he did name the wrong person sometimes, so he took the law into his own hands and violated the Constitution occasionally, "Where there's smoke there's fire." "If you aren't one of them you don't have to worry." Many of the people I spoke with had decided the intimidation of these people whose beliefs were "wrong" was worth the loss of our freedoms, freedoms we took so for granted that we had forgotten their value, freedoms I suspected we didn't understand very well anyway.

One opportunity I had to sample opinions was at Connecticut College. I had been elected an alumnae representative to the Board of Trustees for a five-year term beginning in the fall of 1950, corresponding exactly with the rise and fall of Senator McCarthy, and his shadow fell across every meeting of the Board during those years – at least over the elegant luncheons President Rosemary Park hosted at her house before each monthly meeting. The Board was made up of diverse and sometimes illustrious members. The chairman, William Putnam, a prominent Hartford businessman, would soon have a bridge over the Connecticut River named after him. There were Dr. Allen, chief administrator of Hartford Hospital; Professor Morganau, head of Sloan Physics Laboratory at Yale; Bernard Knollenberg, Yale Librarian; Benjamin Wright, president of Smith College; and Anna Lord Strauss, president of the National League of Voters, to name a few. One of the most interesting members was Helen Buttenwiesser, one of Alger Hiss's lawyers, who was vainly trying to find new evidence to persuade an appeals court to grant Hiss a new trial. Hiss had been convicted of perjury in a case that catapulted Richard Nixon into the Senate and convinced many that there were or had been subversives in the government. This case was used as justification for McCarthy's continuing hunt for dangerous people with dangerous ideas. Poor Miss Park spent a good deal of her time at her luncheons keeping various factions apart. Some wanted to hear from Mrs. Buttenwiesser how her client was faring and what luck she was having. Others were suspicious of her for her obvious belief that Hiss was innocent. He had been in on the formation of the United Nations, hadn't he? That made him untrustworthy from the start.

You might think the issue of subversion among faculty and students at a small college like Connecticut wouldn't raise its head, but in those parlous days, no educational institution felt immune from the rage to root out unpopular ideas. Of course, the more prestigious universities were more newsworthy and therefore more vulnerable. William Buckley, a friend and strong supporter of Senator McCarthy, produced *God and Man at Yale*, an early example of the kind of attacks colleges could expect. The questioning of Harvard faculty members by McCarthy's Senate Investigation Committee made big headlines. Bill Buckley's sister, Aloise Buckley Heath, who lived in our home town, sent a letter to all Smith College alumnae, urging them not to contribute to the annual fund until the college rid itself of several "pinko" faculty members she had disagreed with as an undergraduate.

The Connecticut College faculty had some information that led them to think they and our college might be next. One of McCarthy's staff was a C.C. alumna who, as an undergraduate, had disagreed violently with the head of the Government Department. She leaked the news that the Investigating Committee had its eye on us. At the next trustee meeting, President Park read a statement from the faculty describing how they intended to respond if and when investigators for McCarthy began to investigate them. The statement said, in effect, that the professors planned to answer all questions about themselves, their affiliations, associations, and ideas, but would refuse to answer questions about present or former colleagues and students. Those who signed the document said they were taking such a stand in the interest of academic freedom. There was a minute of silence broken by Chairman Putnam, who scoffed, "There's no such thing as 'academic freedom'," and what followed was the liveliest trustee meeting of the decade. Fortunately, McCarthy and his committee were busy with bigger game and never did find time to disrupt Connecticut College. By the end of my term on the Board, the Senator and his committee were discredited and the search for subversives was essentially over.

LET'S TALK ABOUT IT

I volunteered to head up the League of Women Voter's study of civil liberties. We asked six of our friends in different sections of town to host a series of neighborhood meetings to discuss the League's publications produced for its Freedom Agenda. All during the winter of 1954, we spent two and sometimes three evenings a week on the town, and by "we" I mean at least two League members, a moderator and a resource person. Well, actually the "we" often meant Bud and me. How lucky we agreed and cared strongly about many of the same things! Bud not only filled in when I needed him that winter but he left for posterity his book, *The Enormous Egg*, in which Nate Twitchell from Freedom, New Hampshire, thwarts Senator Granderson, Bud's great caricature of McCarthy, in his attempt to get rid of Nate's pet dinosaur, Uncle Beazley.

We talked with these neighborhood groups about the rise of constitutional governments and the limits of authority granted governments by law, about the concept of an open society which depends on freedom of speech, press, and assembly, and the threats to that kind of society by the various investigating committees the congress had formed. We asked what purposes such committees had and which purposes were legitimate, which were not. We discussed the struggles throughout history to create a fair and equitable system of justice, considering habeas corpus, due process, the right to a speedy trial, and the reason the military had been made subordinate to civil authority. We talked about the damage some investigating committees were doing to our democracy by meting out punishment without observing due process safeguards, contributing further to a fear of unorthodox ideas and unconventional people.

And there in a conspicuous spot at most of our meetings was Aloise Heath taking names. "Now do you all agree with that?" she would ask, pen and notebook at the ready, as we came to a consensus on some idea. She was doing her best to intimidate us and thus scuttle the League's project. Fortunately it didn't work. Neighbors came back in following months to continue studying the rest of the Freedom Agenda pamphlets, and the talk was vigorous, thoughtful, and civil. I remember one dramatic meeting at the home of a friend who had invited a new guest to join her neighbors. He was a relative who worked for the FBI. We were discussing the McCarren Act, the Internal Security Act of 1950, which in one section provided for placing in detention camps persons deemed dangerous to national security in times of national emergency. The FBI man made the mistake of calling the proposed camps "concentration camps" and then, reacting to our strong response, corrected himself. "Detention camps, I mean." "Oh, why didn't you say so then," someone said, seemingly satisfied, but most of us wondered who, in a period of hysterical predictions of disaster, would decide when we were in a state of "national emergency" and who would decide which of us was "dangerous."

Senator McCarthy didn't disclose a single unknown communist, but he did discredit the army, undermined our foreign relations, arbitrarily and illegally declassified classified material, planted the seeds of distrust of government, and eroded our democratic processes and civil liberties. You expect to meet up with characters in political life who will do anything to gain power. It's when a large part of society listens to and agrees with them that you worry.

Did our work that year help our country understand better the nature and value of our traditional freedoms and the threats to those freedoms? We had at least introduced some rational debate into an exaggerated and frenzied view of national security dangers. The League reached quite a few people throughout the country and, as a result, more may have been ready to believe what they saw in the 1954 televised Army vs. McCarthy hearings – a bullying, irresponsible, and dangerous senator, with his unsavory aides, attacking innocent people and valued institutions that got in his way. The mood in the country *did* change, and the Senate finally got up courage to censor their fellow senator. The witch-hunt for subversives subsided, and Bud and I decided we could relax and enjoy a sabbatical year abroad without worrying about the fall of democracy at home.

CHAPTER 17

SUMMERS

None of our four children fits easily into the suburban society they grew up in. They say they were "saved" by the summers we spent at our cabin on Squam Lake in New Hampshire and by the trips we took together. Because Bud taught, we all had long summer vacations, and as soon as school was out in June, we drove north. In the '50s, it took us seven hours to get to our primitive homestead, so we didn't go back and forth very often. We would stay until school opened in September, and our lives there were down-to-earth rustic. We had and still have no running water. We have a privy off in the woods, and we get spring water to drink as well as "walking water" for kitchen use. Someone fills a tank on the outside of the main cabin with pails of water from the lake and, thanks to gravity, water comes out of the faucet at the inside sink. We heat and cook with wood, which means someone must keep the kindling box full, and everyone helps gather, saw, and split larger wood to stack in the woodshed till needed.

We have by this time five sleeping cabins scattered along paths leading away from the main cabin, three of which were built as coming-of-age projects by our children when they were about thirteen years old. They would pick and clear a spot, order the lumber, and build their building according to plans they designed. Bud was ingenious at convincing us that even doing chores was an adventure. Although one or two of our children went through periods of wanting speed and noise, they all settled for the silence and self-propulsion of canoes and now persuade *their* children that motor boats are "square" and canoes and kayaks are the real cool fun.

Our Squam summers were full of climbing, swimming (no breakfast till you had your dip), picnicking, entertaining (the usual number at meals was fourteen or fifteen), and making home movies with plots. The children

Squam
Summers

The Oregon & Santa Fe Trails

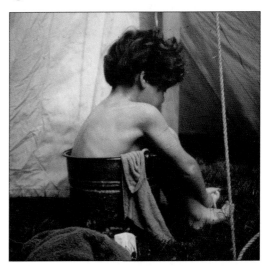

Leaving for the Oregon Trail

always triumphed in those movies, whether they were about Indians, pirates, the first day at school, or hunting a mad mountain man. As the children grew up, we square danced every Friday night in a nearby town in a real barn. We learned you can make do and have fun with very little, a helpful lesson for Dan, who worked in Quaker-sponsored work camps in Poland and Hungary in the summer of 1967, and Tim who taught in Bolivia in the '70s, both able to take crude living arrangements in stride, and especially Kate, who brought up her family in Mexico, often in primitive conditions, without complaining.

Wonderful as our New Hampshire summers were, we sometimes ventured farther afield. In the summer of 1953, we traveled west in a too-small Jeep station wagon, exploring Mark Twain country, visiting the Mormon headquarters in Nauvoo, where Bud and I declined to be "sealed for eternity," then following the Mormon's long march to Salt Lake City, where we had a much-needed change, living for a while with the Parmalees, Bud's sister Dinny and family. Resuming our trip, we drove and walked along the Oregon Trail, sometimes on the very ruts worn into soft sandstone by covered wagons passing through the plains over a hundred years before. We put up tents in the Sierras at the site of the Donnor party's disaster and traveled down the Pacific coast, stopping at the Corwin Butterworth's almond ranch and visiting our Nisei friend, Shizui, in Los Angeles.

We started east by way of the Santa Fe Trail. To be honest, I had too much togetherness that summer. Each day we made breakfast, struck camp, drove about five hours, stopping every hour to throw frisbees or play kick-the-can or have lunch, and before night fell we would find a good camping spot, make supper, up tents, and totter off to bed. It was the five hours cooped up in the Jeep that was murder – too much energy, too little space. Once at 2 A.M. while camping on a Blackfoot Indian reservation, I found myself warming a bottle of eardrops in my armpit to treat our four-year-old's earache, understanding all too well the worries of those earlier pioneer women, trekking westward away from all they knew, nurturing their families through anxious months of a dangerous journey, heading for an unknown future.

The trauma couldn't have gone very deep with me, however. Two years later, we eagerly set out on another considerably longer and more ambitious trip – this time to Europe for a year and a summer.

CHAPTER 18

THE GRAND TOUR

We flew in a prop plane from New York to Manchester, England, on June 12, 1955, with seven pieces of luggage and six handbags to last us for fifteen months of wandering. We had sent some camping gear on a Cunard ship that we would pick up somewhere when a strike against Cunard was settled. The flight was long, hot and uncomfortable, and in Manchester we waited, dazed and disoriented, for a train to London that might go sometime that afternoon in spite of the ongoing strike of the British Railway workers. This sounds like a bad beginning, but we recovered soon after reaching London, which we explored for ten days while waiting for the Volkswagen bus we had ordered to arrive.

Timing is all important for such a venture. Parents have to be young and strong enough to cope, and children have to be young enough to want to stay more or less with their families, yet old enough to get something out of new and strange surroundings. We weren't sure 13, 11, 9, and 6 were the right ages, but now all four say they thrived that year. We did realize when we started

Departure – Uncle Paul, Dan, Bud, Tim, Granny Brooks, Kate, Grampa Brooks, and Aunt Libby in Hartford

that we would be thrown on our own resources and would end up friends for life when we returned to the U.S., or never want to see each other again.

Two other factors of timing we were faced with that year. We arrived in Europe just ten years after the end of World War II. Emotions were still high, much destruction was still evident, and people were poor, struggling to get their countries and themselves back on their feet. From the uncleared rubble we saw in London to the hissing we got in Narvik, Norway, in August of 1956, when we broke out our new Austrian Loden jackets that made us look like a small invading German army, those terrible war years seemed very much present. The VW bus we had picked up in London was a novelty and a German one at that. Not very smart! However, most of the time we were easily spotted as Americans and reaped whatever gratitude or hostility America's current policies were causing or that American soldiers had sown during the war. We also found extremely favorable rates of exchange that year wherever we went. The U.S. had not yet devalued its currency or gone off the gold standard, and we spent less, in spite of all the traveling we did, than we would have if we had stayed home.

THE BRITISH ISLES

The plan we had dreamed up back in Connecticut was to live a while in small villages in various countries, keeping house in whatever accommodations we could find, thinking we could get a taste of different cultures that way. So that first summer, in addition to spending large stretches of time in Slindon, Sussex, imposing on our friends, the Tyrrells, we lived in a croft in the Highlands of western Scotland for three weeks, in view of the Summer Isles – McLeod country. The village had three households, two childless couples in their '60s and a younger family with two young sons. Dolly McLeod's first words when she met us at her doorway, scowling, with arms akimbo, were, "Can you keep your children

Michael and Doris Tyrrell and Kate in Slindon

Camping on moor near site of Lorna Doone

quiet on Sundays?" We looked at our poor weary children and thought we could. Dolly relaxed, welcomed us, and became such a good friend that we had trouble paying our rent when we left.

Strict Presbyterians, Dolly and her husband, Donald, worked hard all week and *rested* on Sundays. Dolly and I shared her kitchen and there was no cooking on the Sabbath. But during the rest of the week, we tried to live their life, brought in peat for their stoves, helped rake up hay into coils before a thunderstorm, joined a larger community to gather in sheep for the annual dipping, and made life-long friends, not only in our village but in a neighboring one, equally tiny, a mile and a half along Loch Broom by cow path. We were plied with vegetables from the McLeod's garden and given milk from their cow. All very pastoral, but winters must be desolate, I thought. During the sheep-dipping, I asked the other Mrs. McLeod, wife of a retired Glasgow policeman, if she missed the city. "Oh, I have my piano," she answered. How exciting! I imagined Mozart or Chopin or perhaps some lilting Scottish folk songs to brighten up those long winter evenings, and I reported the conversation to Dolly. She snorted and said, "Precious little music comes out of that piano. She doesn't know how to play!"

In Ireland we lived for several weeks in a converted store in Spittal, a few miles from Galway. Colin Tyrrell, Dan's age, went with us, seeing his

The McClouds, in Culnacraig ~ sheep-dipping, coiling the hay before a storm

~143~

"Dun Angus" loading for Aran Isles

father's homeland and visiting two of his uncles for the first time. We made friends with Moire Kyne, a wild looking young woman who sold us potatoes and carrots. She brought the vegetables, freshly dug from her garden, in a tote bag, all mixed up with her rosary. She went with us on a trip down Galway Bay and exclaimed at sight of the breakers crashing on the rocks, "Holy mither of God, wouldn't it take the heaarrt out of you!"

One day we took the *Dun Angus* to the Aran Islands, O'Flaherty country, and we saw another aspect of Ireland, a true community that watched out for its own. We gained status with our jaunty cart driver when we agreed to eat dinner at "Mrs. O'Flaherty Pat's" guest house instead of the big hotel. She had prepared a good dinner the previous day, he told us, and none of the tourists had stopped. She wouldn't be able to make ends meet that way, and he obviously cared.

Irish customs and people, at least those on the mainland in Galway County, seemed almost the opposite that of the Highland Scots we had been living with. Men stood idly on street corners, and Sunday was the time to have a good time, meeting friends at pubs, drinking and singing. No reading the Good Book and taking long quiet walks. The Highland Scots and Galway Irish understood each other's Gaelic, but their divergent religions and historical experiences must have made the difference. The Scots had more or less kept their independence, and they boasted of their countrymen who had ruled Britain and the Empire: Ramsey MacDonald, for instance. "He's a guid mann. He eats his porridge!" But the Irish were still speaking bitterly of three hundred years of occupation.

Stonehenge

STRANGERS IN A STRANGE LAND

It was in France we put down our deepest roots that year, staying four months in one village and one month in another. We heard about a place where we might spend the winter from Mme. Trocmé who ran the hostelry we stayed in at Versailles. She and her family had spent vacations in a farmhouse near Lake Annecy in the Haute Savoie, about 50 miles from Geneva across the French border, and she thought it would be available during the off-season. Should she write and inquire? She did and it was. A casual way to find lodgings for six for the winter? Well that was the way we traveled all that year with a few exceptions. We did write ahead for reservations in several cities, for ferries, the Channel crossing, and a February trip to Egypt and Greece where we put ourselves in the hands of The American Express. Otherwise, at tourist bureaus, railroad stations, or maybe a store in a village we liked, we would ask what kinds of accommodations were available, and invariably we found adequate housing.

So in October we found ourselves in Les Moulins, a small medieval village. Most of our neighbors washed their clothes in the public fountain which froze and cracked that winter, the coldest in fifteen years. The village was nestled up against the wall surrounding Saint Bernard's castle. Whenever we used our privy, we could look up at the red-roofed, turreted feudal residence from which St. Bernard escaped the night before his wedding. We stayed in Les Moulins from early October through December and again for a month in the spring, long enough to break through the French suspicion of strangers.

The first to befriend us was Nadia Molino, a little older than Kate, and soon her parents and brother followed. Mr. Molino, an Italian Communist, had left Italy after the war to find a job.

Les Moulins, Chateau St. Bernard

He worked in a factory in Annecy and was the best friend of the one aristocrat in the village, Madame Gavriloff, a countesse, our next door neighbor. Her father had been the French ambassador to Switzerland, and she had married a nephew of the Tsar. She told of escaping from Russia with her two little children during the 1917 Revolution and of the hard times she had experienced since. She certainly seemed poor. The black stockings she wore as she walked her little dog were held together with a mass of darns, and she hadn't paid her rent for two years. Monsieur Gris, another neighbor, her young landlord, a former peasant and now a factory worker and the proud owner of the first washing machine in the village, couldn't put Mme. Gavriloff out of her apartment because of French housing laws, but no rent for M. Gris, no mending of the leaky roof for Mme. G. The gloom of her kitchen on a cold winter night with frost on the inside of her door latch and a big black sooty puddle under her coal stove was something out of Dostoyevsky. The Molinos had befriended Mme. Gavriloff, although they had little in common but humanity. She was ashamed to tell us her daughter was working as a governess, a terrible blow to her aristocratic pride, and she once told us that France hadn't been happy since she'd lost her kings.

We spent a memorable New Years Eve that winter. Until midnight we were with the Molinos in Annecy, where they had recently moved. There were several other guests, an Italian with a story similar to M. Molino's ("No jobs in post-war Italy"), and an amusing Spaniard who had slipped over the frontier to escape Franco. We ate cake and drank coffee and heard about the Spaniard's sister who had starved to death and father who had died in prison. "Why does America help Franco, *le dictateur*?" The Spaniard also livened up the party by graphically and hilariously mimicking the way tourists of different nationalities walk.

We left the Molinos a little before midnight and hurried back to Les Moulins to check on our children and then celebrate more of the New Year with Mme. Gavriloff and her governess daughter. We ate off much-mended delicate doilies "a delightful banquet of jellied vegetables, fruit, tea cakes, etc." to quote from Bud's journal, and talked about the French and the Germans: how the Vichy government had been prodded by the German invaders to fight the *Maquis* just up the road toward La Clusaz, and about the revenge taken on some of the French collaborators, Vichy officials, assassinated in Annecy during the months of chaos at the end of the war. And we discussed Mme. Gavriloff's favorite American book, Kenneth Robert's *Northwest Passage*.

LEARNING TO FIT IN

At first, while we lived in Les Moulins, we held morning classes for our children, but after a month, Nadia took Kate with her to school in Menthon, a quarter of a mile away. (Les Moulins was purely residential.) She learned to read and write in French before she mastered those skills in English. Dan also went to school in town, but only in the afternoons and then only for a month. The Menthon school consisted of two classrooms, one on each side of the town hall. Kate's room was for five to eight-year-olds and Dan's side had pupils up to age twelve. Older children went to Annecy, about five miles north at the end of the lake. We too went to Annecy when Menthon couldn't supply what we needed (a bank, garage, department store) to find household goods like sheets. For our daily needs we struggled to find our way around the little town of Menthon, which boasted a *boulangerie, charcuterie*, a small *epicerie*, and a *Bureau de Poste*. Our high school French courses hadn't taught us words for keeping house, so we lived on soup, bread and cheese until I learned to cope more competently. Once, Bud returned from the store where he'd gone for some eggs, upset because I'd told him to ask for a dozen bears.

Eventually we made quite a few friends. Boys Dan's age, who at first shouted *"Vous avez le derrière du bison"* at us, joined us in our afternoon soccer games, other children roller skated with us and played dolls with Kate. We were even occasionally invited into neighbor's houses for tea or an evening of talk, but most of the time we provided our own diversions. Christmas took all the ingenuity we could muster. Tim and Dan started us off on the first of December by making a candle stand for our kitchen table with three candles stuck into a piece of firewood draped with fresh green holly. There was mistletoe hanging on trees in our back yard and wild red-berried holly for the picking beside the castle wall and we made a wreath. Papa Noël showed up at Kate's and Dan's

Having a look at our next location in the Alps

schoolrooms, bringing presents – puzzles for the boys and dolls for the girls. Kate's good friend Michou got a doll, answering a question Kate had. Well, you couldn't tell by the clothes young children wore or by their unisex haircuts. They all wore blue smocks on top of long warm pants and sturdy boots.

Packages arrived from home and we cooked up a grand banquet for Christmas Eve. We'd found a turkey in Annecy and, since we had no oven, we persuaded the Menthon baker to let us use his after he had finished baking the bread for the day. We paraded the steaming bird through the town back to our farmhouse apartment, ate till we were stuffed, opened presents, sang some songs, played some games and thought longingly of home. Fortunately, we had several things to celebrate. On December 24th, the mailman, wearing his usual black cape and with his moustache dripping in

Tim with broken leg, La Clusaz

the mist, brought us our first copy of *The Enormous Egg.* We were impressed and proud, although in his journal Bud says only, "The book came today – so long since I wrote it, it's an old story." Also, we were planning some new adventures. We would spend January at La Clusaz, a French Alpine village where we'd have lots of skiing and not much tutoring, and in February we would take off for warmer climes – down through Italy to Naples, across the Mediterranean to Egypt, across the eastern Mediterranean to Greece, and back to Naples where we would pick up our car, explore what we hadn't already seen in Italy and maybe Spain, if we had any energy left, and then return to our Les Moulins apartment, probably in April. For the next week we organized and packed, put mothballs in things we could leave behind, wrapped the apartment's water pipes against the cold, told our neighbors we'd see them again soon and, on the 4th of January, took to the road again.

OUR EXOTIC WINTER

Our children were great traveling companions, full of curiosity and inventing lots of ways to make our journeys fun. Of course, we had problems. Tim broke his leg one week into our January ski vacation and missed three glorious weeks on the slopes. He hobbled through Italy and Egypt on an uncomfortable walking cast until we had a private ship ceremony and threw what was left of the cast into the Aegean Sea on our way to Greece. Some of us got stomach troubles and colds, and everyone but Kate got seasick crossing the Mediterranean. Tim was bitten by a jelly fish in Scotland and went to bed for a day. By the second summer, Kate was bored with her clothes and wanted to go home. And once at a campground in Sweden, Lewis Taylor, a West Hartford neighbor and good friend of both Mike and Tim who joined us for the last month and a half of our trip, persuaded Tim to chew some wet tar they found beside a newly paved road. Tim's mouth shut so completely we wondered if he'd need intravenous feeding for the rest of his life. Finally, Bud did some delicate work with a toothbrush dipped in kerosene while we prayed Tim's tooth enamel wouldn't come off too. Fortunately, the only lasting damage was one ruined toothbrush and quite a few frayed nerves.

Most of the time, however, spirits were high. Mike traveled with his head out the VW sunroof in good weather, coming down like an echo to point out a castle or blossoming chestnut tree just seconds after we'd commented on it inside. Once, he pulled his head in and said with surprise, "I think my voice is changing," a full month and a half after the rest of us had noticed. He also came up with a lasting family saying. One bright morning, Bud and I were arguing about something when Mike, looking straight ahead, inter-

rupted with "Isn't the moon beautiful." And in Egypt, he seemed particularly excited by Muslim architecture with its minarets where muezzins called the faithful to prayer.

Egypt was pretty exotic for all of us. Just watching the multitudes thronging the Cairo streets was entertainment enough. Water buffalo, bicycles, donkey carts, delivery boys, pedestrians stepping around puddles and animal droppings, ancient trucks, traffic jams! We climbed the pyramids, took the train up the Nile to Luxor, and then to Aswan, sailing across the river in a *felucca*, admiring the dam in progress. But the most memorable night of our trip was back in Cairo. Sayed, our American Express guide, had persuaded us we could camp out in the Sahara desert in sight of the pyramids as inexpensively as we could in our second class hotel.

We had four tents, just for the six of us: two sleeping tents; one for the kitchen run by a Sudanese named Adam; and a dining tent where Sayed, dressed in his turban and *gallabia*, told us stories about Mohammed while we ate Adams' five-course dinner. We took turns camel-riding while the table was cleared and then were entertained by some musicians from a nearby village. They played odd (to us) instruments: wailing flutes, drums, and tambourines. And an amazing figure in a long red gown with bangles, painted white face, goatlike whiskers, and a tall red cap, scared Kate as he whirled and twitched. But he soon had us all laughing as he impersonated cats, a dog, sheep, goat, and an Arab boasting about his gun which kept failing to go off. In one skit, he started to eat a banana, peel and all, pretending to be blind. That was Dan's kind of humor, and although I think Mr. Red Hat intended to eat only a bite or two, he was so pleased to see Dan falling off his chair with laughter that he proceeded to eat the whole thing.

GREECE AND BEYOND

We crossed the eastern Mediterranean to Piraeus and threw ourselves into the glory that was Greece. We climbed around the Acropolis, in and out of temples, marveling at the Parthenon and the Caryatids. We stumbled over the broken carcasses of giant columns, imagined talking with Socrates in the *agora*, tested the acoustics at Dionysus's theater, and tried to coax some advice from the oracle at Delphi. It was Mycenae, a civilization that had ended in the 13th century B.C., that overwhelmed me. Entering Agamemnon's tomb was wonder enough, but then to come with no warning upon the Lion's Gate with a couple of shepherds eating lunch in the shade of its walls! Why hadn't I somewhere in my education been told of that great structure, one of the world's most impressive artifacts? Take a look at the huge primitive lintel stone and

The Lion's Gate at Mycenae

above it those powerful lions, spectacular even without their golden heads.

We bumped into Martha Graham and her dance group going through the Palace of Knossos in Crete and again at Delphi, but it was not the tourist season. We often felt the places were ours, except in Athens. Several days after we landed, we noticed a tension in the street below our hotel window. The British had kidnapped Archbishop Makarios from Cyprus, an international hot spot at that moment, and the Greeks were angry. We did our best to distance ourselves from the British, to keep a low profile, but the horn of the car we rented shorted and honked loudly every time we turned a corner until we disconnected it completely.

St. Mark's Square, Venice

We took ship through the Corinth Canal and on to Naples where we picked up our VW bus and spent the rest of March exploring Italy. Just a few memorable moments: the children's delight when a repairman rose out of the street in front of the Duomo in Florence, saying, "Mamma mia, mamma mia!"; the hasty retreat we all made from the bell tower in Venice when the Easter Sunday bells began to peal, and the Easter egg pastries and gondolas there. Early in April, we entered Spain, frightened by Franco's policemen with their ominous-looking three-cornered hats. When we reached Pamplona, I declared I was going to stay put for a while to nurse a sinus infection and give myself a breather. The rest of the family could do as they wished. We did slow down, had picnics in the nearby Pyrenees, and felt the chill when some group dared to strike and Franco's menacing police occupied the town.

We spent time back in Menthon in late April, collected the things we'd stored, gave away what we couldn't use, said goodbye to our friends, and in the middle of May started wandering again: through Switzerland, Austria, Germany, and back for a stop with the *Trocmés* in Versailles. From early July through the middle of August, we lived in Scandinavia, the last two weeks in a log house with flowers growing in its sod roof, in the highlands above Torpø, a little town in Norway.

Then across the channel, one more farewell to the Tyrrells, and boarding the *New York* for home.

COMING HOME

We had a leisurely trip home on the *New York*, a converted troopship, that carried mainly student passengers. It took ten days sailing from Southhampton to New York, so there was much good entertainment to keep the natives happy: daily exercises, art lectures, music of all kinds, and no household chores or travel responsibilities for us grownups. The children were a few days late for school, but no one seemed to mind. All four continued into the next grade as if they hadn't missed a year, and, contrary to our expectations, the older they were the easier it was for them to absorb the lost school year. Michael passed Loomis's freshman year final exams in fine style and started there as a sophomore on our return. Kate, having missed first grade, had the hardest time catching up with her classmates and didn't gain academic confidence for some years. She eventually became a good linguist and certainly adaptable to new cultures.

Bud had intended to finish *The Trouble with Jenny's Ear* while we were away but made scant progress. That book wasn't published until 1960, but I think Bud felt our experiences enhanced his teaching. And one of our adventures provided him with the inspiration for his third children's book, *The Narrow Passage*. One cold November weekend trip we took from Les Moulins ended in the Dordogne Valley, where the caves of Lasceaux had been discovered. We stayed in a small hotel, and learned that one of the few other diners had discovered the caves with a school friend fifteen years earlier. He turned up to guide us through *La Grotte* the next morning and, Bud says in his journal, "took us down a flight of stairs into the most magnificent exciting display of primitive art – Beautiful reds, browns, yellows in soft contrast with sharp black – all on white, brown and yellow walls. One couldn't help but be awed by it. 2 diverging passages at the end – overlapping, piled one painting on another – some clumsy, some beautifully deft. The magic of it all."

As for me, I was glad to be home, to catch up with my friends and relations, and – I admit – to live an easier life. My eyes actually teared up when

Kate at the Leaning Tower

I first stepped into our local supermarket. How simple it is to shop when you understand labels and can just pick what you want off the shelves! And when everyone else went off to school, I was free to take on something new. What I wanted most at that time was to understand more history. We'd been surrounded all year by glimpses of momentous events, both past and current. I've already described some of those, but there were many other revealing moments: the cab driver in Cairo gleefully showing us *ex*-king Farouk's palace; the last representative of colonial Britain leaving liberated Egypt on the ship from Alexandria; being among the first tourists to enter Austria as the Russians moved out in 1956; the students and others in Athens protesting the kidnapping of Archbishop Makarios from Cyprus by the British; the Suez conference and crowds of media people and hangers-on in London in August '56, making it almost impossible to find rooms for the seven of us. What *had* happened in the Suez? Well, I wanted to know that and a great deal more, so I enrolled in two courses at Wesleyan University, the start of a Masters degree and maybe a teaching career.

One other significant experience made a lasting impression on us. I've mentioned the Versailles hostel we lived in. We thought we had made reservations at an ordinary lodging for students but discovered it was one of the mills built at the order of Marie Antoinette and, in the 1950s, run by Mme. Magda Trocmé, also an extraordinary person with a distinguished history. By the 1950s, the mill was owned by the Fellowship of Reconciliation, an organization started by the Quakers after World War I to help people of all nationalities and

Salt mine, Saltzburg

Keeping busy on the "New York"

religions. A decade earlier, Mme. Trocmé's husband, André, had been a Protestant pastor in the little Huguenot town of Le Chambon, and the Trocmés, along with their whole village had cooperated in housing thousands of Jews, providing them with counterfeit identity cards, sometimes incorporating them into their homes and school, often helping them over the border into Switzerland. It is estimated the Trocmés and their parishioners saved over 2000, mainly children, in four years of defying the Vichy government and its Nazi masters. We regretted never meeting M. Trocmé, who was away at the time of our stay there, preaching and lecturing about his deeply held belief in non-violence, but Mme. was a fine substitute.

In 1979 a Wesleyan professor, Philip Hallie, wrote a book, *Lest Innocent Blood Be Shed*, about the Trocmés and the community of Le Chambon. We were recovering from the demoralizing period of the Vietnam War, and I bought a copy for each of our children, hoping that it would remind them of our year which, Kate says, cemented our family ties forever, and would give them hope that good is possible, even in the midst of a cruel and devastating war.

We were all settling into our various occupations, getting accustomed to our own culture again. The Brookses helped. "There are three things you should know to be back in the swim," they told us. "Miltown (the first of our mood-altering over-the-counter pills), Elvis Presley and his 'Blue Suede Shoes,' and *My Fair Lady*."

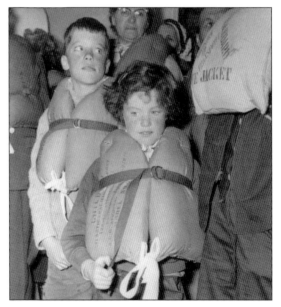

Life boat drill on the "New York"

The Trocmés at La Maison de la Réconciliation, Versailles

CHAPTER 19

LANDING IN PRISON

We had one piece of bad news when we returned to Connecticut. Our friend and family pediatrician, Parker Dooley, was in prison, accused of child-molesting by the parents of the "Wolf Cry Boy," one of the most disturbed of the severely troubled boys Dr. Dooley had agreed to try to help. While we were in Europe, Doc had been convicted and sentenced to a year in Wethersfield Penitentiary, a prison declared outmoded by Alexis de Tocqueville when he toured it in 1833! We visited Doc as soon as we could and found he had already become a guru among the prisoners, as he had on the outside. By the time he had served his sentence, the prison authorities were frantic and eager for him to go. He wrote acerbic letters to the governor and other influential people, describing the inadequacies of prison health care, encouraged inmates to become involved citizens of their community and think for themselves, and arranged for his friends (us, for example) to become active in prison affairs. And it was not only his fellow inmates who turned to him for advice and guidance. After Doc's release and return to Kent, one of the prison guards brought his disturbed son to Doc's cabin for help, and one of the deputy wardens, needing help himself, stayed several weeks with his former prisoner.

So we were introduced to Herb Brown, picked for us by Doc because he could still "relate." Some of the inmates had been so damaged by life they were unreachable, but Herb became a good friend, and we visited and wrote to him for the next eight years. In that way we were able to follow the temperature inside the prison, become acquainted with the wardens, watch the good effects of the inmate-run school on morale, and in general see the criminal justice system from the bottom up.

One rare time, we sat beside Herb at a graduation ceremony while

Parker Dooley, MD, ca. 1947

he told us about the various inmates and their crimes. The one getting the model prisoner award had murdered his wife and his feelings of guilt cried out in every move of his body. Another was a Harvard graduate, a bad-check-passer but a gifted linguist, who was instrumental in organizing and teaching in the prison school. A third, Parker Young, a trim African American from a prominent family, was there for breaking and entering, a highly valued manager of the prison industrial program welcomed back whenever he reentered the prison system. The two we got to know best, Herb Brown and Parker Young, were both inveterate criminals, recidivists, in prison from a young age. They both spent Thanksgiving with us at different times, and both stayed out of prison upon completing the sentences they were serving after we got to know them. Parker who was on the lam for about two years during the time we knew him, violating parole, of course, met a college professor and when next out, married her. She wrote us when he died and told of their "ten glorious years" together. Herb and I still exchange Christmas cards and I occasionally get a Mother's Day card or a phone call from California, where he has retired.

Bud and I learned a lot about the many irrationalities and counter-productive effects of our judicial system. We served a long time on the boards of the Connecticut Prison Association and Families In Crisis, which commissioned Bud to write a children's book, in hopes that talking and reading about prisons in an honest way would help families weather the catastrophe of having a close relative in prison. His *Visit to the Big House* was published by Houghton Mifflin and I believe sold quite well, though it must have had a limited audience.

I often wonder if the effort we and others put into trying to improve the prison system did any good. The great increase in the prison population, mainly caused by the drug "war," has overwhelmed most attempts to make a difference. At least a few prisoners' lives got better and more of us know what prisons are like and how they function. Perhaps that is as much as we could have expected.

Doc Dooley died of pancreatic cancer several years after getting out of prison and was mourned by almost all who knew him, especially by those desperately disturbed boys, including the Wolf Cry Boy Doc had brought back from the edge.

CHAPTER 20

THE END OF AN ERA

The decade of the '50s is stamped on my memory because of a more personal sorrow. Mother died suddenly of a brain aneurism in May of 1957 at the young age of 64, while she was still vitally active with music and friends. She had seemed as vigorous as usual at choir rehearsal the night before. The day before that she and I had driven to Wilson together to deliver a birthday cake she had made for an old friend. We enjoyed being together and I didn't detect any hint of sickness or any lessening of her enthusiasm for life. Mother and Dad had moved to a house in West Hartford about five minutes away from us and had become very much a part of our lives. Miraculously, neither ever gave us unasked advice or criticized our child-rearing. Once I was a mother myself, Mother treated me as an equal, and I lost a friend when she died as well as the parent most entwined in my life, the person I identified with most. So I felt not only grief for our loss but a sudden vulnerability, the first taste of my own mortality.

Kate had a special connection with her grandmother and still speaks of her with love, and all the children felt the hole in our family fabric, especially when Dad came to dinner alone without the partner who had always before camouflaged his lack of social ease. But it was Dad, of course, who was most overwhelmed – and surprised. He was ten years older than Mother, and it never crossed his mind that she would die first. One poignant moment at the funeral home, when we last saw Mother's body, showed me how much he still cared for her in spite of their rocky marriage, and illustrated once more the nature of their relationship. Many years earlier, jewelry stores had run ads promoting platinum as the modern, classy setting for engagement and wedding rings. They offered to exchange "old fashioned" gold rings for resetting diamonds and wedding bands in the more stylish metal, and Mother bit. I didn't know at the time that Dad had retrieved from the jeweler the ring he had given Mother when they were married. In the last drama of their lives together, Dad look off the platinum and put on the gold, kissed her, and said a long, lingering goodbye.

Dad was a vigorous 74, without an anchor, so we persuaded him to join me at Wesleyan, his Alma Mater, where he could take enough courses, one at a time, to make up the credits he needed to graduate. The Philosophy Department accepted him, and in 1960 he marched with the University's senior class to get his diploma, 45 years late, with children and grandchildren cheering him on. That proved to be a rare burst of energy, however, and he seemed gradually to give in to loneliness and give up on life. He was always good-natured, even-tempered, and easy to live with, making it possible for Doug and, later, cousin Rachel with her two children to use his house as a haven. However, we were no substitute for what he had lost, and he died of pneumonia, the old man's friend, twelve years after Mother, at age 87.

John Lee Brooks
1882 - 1969

Genevieve Ford Brooks
1893 - 1957

CHAPTER 21

PREPARING FOR WHAT COMES NEXT

I was granted a Masters of Arts degree in 1959, in the first class to which Wesleyan gave women graduate degrees in areas other than education. There were few of us women, and I usually found myself the lone female in a class, and ten to fifteen years older than my fellow students. I enjoyed matching wits with my young male classmates, but it wasn't just age and gender that made my graduate studies unlike my undergraduate work at Connecticut College during the '30s. Underneath the familiar high spirits of the young, I sensed a wholly different mood, an undercurrent of pessimism perhaps, a loss of innocence, historically speaking, a recognition that events and people were more complicated than we had once thought.

In the intervening years, we had experienced several devastating wars, World War II and the Korean War. We knew about the Holocaust with its concentration camps and gas chambers, and had to face up to the development and use of nuclear bombs. We were aware of the immense slaughter these weapons had produced, and I believe no one since the 1940s has been able to have the same lighthearted response to life that we once had. What I think I sensed was a feeling the rest of the world had long been familiar with: fear, yes, but also a kind of subliminal state of mourning, what someone called "an unresolved historical grief."

It was the younger professors, some of whom were Europeans, who were most challenging and relevant. My advisor was Sigmund Neuman, who had escaped from Nazi Germany during the '30s and who required all of his students to read "The Grand Inquisitor," that marvelous and chilling chapter in Dostoyevsky's *The Brothers Karamazov*. One memorable lecture course I had was Russian History, taught by a White Russian, but the most mind-stretching course was taught by Carl Schorske, who later wrote a Pulitzer Prize-winning book, *Fin de Siècle Vienna*, a history of the decadence in turn-of-the-century Vienna.

My focus at Wesleyan was mainly on 18th and 19th Century European history. My thesis on George Sorel, an early 20th Century Syndicalist, was accepted (I had learned from my senior thesis disaster), and I survived formidable orals in front of an all-male panel of scowling professors. When I saw I would graduate, I sent out résumés to various private schools in the area, knowing I didn't have any education courses or the credentials to teach in the public school system. I was late in applying for a teaching job and was surprised to be hired at the last minute by Ethel Walker School, a girls' school in a nearby town, to fill in for someone who had developed a serious illness. I would be teaching two courses, Ancient and Medieval History, neither of which I had thought much about since elementary school when we dabbled in those wonderful Greek myths. Still I looked forward to the fall and my first paying job since graduating from Connecticut College nineteen years earlier.

Part III

What on Earth Did You Find To Do?

Careers & Causes

"What? You've lived all your life in Connecticut? What on earth did you find to do?"

Comment from a young American woman enroute to the 1995 UN Conference on Women in China

CHAPTER 22

TEACHING HISTORY

The first two years of my rather brief career as a teacher were not happy ones. Ethel Walker still had much of the "finishing school" atmosphere about it in those days, with a discouragingly homogeneous student body – all girls, to begin with. Someone said there wasn't even a male dog on campus. The one male faculty member, in addition to the riding master, was hired the same year I was to solve an emergency in the Classics Department. To my great surprise, fascination, and apprehension, the newcomer was our old acquaintance, that Harvard linguist we had met in prison, fresh out on parole. How much did the president of the school know about him? Or the trustees? Was I the only one aware of his recent past? Should I say something about it? At least his MO, passing bad checks, wasn't a threat to the students, just to the reputation of the school. He occasionally taught in a classroom next to mine and peals of laughter came through the wall. Latin couldn't be that funny. Was he treating them to a bit of jailhouse humor? Whatever it was, the girls coming out of his classes were in much better spirits than those leaving mine.

Unfortunately, his problems caught up with him. His absences increased as did the wildness of his excuses. How often can you attend your grandmother's funeral? After several months, the school was notified by the police that he was back in prison for violating parole. He had found a nice woman to live with, and the Ethel Walker income should have helped, but evidently he couldn't resist booze and blank checks.

Almost all of the girls at Ethel Walker were Wasps – no African-Americans and no Jews. One saving spot of diversity came from a small group of students from Colombia, wealthy like the others but Roman Catholics well versed in and serious about their beliefs, their intellectual background more European than American. In one of our first Medieval History classes, we were discussing early religious influences on Jesus, the pre-Christian milieu in Jerusalem. "Mrs. Butterworth," said one of the Colombians, "you don't think Jesus was influenced by anyone, do you?" Now there was a challenge! That same girl, later in the year, decided to do a research project on the Spanish Inquisition. She made class fun but, beyond the Colombian group, there were few intellectual sparks to be found.

I decided to move on when the school president showed slides of a tour of alumnae she had made. She quoted many of the Ethel Walker graduates as saying how grateful they were for the good education they had received, how well they had been taught to pour tea, how excellently they had been trained to be executives' wives. I applied to my alma mater, Chaffee School in Windsor, was hired, and taught for another eight years there and at Loomis, Chaffee's brother school about three miles away. I suddenly felt at home. At Chaffee, students and faculty lived off campus and brought to school different family experiences. It was a much more diverse group in every way, and on the whole the girls and boys I taught seemed eager to learn.

Chaffee School Colleagues 1962 - 1969 as we looked 10 years later

Meanwhile, Mike started college at Dartmouth. I thought he would do better at a place like Swarthmore, but Dartmouth and New Hampshire were more familiar. Besides, John Kemeny, recently made chair of the Math Department, wrote a recruiting letter to Mike. Recruiting for an academic subject, not just sports! Mike had just turned 17, too young for college, but off he went.

Mike graduating from Loomis in 1959, ready for Dartmouth?

Since we had an empty bed, we offered to house a foreign exchange student who would be a senior at Loomis. He and Tim, a sophomore there, could go to school together. The student turned out to be Detlef Leenen from Germany who fit into our family remarkably well. We saw our country in another dimension through his eyes that year He and his whole family continue to be close friends. He has become a distinguished jurist, so his year in the States obviously didn't hinder his career.

Bud's second children's book, *The Trouble with Jenny's ear,* was published that winter, winning the Herald Tribune Spring Book Award. Jenny is a six-year-old with principles. Her two older brothers get much too enthusiastic about electronics, wiring their house to listen in on private conversations and broadcasting them to the public until Jenny develops a bad earache. The ache goes away, but she is left with a remarkable new ability: she can hear people's thoughts. Her brothers persuade Jenny to enter a quiz show to make enough money

AFS Exchange Student Detlef Leenen graduating from Loomis 1960

to buy their favorite sliding hill and save it from development. Jenny does win a lot of money but soon insists they give it back because she realizes she had won it under false pretences. She hadn't really known the answers but had only repeated the thoughts of the quiz master. She'd been a fake!

Think of the serendipitous timing of the publication of that book. It was at the printers when Charles van Doren's cheating on the quiz show *Twenty One* was discovered. On top of this, Rita van Doren, Charles's aunt, had to present the award to Bud at the ceremony we went to in New York that spring. Some young people claim Charles was their hero and the revelation of his fraudulence was the beginning of their cynicism. There would be a great many more deceits to disillusion them before the decade was over.

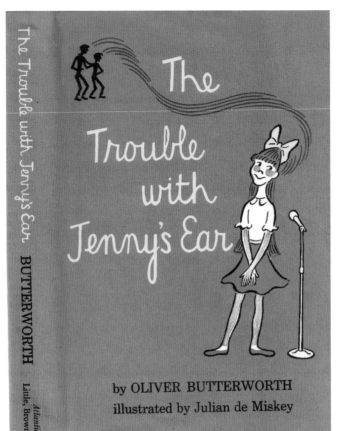

The Trouble with Jenny's Ear

by OLIVER BUTTERWORTH

illustrated by Julian de Miskey

CHAPTER 23

THE SEESAW DECADE

The 1960's was the defining decade of the century for me as well as for the country. How can I – how can anyone convey the emotional havoc of those times to a generation which didn't live through them? In the beginning, there were great hopes and idealism: Kennedy's election and the formation of the Alliance for progress and the Peace Corps. "Ask not what your country can do for you but what you can do for your country." And there was confidence at first that our democracy was getting stronger, that together we could rectify the injustices of segregation through the civil rights movement. Yet by the end of the decade, there was growing cynicism and despair and a realization that the men making decisions for us were not only fallible but even immoral. Some early clouds on the horizon should have warned us of the coming storms. The Bay of Pigs, for example. Who got the idea the Cuban people would rise up to support the invaders, old Batista supporters? Certainly, the argument goes, any rational people would overthrow their government, given the chance to join the "free world." We would be lost in Vietnam because of this and other false assumptions before the decade ended.

In the summer of 1962, we took one more family trip, knowing our children would soon be having their own adventures that wouldn't necessarily include us. We spent a month in Alaska, two weeks of which were at Barrow, the most northern settlement in the western hemisphere. It was then a community of 1500 Inuits and 8 Caucasians. We found lodging with the Presbyterian minister's family and as a result had entree to many neighbors and their stories. The young minister's wife with three young children was lonely, and we had parties for one excuse or another every night. We were taught to raise bean sprouts before they became the rage in the lower 48, and discovered caribou and sprouts made a delicious sandwich. Lucky Tim got a chance to fly with Rev. Chambers in his small plane, which his wife claimed came first in his three great loves – plane, God, and family – to deliver provisions to some caribou hunters far out in the tundra. Mike's Barrow adventure was on foot. He decided to walk to the monument commemorating Wiley Post and Will Rogers, about 10 miles down the coast where they had died in a plane crash in 1935. He took off early one morning and didn't get back until late that evening. I began to worry and asked people coming from the direction he'd taken if they had seen him. Nobody had, but one asked with concern if he had a gun to protect himself from polar bears. Of course he didn't, and I doubted he would have known how to use it if he had. You can imagine our relief when he came limping home around 9 o'clock, still in daylight so far above the Arctic Circle.

We were surprised to learn that Alaska had been divided up between various Christian denominations. All Inuits born in the Barrow region were automatically Presbyterians, and the Baptists, Roman Catholics, and others each had their sections of Alaska. Rev. Chambers was head of the Presbyterians and had ordained an Inuit native, whose family we got to know. One story we heard illustrates the confusion that was inevitable under these circumstances. In the Inuit community, it had previously been the custom for a couple contemplating marriage to have a child before the ceremony. I assume this provided evidence the couple was fertile and the girl would make a good mother. Often this first child was given to an older childless couple in the family but was brought up knowing who its real parents were. Christianity, however, disrupted that local custom, along with many others. One young father we heard about, when told having a child out of wedlock was a sin and therefore he and the mother would go to hell, was bitter. "You mean that if like our forefathers we didn't know that was a sin, we wouldn't go to Hell? Then why did you tell us?"

We marveled at the skills we saw for surviving in that hostile land, in a town built on permafrost, perched on the shore of the Bering Sea that was open only a few weeks a year for the one ship, the *Lone Star*, to deliver a year's supply of things too uneconomical to transport by plane. Little six-year-olds were already able to hit floating tin cans and flying birds with their homemade

Kate & Tim playing with curious children outside the one hotel in town

sling shots. They built little fires of driftwood and cooked the birds where they fell. We were impressed with the appropriate clothing the Inuits had devised, parkas of padded cloth or skins that we borrowed that August because it was too cold for the winter garments we had brought from home, and the wonderfully comfortable mukluks, boots of skin and fur stuffed with grass, that came up to the knees. They had added motors to their skin Umiaks, and Evenrude, like Kleenex had become a generic term. "What kind of an Evenrude do you have?" But they still hunted whales, walruses, seals and caribou and carved them up with their ulu knives to be stored in their iceboxes, dugout holes in the permafrost.

The town had a traditional council of both men and women.

In Barrow, posing for our 1962 Christmas card

It met while we were there and voted to continue being a dry town and to allow a gas pipeline to serve their houses. Such a change had been stopped before because of fear of fire and the danger to children who were seldom disciplined. The environment did the disciplining for them. Nobody had to remind their offspring to wear their mukluks when they went out. We were amused at the notice posted at the school declaring that the aim of the U.S. Department of Indian Affairs which ran the school was to teach Native Americans to adapt to their environment. We could see the adapting being taught was to a different and more dominant culture – ours.

*Using her ulu knife on fresh walrus meat, readying it for
permafrost deep-freeze storage*

CHAPTER 24

MAKING STATE HISTORY

In the fall of 1962, Bud and I participated in one more project initiated by the League of Women Voters. We were part of a suit, Butterworth et al. vs. Dempsey et al., brought by ten of us against Connecticut's governing officers "on the grounds of a denial of equal protection of the laws by reason of the inequalities in representation in both houses of the General Assembly." The League and various political scientists had tried in vain for many years to get the legislature to reapportion the existing legislative districts. By the 1960's, the malapportionment gave overwhelming political power to small towns and our argument was that such inequalities made it difficult for cities to get their

BRIDGEPORT SUNDAY POST

SECTION—C   BRIDGEPORT SUNDAY POST, JANUARY 9, 1966

Oliver Butterworth Sued for Reapportionment

Name Inscribed in State History

By BETTY TYLER

Oliver Butterworth's name has gone down in Connecticut history but few Nutmeggers outside of the Hartford area know who he is.

Oliver Butterworth et al sued Governor John Dempsey — and won — in the U. S. District court case which brought about reapportionment of the state's legislative districts and, backed by approval of a new Constitution for the state, led to the first major change in the composition of the House since 1818.

The el al included his wife, Miriam, and eight others.

Both Are Teachers

Who are the Butterworths? Both are teachers, he of English at Hartford College, for Women, enrollment 200 students, and she a teacher of American history at the private Chaffee school in Windsor, enrollment 120. He also writes children's books and their hobby is mountain climbing. They are the parents of four children, three of them currently in college and one at Chaffee school.

Though both are Democrats, they have been politically inactive — and the sponsors of the suit, the League of Women Voters of Connecticut, wanted it

went into effect in 1818 had provided for one representative in the lower House for each town under 5,000 and two for each town with population exceeding 5,000. However, some towns which had had two representatives at the time of the adoption of the Constitution were allowed to keep two.

"The result was," Mr. Butterworth said, "that the vote of a resident of the town of Union weighed 424 times as heavily as the vote of a resident of Hartford."

The small towns had the maj-

needs attended to and for states to solve many of their problems. Our case was filed in December of 1962 and was based on a Federal Supreme Court decision, Baker vs. Carr, stating that a legislative body that didn't provide for equal voting rights, based on the principle of one man one vote, violates the 14th Amendment to the Constitution. The three-judge panel voted two to one in our favor and the result was the first Connecticut Constitutional Convention to be held since 1818. Later I heard leaders in both parties say that taking part in that convention, where they really did rise above partisanship and did adopt a constitutional amendment which provided a fair reapportionment process, was the high point in their political careers.

The outcome wasn't exactly as we had anticipated. The suburbs seemed to garner more political power than the cities, but the control and resistance to change of the agriculturally oriented, conservative smaller towns were broken. This case fit well into my U.S. History courses at Chaffee. So history is alive after all! That was the last action I took with the League. I admired their methods, their calm, orderly, and careful preparations and logical conclusions. But by the mid '60's, our world seemed to be oscillating out of control and in need of faster, more direct political action.

Tim and crew at the Eastern Sprints in Worcester, MA

In the fall of 1962, Tim went off to college. Dartmouth again, although I hoped he would pick Earlham in Indiana. Someone ought to break out of New England! Tim followed in Bud's footsteps by majoring in English and becoming an oarsman. Crew, the quintessential team sport, and the comradeship of those big men who spent their afternoons and weekends pulling together, seemed made for him.

And in the fall of '64, Dan followed his father and two older brothers to Hanover. I had no other suggestions for him, was just grateful that he had filled out at least one college

Dan's School Picture

application and surprised he was accepted. He was a late bloomer, but he really had bloomed during his last years in high school. He still was more flighty than Mike and Tim. In his early years at Dartmouth, he joined a fraternity, the first of the three to do so, seemed always on the edge of disaster: riding just behind another car that crashed in a fatal accident; bursting into flames at the freshmen bonfire ritual; squeaking through semesters with barely passing grades. When did he ever study? Fortunately, he continued to grow and became engrossed in history, in which he majored. By his senior year, the outside world, experience, and time had sobered him, perhaps even more than we wished.

~177~

CHAPTER 25

MORE CLOUDS ON THE HORIZON

Also in the fall of 1962, our government discovered the Soviets were installing nuclear missiles in Cuba, ninety miles off the coast of Florida, and the crisis that followed, the nearness of nuclear war, shook us all. Luckily for the world, Kennedy stayed relatively calm. The installations were cancelled, but in the process we began to imagine how the Soviets felt with *our* nuclear weapons in near-by Turkey aimed at *their* cities. We also began to hear rumors that our government was plotting to kill Castro. How secure was a future based on threats and obvious violations of international law? To our great shock and sorrow, just a year later, it was Kennedy who was assassinated, not Castro.

It was school-aged children who were most deeply troubled by the close call with Cuba. They were the ones who practiced getting under their desks for protection against a nuclear attack, but the smart ones knew desks weren't adequate shelter from that kind of bomb. Dan remembers a biology class when, in the middle of a long, complex explanation, one of the girls asked, "Why should we learn all that when we're going to die soon anyway?" Dan says the teacher answered, "We have to pretend we're going to live and continue to do our work." Even suburban children felt they lived in a vulnerable world. Our children were told that Hartford would be one of the prime targets if war broke out, and Kate says she decided to get out as soon as she could find a way. Was that one of the reasons she married Fernando Valdez and lived for fifteen years in Guadalajara, where she had three children? Was that one of the reasons that impelled one of our nephews to become a born-again Christian? He was more terrified of The Bomb than anyone else I knew, but now he believes in Armageddon, when he and his present family, all believers, will be saved.

Was the threat of a nuclear war a factor in the sexual revolution and the big rise in drug use? Life is short; let's live it up while we can! It was our younger two who seemed most affected by the missile crisis. However, we all learned that the splitting of the atom made possible nuclear annihilation and that these new weapons of mass destruction are a whole different kettle of fish from conventional weapons. The crisis was a potent lesson for our United States History course, too, and, from that time on, we spent a third of the year in my classes studying foreign relations with an emphasis on Latin America.

Teaching is a great way to educate the teacher. To mention just a few moments of revelation for me, I once asked my class what they already knew about Andrew Jackson, thinking they might talk about the War of 1812 or the spoils system, or Jackson's fight with Nicolas Biddle over the federal bank. As we began to study that era, I wanted to know what, if anything, stuck in their minds, myths or facts, from elementary school history courses. Only one girl waved her hand, an obnoxious, chauvinistic, German exchange student, very defensive of her country's recent past. "He practiced genocide on the Indians," she said. What a difference a word makes! Well, class, does our country, too, have that blot on our escutcheon?

Another time, I invited John Rogers, a local historian of African American history, to speak to my classes. We were studying the period of Reconstruction at the time, and I had been teaching about carpetbaggers and scalawags, as emphasized in the text books I was using. Also, we had been reading about the failures of post Civil War governments in the former Confederate states until the 1870's, when the federal government pulled out of the South and politics there returned to "normal." As we drove through Windsor, Mr. Rogers pointed to the old Congregational church where all Chaffee graduations were held and remarked on its policy of excluding blacks as members until the mid-1950's just ten years earlier. As far as Reconstruction was concerned, he declared, "that was the period of the greatest outpouring of love our country has ever known. A tremendous number of young lawyers and teachers gave up their jobs in the North to try to get justice and education for the newly emancipated slaves."

Since that time, there has been much new research and new histories have appeared, altering our understanding of that post-war era. The civil rights movement of the 1960's prodded historians to take another look at a period that ended with de facto segregation in the North and Jim Crow laws in the South, ex-slaves virtually re-enslaved as sharecroppers, disenfranchised by poll taxes, intimidation, and other discriminatory methods. New studies have shown the post-war state governments in the South weren't so corrupt after all, not when compared to Grant's administration or northern states' governments of the time. The first public school systems and judicial reforms came out of those integrated legislatures. But they were all too short-lived. For Southerners, giving the vote and education to blacks was the real scandal, and they were the ones who wrote the first histories of the period. I began to think that although Robert E. Lee had surrendered on the battle-field, the South had won the war of historical perception.

"ALL THESE GIRLS" might well have been reaction of U. S. Congressman Thomas J. Meskill when students of Chaffee School visited during recent trip to Washington. From left are: Mrs. Oliver Butterworth, class teacher; Mrs. Cherry Howard, who accompanied class; Deborah Coburn, Jean Liscord and Toni Treadway of Windsor; Debby Ward-ner, Jane Hogeman and Gail Smith of West Hartford; Susan Carlson, Hartford; Barbara Dickle, New Britain.

Mims taking students on a field trip to Washington

CHAPTER 26

THE CIVIL RIGHTS MOVEMENT COMES TO CONNECTICUT

In the 1960s, anyone with half an ear to the political ground could hear the rumblings of a rebellion against racial segregation and our country's pervasive discrimination against people of color. Rosa Parks' refusal to give up her seat on the bus to a white man had sparked an increasing resolve in the black community to break out of their demeaning status in our society. Martin Luther King, Jr., a highly respected theologian, had emerged as a forceful, dedicated leader of the movement, preaching non-violence, searching for ways to achieve justice. Thousands of people, many of them students, went south to join the sit-ins and marches to protest Jim Crow, three quarters of a century late but bolstered by the Supreme Court decision, Brown vs. Board of Education, that stated what we all knew: that "separate but equal" is never equal.

None of our family went south to help out, but we, too, were a modest part of the civil rights movement. One summer we had a two- week "camp" at Squam. There were only four

Rosa Richards, 8-year-old "camper" doing chores at Squam

campers, two sets of Afro-American sisters from Hartford, two 12-year-olds and two 8's. One set was a pair of adopted daughters of a friend who had taught Dan and Kate at Quaker Lane Nursery School, and the other two were friends of theirs. We taught swimming and canoeing, roasted marshmallows and sometimes of

Anna Bing, left – a part of our family 1963 - 1966

a morning found two giggling eight-year-olds in bed with us. We learned about hair, helped Eugenia with some homework, and felt a twinge when they announced that the best time they'd had all summer was the 20-minute motor boat ride Uncle Paul had given them. I've since reconnected with Rosa, one of the eight-year-olds, and she has forgotten the motor boat, now telling everyone how I taught her how to swim.

More constructive was adding Anna Bing from Beaufort, South Carolina, to our household in the fall of 1964. She and we were part of a Quaker program called the Southern Student Project, a forerunner of the ABC (A Better Chance) program that recruited northern families to host good students from segregated southern schools for their junior and senior high school years. The aim was to prepare competent Blacks for better colleges, better jobs, and better lives – a very small-scale attempt to achieve more equality of opportunity. Anna arrived on a weekend, a few days before she was to start school at Conard High School, from which Dan had recently graduated. She doubled the Black population there that fall.

Michael had left for Stanford in California to begin his second year of graduate school. Kate would soon be busing to Windsor for her sophomore year at Chaffee School, where I was teaching, and Tim and Dan were lolling around the living room after dinner, rough-housing with some old friends during Anna's first evening with us – before taking off for Dartmouth. At one point during the evening, Anna abruptly left the living room, went into her room and shut the door. Suddenly homesick? Overwhelmed by so many white people around? Think of the courage it took to brave so many strange and what must have been perceived as dangerous experiences! The next morning, just as we all sat down to Sunday breakfast – eggs and bacon and coffee cake fresh from the oven – a Jehovah's Witness and his little boy arrived at the door. I explained we couldn't listen to them then, and as they walked back down the driveway, Anna said, "At our house we never turn away a man of God." I could see one thing we needn't worry about was a crushed, intimidated spirit, and I began to think we might learn more from Anna than she from us.

Anna was bright, knew how to study, had usually been top student in her class, and was exceptionally self-possessed. Most of the other students in the Friends' Southern Program came from middle class families, but Anna's father had only a third grade education and had been a farmer until he became too ill to work. Then the family moved into Beaufort, where her mother supported the family doing domestic work. I've never met Anna's mother, but I know I would like her – a strong, resourceful woman who had finished 8th Grade in a segregated school and was a devout Pentecostal.

The Bings' minister, Reverend Ike (Ikeroder) said Mrs. Bing was his favorite cook and often ate Sunday dinner with them when he was in Beaufort. He had a second church in Boston, so Anna, who liked and trusted him very much, presumably felt some sense of security knowing he was often within counseling distance. We met Rev. Ike when he came to Anna's graduation and found him a bright, thoughtful theologian who obviously cared about Anna and her family. Eight years later, Rev. Ike's picture was on the front page of a Sunday *New York Times* magazine section. The story inside told of his conversion to a more materialistic religion. When Anna was with us, we knew Rev. Ike was raising money from his congregation and the wider audience of his Boston radio station by selling prayer shawls and other magical icons to help his flock pick the right lottery number or overcome some sickness. By the time he was featured in *The Times*, however, he had abandoned any theological talk and simply preached getting rich. He was quoted as saying, "The best thing you can do for the poor is not to be one of them." I wondered what Anna and her mother thought of their minister's new revelations, but he was at last in tune with the larger community's worship of the bottom line.

Our responsibilities under the Quaker program were to send Anna home for Christmas and summer vacations and to arrange for her to attend a church of her choice. We found a Pentecostal church in Hartford, with services held in the minister's living room. Bud and I went there with Anna several times and came home full of The Spirit. There was a good deal of shouting, laying on of hands, and belting out of hymns. Anna went to Quaker Meeting with us once and afterwards said, "What those people need is more noise."

Anna found friends at Conard, girls not very attractive to high school boys nor to the in-group girls, but solid and kind, the sort you'd be surprised and impressed with at your 25th reunion. Kate was not pleased when Anna tried to convert her to Pentecostal beliefs, but otherwise they got along well with each other, and not much later Kate was Anna's maid of honor at her wedding. As a family, we gained some sensitivity to racial relations, having Anna so much a part of our world. I even found myself looking uneasily around when we went out in public, feeling a little alarmed if we were the only Black family there.

We learned something about education and affirmative action through Anna, too. She made the honor roll at Conard and was elected to their Honor Society, but she did poorly on her SATs. We realized then that those tests don't test ability. What they test is background. Anna had no uncle or neighbor who was a doctor or lawyer or scientist. She had not heard standard English spoken at home or at her previous schools. She had never heard of Hinduism or Buddhism or Judaism.

Colleges in those days were infected with the idealism of the civil rights movement and took seriously their responsibility to educate all parts of our society. so in spite of low SATs, Anna was offered full scholarships at Oberlin, University of Connecticut, and Earlham, all of which felt Anna was someone they were eager to work with. She chose Earlham at our urging. We had visited it on a college tour and she'd seemed to like it. It had a somewhat religious aura about it, having been started by Quakers, and the college offered her a six-week summer program. She was to tutor some high schoolers and at the same time get some help with English herself.

Well, Anna's father died, she left the summer program after five weeks, and she never went back. She met an old school friend, a paratrooper in the U.S. Army, and decided to get married. "Aren't you disappointed?" our friends asked. We weren't really. We had begun to wonder if Anna would be able to juggle her two worlds.

With a college education, could she ever have gone home again? We

Anna Bing graduating from Conard High School in June, 1966; Funeral Sevice of Anna's Mother

In Loving Memory

Of

Mother Anna Florence Russell Bing
March 29, 1909-February 12, 1997

Services
United Church Of Jesus Christ
For All People
1:00 P.M. - Monday, February 17, 1997

Elder Arthur Thomas, Pastor
Pastor Josephine Bostick, Officiating

didn't need to worry. Anna had spunk enough to manage her own life. A few years and one son later, she wrote from Germany that little Jonathan loved visiting Neuschwanstein, and soon Anna and her husband came back to the States. They both earned bachelor *and* masters degrees, settled in Anchorage, Alaska, and had three more children. There, Anna has been a school principal for twenty years. Who's disappointed?

CHAPTER 27

FLYING THE COOP

Anna's graduation was only one celebration in the very busy summer of 1966. Tim graduated from Dartmouth, and he and Sue Hallock, a graduate of Hartford College and Mount Holyoke, were married that same June. Much of the planning for the wedding came out of our house because Sue's family had recently moved to Minnesota. We listened to arguments over whether Tim should buy a new pair of shoes with unscratched soles (no) or a new "going away" jacket. (Well yes, if it means so much to you.) They took off for Europe and, when they returned, went to North Carolina where Tim did graduate work in English and Sue taught in a formerly segregated school. New laws mandated integration or the loss of funding. Since no white child would attend the school, Sue integrated the faculty and saved the funding. "Don't ever stop at that garage, little lady. It's the headquarters for the KKK and they have their eyes on you!"

In July, Mike married Carol Hastings, a classmate of Sue's at both Hartford College and Mount Holyoke. Mike and Carol's celebration was more modest than Tim and Sue's, but again we wondered how compatible those

Michael & Carol's wedding reception at Sunset Farm

two young people really were. After their wedding, the Mike Butterworths drove back to California, to Palo Alto, where Mike was in graduate school studying Math at Stanford. In the fall, Dan went back to Dartmouth for his junior year, leaving Kate to start her senior year at Chaffee, an only child ready for our undiluted attention at last.

I'm sad to say that Kate was not happy at Chaffee. She needed more confidence in herself, and she didn't get it there. Her advisor once told her

Michael & Carol off to California

she "had no aptitude for languages." Well, she learned Spanish in Mexico when she needed it, became proficient in linguistics before moving back to Connecticut with her family, and got a job teaching Spanish at a prestigious language school in West Hartford. A few years after she moved North, Bud, my brother Doug, and I thought it would be fun to have her tutor us at her school. It *was* fun, and she was the best language teacher any of us had ever had. Would she have thrived more at our local high school? She made some good friends at Chaffee and absorbed an excellent education that has been of good service to her ever since, but she says she felt a weight all the time she was there. It was obviously difficult for her to be a stu-

*Kate graduating from
Chaffee School*

Street in Morelia, Michuachan, Mexico

dent in the school, such a small one too, where her mother taught. When it came time to apply to colleges, she hunkered down in her stubborn way. She had had enough of academics. No more conventional schooling for her! Yet what were the alternatives? She needed most of all to get away from her omnipresent parents, but from our point of view, she seemed unready to cope in some big city apartment, alone. Looking back, I can see we were too protective. She was eighteen, for heaven's sake. She says she had a fantasy of moving to Boston, finding a factory job, and living on her own in a world more real than ours. That wouldn't have been a bad choice.

Just as time for applying to colleges was running out, we met with a young recruiter for an experimental college called The Friends World Institute. Its program included one semester in the U.S., getting some perspective on our own society, and then, in subsequent semesters, living with families in various parts of the world, learning by experiencing. There was a headquarters in Morelia in Michoacán, Mexico, one in Nairobi, Kenya, one in Japan, etc. That struck a cord with Kate, and in the fall of '67, we drove her to the U.S. "campus" of FWI at Mitchell Field in Westbury, Long Island. The dorms were old army barracks, and Kate looked happy.

Here's a taste of Kate's college experience: for two weeks before Christmas vacation, she and two classmates lived and worked in Decoy, Kentucky, a tiny Appalachian spot, an abandoned strip-mining town with ruined land and a constant smell of coal. Of the ten families left, only three were not living on federal aid: the teacher, the policeman, and the local moon shiner. The three FWI girls lived in the schoolhouse. Two of them did some teaching, and Kate joined some Decoy women, sewing braided rugs on a treadle sewing machine. In early February of 1968, part of Kate's class drove to Mexico and settled with families in Michoacán's capital, Morelia, to study at the university there. In March, we visited her and met the family with whom she and roommate Ann Wyllis lived. Once, when no one else was around, Kate showed us the servants' quarters, very like a chicken coop. That was where two young Indian girls, about 10 and 12 years old, treated essentially as slaves, spent their "free" time. Kate was understanding a lot more than an orthodox academic program could have taught her, although she was getting some of that, too, with lectures on Mexican history and society, along with large doses of language training. Here at last was one of our children who had broken out of New England – in a big way!

Kate's class studying in Mexico

CHAPTER 28

JUSTICE INTERRUPTED

Some of the most effective teaching I did in those years was not in Connecticut but in Washington, D.C. Every spring I took my U.S. History classes to our nation's capital for several days, asking a few mothers along as chaperones. The classes divided themselves into three or four groups around subjects they wanted to explore. Each group made appointments with Washington pros who were working on their issue, perhaps a congressman or someone in a think tank. If we were lucky, a parent would have access to an old friend in the President's cabinet or an undersecretary in some governmental department.

In 1965, we hit the jackpot. We had an appointment with Supreme Court Justice "Wizzer" White AND Attorney General Nicholas Katzenbach. In fact, some of us were sitting in the Attorney General's office when a call came in from John Dorr, Mr. Katzenbach's representative, reporting on what was happening in Selma, Alabama, where the state and local police with billy clubs and bullwhips were beating the protest marchers led by Martin Luther King, Jr.. The protesters were insisting, non-violently, that Blacks be allowed to vote. That Monday evening, we watched on our hotel televisions while President Johnson presented the Voting Rights Act to a joint session of Congress. We saw not only the President but the nine members of the Supreme Court – Look! There's Wizzer White! – and the members of Johnson's cabinet – Look! There he is! There's Nicholas Katzenbach! And there was the Connecticut delegation, some of whom we had met with, too. We had been at the right places at the right time. Johnson was announcing a bill he would submit to congress the next day which, among other things, would "establish a simple uniform standard" for voter registration, "send federal officials empowered to register Negroes wherever state officials refused to register them…and ensure that properly registered individuals are not prohibited from voting…" He promised that protests, such as the one in Selma, would get full protection from the federal government. And he recognized that civil legislation is not enough. To be a productive citizen "requires a trained mind and a healthy body…a decent home and a chance to find a job, and the opportunity to escape from the clutches of poverty." He was setting out his vision of The Great Society in words that reminded us what it is that makes us proud to be Americans.

Anyone anywhere in the world can be and probably is patriotic, proud to be a citizen of whatever country he belongs to. Some are proud of their country's power or military might or its beauty or wealth. Americans, young people especially, believe our country, with all its mistakes, stands for something more, something unique: for the idea that all men are created equal and that government should be by the consent of the governed. Johnson's speech confirmed that belief. The civil right's struggle of the past several years, seen on television and in the press, had convinced most of us that blacks were still shamefully oppressed one hundred years after emancipation. "Their cause must be our cause too," Johnson said "…It is all of us who must overcome the crippling legacy of bigotry and injustice." I was particularly pleased with the President's words on the violence that accompanied the struggle for rights, violence which up to that time had come almost exclusively from police and opponents of desegregation. "We will not seek the peace of suppressed rights," we heard him say, "or the order imposed by fear, or the unity that stifles protest, for peace cannot be purchased at the cost of liberty."

It was a great speech. I think the most inspiring one I have ever heard, and, as it turned out, the high point of the decade. However, it was fatally marred by what was happening in Vietnam. On March 2nd, a week or two before we listened to Johnson's commitment to civil rights for *all* Americans, U.S. planes began their first attack in the sustained bombing of North Vietnam, a sign that a negotiated peace was not in the wind and that the war in Southeast Asia was expanding.

I was reminded of a revealing moment on our Washington trip of the previous year. I had slipped away from my students and sat for a few minutes in the Senate balcony to listen to a debate. Tom Dodd, one of Connecticut's senators, had the floor and was railing about the situation in Vietnam. He was denouncing the Vietcong for killing an American advisor. I watched Oregon Senator Wayne Morse rise to get attention. "Will the Senator yield?" Senator Dodd yielded. "If you don't want our men killed there, bring them home!" Morse said and sat down. Made sense to me.

As we know, our advisors and Green Berets and marines were not brought home, but instead were augmented. In August of 1964, during the presidential campaign, Congress passed the Tonkin Gulf Resolution at Johnson's request in response to an unverified incident, an alleged unprovoked attack on two U.S. destroyers. Our ships were actually providing electronic espionage and other support for the U.S.-equipped South Vietnam Navy that had attacked the North Vietnam coast. Yet, the resolution was subsequently interpreted by Johnson as Congressional carte blanche approval for whatever action he decided to take, and among other things, he used it as authorization for the March 1965 sustained bombing of the North.

The heroic, often dangerous, dedication of those in the civil rights movement, and the Johnson Administration's obviously sincere commitment to progress as shown in the Civil Rights Act of 1964 and the Voting Rights Act of 1965 made significant changes in the law and looked wondrously hopeful. But follow-up enforcement and further necessary reforms were lost in the growing obsession with Vietnam. The White backlash to Black gains in political power and desegregation grew, and Black leadership became more militant. Segregationist Alabama Governor George Wallace, of Selma fame, declared his candidacy for President in the 1968 campaign and was finding supporters all across the country. Our personal efforts, too, by that time were becoming focused on Vietnam. The hopes of overcoming the injustices of racism floundered once more on our country's deep-seated prejudices and the effects of the growing militarization of our society.

CHAPTER 29

WE ALL FALL DOWN

In the presidential election of 1964 between Johnson and Goldwater, I argued for Johnson with anyone who would listen. Goldwater was far too much the Cold War militant, too extreme. Johnson at least seemed a reluctant aggressor in Southeast Asia and, with his civil rights agenda, he had the incentive and the possibility of de-escalating our involvement in Vietnam. The bombing of the North he ordered in March of 1965, just two months after he had been inaugurated president in his own right, felt to me like a personal betrayal. I had decided by this time that our whole intervention there was based on false assumptions, at least as they were articulated to us by our government. Here are a few:

1. Vietnam was two separate countries, North and South, and we intervened to save the South from the North.

2. Communism is a monolithic movement, connected in a worldwide conspiracy.

3. Given enough arms and money, the people our government backed in Vietnam, most of them former collaborators of the French or Japanese, most of them Catholic in a Buddhist country, and most militarists from elite families, could win the hearts and minds of the Vietnamese people.

4. The war was between Communism and the Free World, not an occupied people insisting on their sovereignty against a colonial power.

5. Widening the war (into the North, Laos, and Cambodia) would shorten it.

I could go on with many more examples of what seemed to me misjudgments, dangerous misapprehensions on the part of those who supported and conducted the war. Most of the explanations we were given for our escalating intervention sounded so hollow that we began to suspect the real reasons were to protect the credibility of the men who got us there.

My understandings came from sources outside the mainstream press. Since college, I had subscribed to *Christianity and Crisis,* a monthly magazine started by the theologian, Reinhold Niebuhr. I read *The Nation* and *The New Republic, The Atlantic* and *The New Yorker.* All of these, and some smaller, more temporary magazines I subscribed to like *Citizen Soldiers,* put out by Vietnam Veterans Against the War, and *Clergy and Laity Against the War,* published convincing articles on the roots of American involvement and conduct in Southeast Asia, as well as the progress of the fighting. The most authoritative information I received came from George Kahin's *The United States in Vietnam* (1967), which included copies of documents such as the treaty signed after the French de-

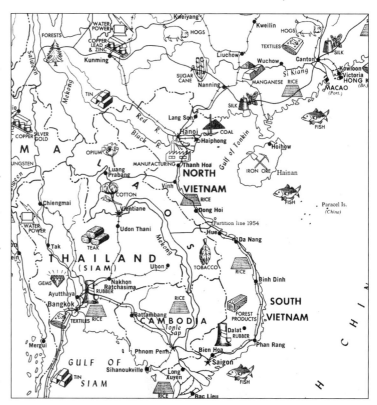

What's in a name? The cease-fire line at the 17th parallel did not create two countries.

feat at Dienbienphu. All of these created a perception altogether contrary to official information.

How can one judge which view of reality is right? I decided the way to test one's assumptions, especially dissenting ones, against others' is to watch how events play out. There are some facts that can be verified. Beyond that, you look to see if the results of certain U.S. actions conform to the government's version of reality or to the fears of us dissenters. And time after time, our assumptions were confirmed. I was not happy to find we seemed to know more about the nature of the war than Johnson and his advisors, or more than they were willing to admit to, anyway. Policies were being made on the basis of false assumptions, and those policies were for many matters of life and death.

In the fall of 1967, Helen Parker, a Chaffee colleague, and I went to Washington for a day-long conference at the State Department. Invitations had been sent to heads of secondary schools and their history departments to meet with VIPs for briefings on the Vietnam War. The government hoped to influence educators, who in turn would persuade their agitating and alienated students of the necessity for our actions in Southeast Asia. We sat in a big auditorium at the State Department, listening to Dean Rusk, Max Frankel and William Bundy. They warned of the domino effects of pulling out, explained the importance to our reputation of staying in, and assured us the U.S. and our allies were on the verge of victory. The country as a whole was way past those Washington pols. All of these arguments had been heard and dissected and discredited. We didn't believe them.

By the time of the 1968 presidential election campaign, a large majority of Americans were intensely against the war, a good many of them because they could see no benefits from it that would justify the costs. And the costs were horrendous. In the 1950's, we were already substantially funding the French Vietnam War efforts. Then in 1955, we gave an initial economic grant of $322.4 million to Diem, the U.S.-installed president of South Vietnam, and from 1955 through 1961, $1,447 million more. Also, the U.S. contributed another $508 million in military grants in the same time period. Translated into today's dollar, these were big bucks. Add to this, payments to our own soldiers, advisors, counter-insurgency experts, and pilots, and helicopters, and… The non-military costs were the greatest and eventually were unbearable – 55,000 Americans killed and many more injured.

In addition to the costs, many Americans thought the war was immoral, and a large part of the country couldn't see any threat to us from Vietnam. We further believed a country has no right to ask its citizens to make supreme sacrifices except under extreme circumstances, yet men between the ages of 18 and 29 were being asked to sacrifice a great deal. These young men found they had no good choices: they could fight in a war they never quite believed in, they could get medical exemptions, or they could become conscientious objectors, but these choices always had behind them a lurking question of motive. Or they could go to prison or to Canada or underground. We knew men who made each of these choices and none was proud of his decision. Some of draft age escaped induction because they were doing graduate work or were married or had begun families, but even these felt guilt at not suffering like their peers.

The men I felt most sorry for were the ones who fought, who were taught to kill and found they were killing women and children and old men, destroying whole villages, killing more non-combatants than enemy soldiers. The nature of war has changed. In World War I, civilians made up about 17% of the casualties, but by the time of Vietnam, the proportion of civilians killed and injured was as high as 85% or 90%. And it was not soldiers who became refugees or were forced out of their homes, carrying their children and as many of their belongings as their backs could bear, seeking sanctuary. "We had to destroy the village to save it," was one general's revealing statement. Some GIs did terrible things, often out of fear, often because that is what war now is with the expanded destructiveness of modern weapons, but whatever the explanation, they can't forget torn bodies of women and children, the smell of burning flesh from napalm, the lifting of normal restraints that happen in all wars, but more so in this war against Asians, against "Gooks." Many of our soldiers learned to drown their sorrows in alcohol and numb their fears with heroin.

Most who write about the costs of the Vietnam War forget to mention the cost to the Vietnamese and Cambodians. The devastation of neutral Cambodia is seldom mentioned. We don't think much about the Asian dead and injured and missing in action. What ends could you possibly find that would justify the means we used in Southeast Asia? I began to believe that war in general has become counter-productive, that war is obsolete.

To express our growing dismay, our aversion to our country's Vietnam policy, we demonstrated, set up draft-counseling sessions, delivered to our congressmen thousands and thousands of signatures on petitions to end the war – showed in every way we could think of that a large majority of fellow Americans wanted out. You would think in a democracy such wide-spread disaffection would be enough to effect a change of policies, but the escalation (more troops, increased bombing) continued as if our cries of "stop" were not heard. We would have to take other actions to get our government to listen. In early January, we were presented with a chance for a more effective challenge to President Johnson and the war. We took it.

CHAPTER 30

HOPE DEFERRED

Early in December of 1967, an anti-war Democrat, Senator Eugene McCarthy from Minnesota, whom most of us had never heard of, declared he was challenging President Johnson for the nomination of our party in the 1968 elections and would begin to campaign in the New Hampshire primary. About a month later, Bud and I went to a meeting called by Reverend Joseph Duffey, an acquaintance of ours at the Hartford Seminary. The purpose of the meeting was to hear Geoff Cowan, a Yale law student, describe how we Democrats who wanted to stop the war could use Connecticut's arcane party rules to get pro-McCarthy delegates to the August Democratic National Convention in Chicago. We had no presidential primary in our state, no democratic way to express our interests and frustrations within the parties. Both parties, Republican and Democrat, were closed clubs, with jobs and prestige, sometimes power, to dispense. Delegates to national conventions were selected for faithful service to their respective party as part of the patronage system, and they went to have a good time, willing to vote as their leaders told them.

However, Geoff had found a chink in that armor. There was a way to get pro-McCarthy delegates to the *state* convention which in turn would elect delegates to the *national* convention where the presidential nominee would be named. In towns with a population under 5,000 it was comparably easy. Any Democrat could attend the open caucuses where delegates to the state convention were chosen. McCarthy people just needed to identify and then get their followers to the caucuses. In larger towns and cities, the process was more complicated. McCarthy Democrats could pay a fee, file a slate of del-

*Tim meeting Gene McCarthy during his
New Hampshire campaign*

egates to oppose the slate chosen by the party's town committee, gather signatures of 5 percent of registered Connecticut Democrats on a petition supporting the McCarthy slate, then campaign for victory in a primary which was set for April 7th, less than three months away.

By organizing town by town, we might get enough McCarthy delegates to the Hartford convention in June to persuade the regulars to include some of us on the Connecticut delegation going to Chicago in August.

We got to know well most of the McCarthy supporters from all parts of the state at that crowded January meeting, and some became good and lasting friends. We were ready to try Geoff's suggestion, difficult and useless as it might seem. When Joe Duffey came up to me after the meeting and asked me to organize West Hartford, I looked around, hoping to see someone I could corral to do the job. No, not within striking distance. I caught Bud's eye and knew he felt as strongly as I did and would help as he had during another McCarthy period. So, yes. The answer was yes.

I announced in the paper that a West Hartford McCarthy for President Committee to select a challenge slate to the June State Convention was being formed and invited anyone interested to a meeting at our house. Over 50 people came! We soon elected a chair (me), secretary, and treasurer, and picked 21 of us to make up an opposition slate. Dr. Robert Hepburn, Katherine's brother, was one of us, so we called ourselves the Hepburn slate, hoping to be identified with our town's favorite celebrity. A friend offered a part of his office for our headquarters. We filed with the registrar of voters, picked up petitions and began collecting signatures, going house to house, explaining, cajoling, answering questions and urging anti-war unaffiliated voters to register as Democrats so they could vote for us in April. We had a lot of explaining to do, telling why we were trying to go to one convention in order to go to another. No one in town had participated in that kind of process before. Ordinarily, choosing candidates was done by the "machine" behind closed doors. The one formal political act possible at that time for the ordinary Connecticut voter was to choose in the polling booth between two presidential candidates chosen "in smoke-filled rooms" by party insiders. We persuaded about 1000 unaffiliated voters to become Democrats and in the process shifted the political balance in our town.

As the deadline for filing our petitions approached, I began to get calls from the Democratic town chairman. "We understand your concerns," he said. "We could substitute you, Mrs. Butterworth, for one of our delegates and then you would be represented at the convention."

"Out of the question," I answered.

The next call was, "How about two?" The offer got up to eight – eight out of twenty-one, and I decided to go for a long walk. Not that we expected to win. In fact, in those days of attempted negotiations, we were sure we would lose. But we did hope to have a few weeks of talking about the issues and being listened to. We would have lost that opportunity if a few of us had been absorbed into the "regulars'" delegation. We hoped to influence public opinion and to send a message, not only to the public about the war but to party insiders about the closed political system (the very one we were trying to use). We wanted to state forcefully that it was undemocratic and would have to change. Our long-shot campaign we saw as the means toward those ends.

CHAPTER 31

THE CONNECTICUT
PRE-CONVENTION CAMPAIGN

In every campaign I've worked on, events in the outside world have influenced the outcome in ways that could not be predicted or controlled, and our primary challenge was no exception. When McCarthy came within 230 votes of President Johnson and gained 20 of the elected delegates in the New Hampshire March primary, our fortunes rose: McCarthy looked like a feasible candidate. Four days later, when Robert Kennedy, also strongly anti-war, declared his candidacy, our fortunes dipped. And when Johnson, realizing that he was about to lose big in the Wisconsin primary, withdrew from the race at the end of March, our chances really fell. Wasn't that what the McCarthy campaign was all about, getting rid of Johnson? We'd already won, hadn't we? Besides, some of the delegates on the regulars' slate let it be known they were for Kennedy, so the McCarthy vote was no longer necessary. We managed to maneuver through those obstacles, and as the primary date came closer, we began to imagine we might actually win. There was much *esprit de corps* in our Farmington Avenue office. We made close friends of fellow workers. Generational differences disappeared as young people poured in to help get out the vote, sharing moments of hilarity, discouragements, and hopes. But there were still a few more shocks ahead.

About a week before the primary vote, we discovered another section in party rules that we thought would affect our campaign. Not only would the winning slate go to the state convention, but it would also choose two representatives to the State Central Committee, the highest political body where presumably important decisions were made. West Hartford was the political base for Katherine Quinn, the vice-chair of the Democratic State

Central Committee, Chairman John Bailey's "right hand woman," and if we won, we would have her political fate in our hands. That was amusing but hardly the important issue, so we put it out of our minds and concentrated on getting out the vote. Later we tried to barter for another McCarthy delegate to the Chicago convention in return for voting Katie Quinn another two years on the Central Committee, but no dice. Miss Quinn was not for sale. "To the victors belong the spoils," she told us, sounding reconciled, But I know she never forgot and her friends never forgave.

On April 4th, three days before the primary, Martin Luther King, Jr. was killed by a white man's bullet while he was helping Memphis garbage men gain a living wage. I felt a sinking in the pit of my stomach, the first emotionally depressing blow of the campaign but not the last. A man who preached non-violence to achieve desegregation and economic opportunity, a

MILES OF A WINNER—West Hartford primary results ire in and it's happiness in West Hartford. McCarthy Committee Chairman Mrs. Miriam B. Butterworth is flanked by State Chairman, the Rev. Joseph Duffey of Hartford, left, and Dr. Robert H. Hepburn, who headed the slate.—[Times Photo, David Ploss

from Hartford Times, 4/11 1968

man who opposed the Vietnam War, understanding the connection between our foreign policies and our domestic hopes and needs, a man of much influence and an extraordinary communicator, a man who worked for the things we were working for, was no more. Neither we nor the country could afford that loss. King's death sparked wide-spread rioting. About a hundred cities were trashed and burned, one of which was a section of Hartford. In Chicago, Mayor Daley told the police to shoot to kill arsonists and shoot to maim looters. In a few months the campaign for the presidential nomination would reach its climax in Chicago with Mayor Daley and his revved up police as convention hosts. We new-comers were learning that if politics was a game, it could be a deadly one. For a few days, the heart went out of our efforts, but then we pulled ourselves together, regained some of our *joie de vivre*, and went back to work.

Well, we won – by 156 votes! Along with New Britain, New Haven, Stamford, and some smaller towns, West Hartford would present a dissenting voice at Hartford in June. It was a great triumph and a rare one that year, but there are other bonuses than winning when you work on causes you feel deeply about. You make close friends and you feel a good deal of creative energy beginning to flow, encouraged by heightened emotions and an appreciative built-in audience. Some people fell in love. Others wrote songs or poetry. Somebody decided we needed a place to express our exuberance as well as our woes, a place for fund-raising, too, and found a sympathetic East Hartford nightclub owner who agreed to rent us his place every Friday. So once a week we had a nightclub of our own, Eugene East, where McCarthy supporters met and sang and talked, and where we had some really elegant entertainment: folk singers, story tellers, jazz players. The evening I remember best was spent with John Henry Faulk, a famous monologist who had been blacklisted years before for refusing to answer questions from the House Un-American Activities Committee. He was one of the few who had filed and won a libel suit against those who had ruined his career. The night he came to Eugene East, he told a long story about his fictitious Aunt Em who lived in the Texas boondocks. He had visited her "just last week" and she had greeted him with, "John Henry. Why cain't yew let Lyndon fight his war in peace?"

We needed those moments of merriment. A few weeks before the June convention in Hartford, the country was shaken by one more trauma. Robert Kennedy, too, was assassinated. One more Kennedy, one more possible avenue for changing our country's direction was snuffed out. Although we were McCarthy delegates, we were prepared to join forces with the Kennedy delegates if their candidate turned out to be stronger than ours. Now that was no longer an option. Senator George McGovern stepped in to hold the demoralized Kennedy delegation together, but the contest for the Democratic nominee for president had become essentially between Vice-President Humphrey, whom President Johnson could ensure would continue his war policies, and McCarthy, whose campaign had been weakened by some bruising contests with Robert Kennedy.

At the Hartford state convention, about a quarter of the delegates were for McCarthy, and we believed Connecticut's delegation to Chicago should reflect the preferences shown by the rank and file Democrats whenever they had been given the chance to choose. By that calculation, 11 or 12 delegates would have been added to McCarthy's strength at the National Convention. It gave me much pleasure to answer, when West Hartford's name was called, "21 votes yes" for the motion in favor of proportional representation, though we lost. We were given seven seats at first. When you remember all the powerful Democrats in the state and the party (the Governor, Secretary of State, Senate Majority Leader, and U.S. Congressmen, for instance), and when you consider that John Bailey, our state chair, was also national chair of the party that year, ensuring that Connecticut would be an important and conspicuous state in Chicago, I suppose it is surprising that we ended up with as many places as we did.

Paul Dwyer came up from New York and Dick Goodwin flew in from McCarthy's national headquarters to help our McCarthy state co-chairs, Joe Duffey and Anne Wexler, negotiate with John Bailey; and we were allotted two more spots on the delegation. One came from Senator Ribicoff, who wanted to heal the obvious rift in Connecticut's ranks. Ribicoff was up for reelection himself and would be in Chicago anyway to nominate George McGovern for the Kennedy delegates, but we appreciated his sympathetic gesture. Nine seats were still too few for some, and did not prevent almost a quarter of the convention from walking out in protest. As we started out the door, we heard the priest giving the final benediction say, "Remember, in Heaven there is neither Republican nor Democrat."

"Amen to that," we answered.

McCarthy himself put pressure on our negotiators to take the nine seats we were finally offered at the Connecticut convention. He needed as many delegates in Chicago as he could get. I was one of the nine. The others were Joe Duffey and Anne Wexler, the co-chairs of our state committee; Bill Jones, a young Black activist from New Haven; Stephanie May, a creative, irreverent housewife who had already put in years working for a nuclear test ban; two effective long-time peace activists from downstate; Paul Newman and Arthur Miller, who had enough celebrity status to sway their fans at the convention, perhaps. Heady company! We also had nine alternatives: a lawyer, several professors, and one writer of children's books who later wrote about circuses and persuaded his wife to give up their suburban life to join the lion tamers, clowns and acrobats. The others on the delegation were mainly big names in Connecticut politics: Governor Dempsey; state and national chairman, John Bailey; Senator Tom Dodd; ex-senator William Benton; my Chaffee School classmate, Secretary of State Ella Grasso, who would later become Governor; a handful of state congress people; and a number of other local and state heavies.

I became acquainted with many of the regulars at the state convention, and as the McCarthy representative on the Connecticut Platform Committee, I met some of the national cast of characters, too. The last weekend in June, I flew to Chicago to a hastily called meeting of the newly formed Coalition for an Open Convention. About 1500 from 39 states showed up: Kennedy and McCarthy delegates, members of the Black Caucus and student groups, and California field workers, all trying to find a way out of the disastrous campaign they saw coming. It would inevitably be Hubert Humphrey, Johnson's surrogate, who would continue Johnson's Vietnam policies, versus Nixon, neither wanting to end the war. It was a discouraging picture. In Chicago that week-end, the Kennedy people were still in shock. It was just three weeks since Bobby had been cruelly assassinated, and his people exuded anger, numbness and resentment. They were in no mood to switch to McCarthy.

We McCarthyites knew we didn't have the votes to nominate our candidate or even to influence the platform in an anti-war direction. Al Lowenstein, whom we had met at Eugene East one exciting evening; Sandy Gottlieb, head of the National Committee for a Sane Nuclear Policy, whom I would see more of in the '70's and '80's; and a very young but already charismatic Jesse Jackson – all were there, hunting for some new idea to retrieve a disintegrating situation. The whole gathering seemed to be foundering until late Saturday night when suddenly the mood changed. Those dissenters turned to what they knew best. They would organize their people to swell the ranks of the convention demonstrators. They'd get 100,000 – no, 150,000 people – housing for a million! And the weekend was over, a weekend fundamentally adrift with a thin overlay of hope.

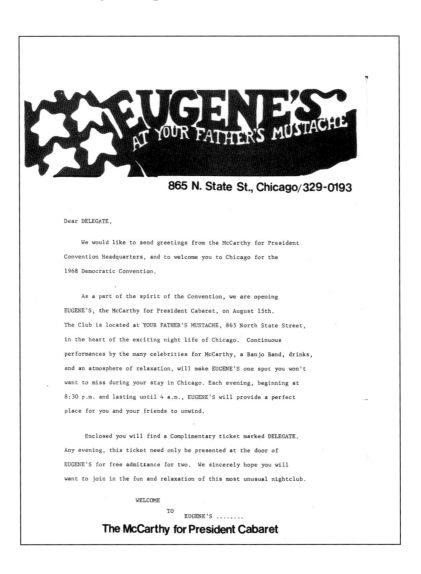

The McCarthy campaign established cabarets around the country
for a new kind of campaign rally.

CHAPTER 32

THE WAR COMES HOME

The Free University - ". . . an effort to form a new politics, a new economics, a new religion, a new education: a new vision of humanity."

In the midst of all this, we were teachers and parents still – and still sons and daughters. In June of 1969, my poor father died of pneumonia. He had lived in a nursing home for about a year, and although he got good care and Doug and I visited almost every day, he was ready to leave. Even at the end of his life he was undemanding and considerate, but he was not happy. He gave us the impression he was only waiting for the end.

Mike and Carol were studying and working in California. Mike had become involved in an innovative project called the Palo Alto Free University, a cooperative volunteer venture where anyone could offer and take imaginative courses in almost anything. Mike sent us their periodic descriptions of course offerings, large attractive booklets looking something like the later Whole Earth catalogues, and I loved to read them. There were the expected sensitivity sessions offered by various youths who wanted more sexual opportunities, courses exploring surrounding flora and fauna, and courses in dance, meditation, martial arts, and in U.S. foreign policy and Eastern religions. One course was labeled *How To Give Away Bread*. First you learn how to mix the dough, letting it rise while thinking high thoughts, and then you learn how to express love by giving the baked loaves to passers-by. I hope someone has an entire set of those remarkable publications. They contain a complete and authentic picture of a battered generation, idealistic, disillusioned, hopeful and despairing, caring and self-absorbed.

E. Brook Butterworth, 1st grandchild, in our home-made teepee – her father, Tim, taking the picture?

After the start of the lottery, Mike's draft number was called. However, before he was given his physical, he was kicked out of the recruiting center for distributing anti-war literature. He passed a rescheduled physical six weeks later, by which time they found him "too old" for the army. Maybe they didn't want a 27-year-old dissident creating trouble in a troubled army.

Tim had begun to teach at a private school in Vermont. He and Sue had

A serious Dan

their first child, our first grandchild, in July of 1968, a daughter called Brook who holds a special place in my heart. She was with us in 1990 when Bud died and continued to live with me for the next year, helping with correspondence, going through papers, cooking vegetarian meals. She was good company when I needed it most. Her birth afforded Tim another exemption from the draft, and the course his life had taken – college, graduate school, having a family – meant he never did receive an induction notice.

Dan and Kate's paths were not so smooth, and I think they remember the summer of 1968 with more anguish than the rest of us. In April before graduation, Dan and his classmates were ordered to take their physical exams at a selective service center in New Hampshire. Getting the preliminaries over with would speed up the process of induction for local draft boards when the graduates got home in June. The military needed more bodies fast. Dan didn't intend to fight in Vietnam and applied for conscientious objector status. He came from a long line of CO's – Quaker ancestors from generations back, including father, uncle, and grandfather. He was angry at our government by that time and didn't make it easy for the recruiter who asked, "Have you had any contact with communists, either here or abroad?" " Oh yes I have," happily answered Dan. "All last summer I worked in Poland and Hungary, and most of the people I worked with were communists." That was true. In the summer of 1967, Dan had applied to the American Friends Service Committee for some work camp experience, and they had placed him in two month-long programs in those two Communist countries. In the induction center, Dan made as much as he could of those contacts. The befuddled political officer called his Washington back-up officer, who flew in to interrogate Dan further. Dan, it was finally decided, was unsullied enough to fight, but the CO issue was still unresolved, and that was referred to Dan's Hartford draft board for further action.

In June, we drove north to Dartmouth for Dan's graduation, still stewing about the political maneuvering in Connecticut, not knowing we were heading for a historical event. At the ceremony, Dan sat with the group of graduates wearing black armbands, and we noticed his hair was longer than most; the longer the hair, in those days, the stronger the protest. We found the family section on the Hanover Green and sank back in our seats, expecting to sit through the usual bland ritual. We didn't relax long, however. We all sat up and paid attention when the class valedictorian, James Newton, began to speak. In my roles of teacher, teacher's wife, student, and mother of students, I've heard countless graduation speeches and forgotten them all except the one we heard that bright June day. Jamie Newton began calmly enough. He said the Class of '68 could not look forward to the kind of life earlier Dartmouh graduates had expected "because the larger society is in turmoil." What was most important domestically, he stated, was "to respond to the needs of our repressed minorities. We who are white must also realize that to evade the responsibility of reform is to passively aggravate the conditions that must be transformed if this society is to be worth living in." It was perhaps a little daring to be so concerned about civil rights at a Dartmouth graduation, but parents might assume their offspring weren't listening. A little head-in-the-clouds idealism probably wouldn't hurt.

When Newton started to talk about Vietnam, however, we parents knew every one of our sons was listening. "Most of us who graduate today will find our career plans...our attempts to respond to the needs of this nation will be interrupted by a notice to report for induction... Many of those drafted will be ordered to join in the military effort in Asia. I urge you to make full use of the academic skills you have gained at Dartmouth College before you accept that government imperative. Study the history of the Vietnam War and study its conduct. Study the impact it is having on Asian societies, on Asian attitudes toward America, and on America's conception of herself. Men of the Class of 1968...before you set off to participate in the devastation of that small country, Vietnam, and to risk your lives into the bargain, consider what you are about... It is my conclusion that the Vietnam

War is a colossal stupidity, a vast international atrocity, and an expensive lesson in the futility of modern aggressive imperialism – for, thank God, we are losing that war."

At this point, there were loud boos and cries of "treason" from many of the parents while some of us and most of the graduates gave Jamie a standing ovation. When things quieted down, Newton went on with his speech and soon was rousing his audience again. "Men of the Class of 1968…use the skills you have gained here as you plan your course of action. We must find our place in an on-going universal struggle for freedom and human dignity. I urge you to refuse to fight in Vietnam when that call comes for you. Take the path that seems appropriate for you. It may be conscientious objection, draft resistance, or escape to a country of greater freedom in the north…." At this, more boos and another standing ovation. It was an astonishing performance. Who else could have spoken more gripping words to a more attentive audience? Certainly not poor Senator Jacob Javits who got up next to give the main address. I don't know what he planned to say. Perhaps it was a strong patriotic appeal to those graduates or a standard exhortation to remember their obligations while embracing with enthusiasm the exciting prospects of their promising futures. Whatever that speech was, he knew he couldn't give it. Instead, he stumbled badly over some extemporaneous remarks that he tried to make appropriate to the emotions he was confronting. He was bound to fail, but it didn't matter. Nobody was listening.

The Hartford area draft board called Dan in soon after he got home to explain why he should be granted CO status. His request was denied. He appealed that decision and for almost two years he was in limbo, waiting to be called for a second hearing. By the spring of '70, fewer combatants were being sent to Vietnam and the board reversed itself. They must have understood that Dan was a serious objector and he, too, was the kind of trouble the army could do without.

Shortly after Dan's graduation, Kate came back from her semester in Mexico, trailed by a young Mexican named Fernando Valdez. We couldn't communicate with him because we spoke no Spanish and he spoke no English. Kate announced they planned to get married. Oh, Katie, Katie! What can you possibly know about him? What could *we* possibly know about him? How old was he, for instance? Kate said twenty, a year older than she, but he looked about sixteen to us. He hadn't been in the picture in March when we visited her during spring vacation, so they hadn't known each other for more than a few months. How could they even imagine what they were getting into? What could they do to support themselves? The family gathered at Squam in July, and Fernando was naturally scrutinized. He seemed affable enough and he liked cars, but beyond that he remained a mystery. We finally persuaded Kate to wait a year and continue on with her class to Kenya for the next semester. We promised she could go back to Mexico in the spring and then they could decide what they wanted to do. At least they would be a little older and maybe more mature. Fernando said *hasta luego* in August. Knowing Kate, we guessed we would see a good deal more of him, and we did. And because of him, our world, which up to then had been predominately European-centered, was widened to take in another language and another culture, that of the Hispanic societies south of our border.

CHAPTER 33

THE CHICAGO DEBACLE

Very little organizing was necessary in those days to get out a protest crowd. Take out ads announcing time, place, and purpose, and people around the country would do their own organizing. By August, however, Lowenstein and the others in the Coalition for an Open Convention sensed there would be big trouble in Chicago and warned their followers to stay away. In all, only about 10,000 protesters showed up during convention week, not even a twentieth of those expected at one time, but that was enough to arouse Daley and his police. The result was chaos.

As an official delegate to the convention, I was able to get a suite in the hotel with the rest of the Connecticut delegation. On August 26th, Bud, Kate, Dan, two young friends and I stepped out of O'Hare Airport into occupied Chicago – police everywhere, guns, barbed wire, police escorts, all presumably to protect us from the gathering mob of young people. It was hard to believe. What had our democracy come to if presidential nominations had to be conducted in armed camps? For four days, I was a part of the unfolding drama at the convention hall in the International Amphitheater while Bud, our two children and their friends were witnesses to the street theater going on in the parks and the streets of Chicago. At the end of the day, we would share our experiences, none of us having anything optimistic to report.

Those of us trying to move the country out of the Vietnam War by means of political action had chosen the Democratic Party. It was certainly more accessible to dissenting ideas than the Republican Party, which seemed permanently captured by what President Eisenhower called the military industrial complex. But our party, too, was stacked against us. Our primary challenges over the past six months proved that as many as 75% of the country wanted our troops out of Southeast Asia, yet we arrived at the convention knowing that Humphrey, who was irrevocably tied to Johnson's policies of military escalation, already had 1450 delegates pledged to him, 128 more than needed to get the nomination. Only about a third of the delegates had been chosen through primaries, the rest – rewarded for long and faithful service – had been chosen by party officials, the regulars.

As the regulars were inevitably tied to the Democrat in power, there weren't many options open to us. What about credentials? Fifteen delegations were challenged, those in the South on the basis of racial discrimination and lack of loyalty. Were Blacks able to participate freely in the political process that chose the delegations? Were white delegates going to vote for the Democratic nominee, or did they plan to vote for George Wallace, who had bolted the party? Mississippi was blatantly out of compliance with the rules defined in the Call to the Convention, and the challenge slate was seated. The challenge in Georgia was led by Julian Bond, an articulate young legislator who earlier in August had organized an alternate state convention. Bond's slate was much more democratically selected than that led by the Georgia Governor, Lester Maddox, a ranting racist type I had not encountered before. We had visits from Julian Bond, Andrew Young, and Gov. Maddox. Such a study in contrasts! Two educated, sophisticated, rational Black men and a crude, ideologically biased segregationist. The Georgia challenge ended in a compromise – half of each delegation was seated. The rest of the credential challenges were dismissed.

Another fight was against the unit rule. Until then, many state party rules included a provision that, at conventions, every state delegation had to vote unanimously – however the majority decided. Connecticut's unit rule had been suspended earlier in the year as a result of our primaries. Now the convention discarded the unit rule for all delegations at this and subsequent conventions – a victory, but the only one we were to have all week.

The crucial issue became the wording of the platform plank on the Vietnam War. Much of the platform was accepted without argument. On Wednesday, the convention heard discussions on issues that were not resolved. For days, representatives of various factions – the McCarthys, Kennedys, Humphreys, Southerners and Northerners – had met to find some compromise language on Vietnam that everyone could accept. During the negotiations, the peace delegates gave up asking for a South Vietnamese coalition government that might have been able to negotiate a cease fire at the bogged-down peace talks in Paris. They dropped the words "civil war" so the Johnson administration could maintain the fiction of a war of aggression from the North. What they couldn't give up was a call for the unconditional cessation of the bombing of the North. We believed such a pledge was absolutely essential if meaningful cease-fire talks were to begin. (Our negotiator in Paris asked a North Vietnamese negotiator what actions they would give up if we stopped bombing them. "We'll promise not to bomb your country if you stop bombing ours," he answered.) Ella Grasso was one of the regulars trying to find a compromise plank. I met her on the street once during this process, and she sounded almost up-beat. She thought they had worked out an agreement, but she was wrong. President Johnson, and therefore the Humphrey delegates, would not accept the compromise, so the majority plank gave no hint of a possible change that might bring an end to the war.

We listened to three hours of debate on the implications of the two planks and then retired to a room assigned to the Connecticut delegation for a vote. As we were leaving the convention hall, the daughter of one of our delegates asked me to watch how her father voted. He had promised to vote for the compromise plank and she was checking up on him. I remember that caucus for the impassioned speech made by Irving Stolberg, one of our McCarthy alternates. How could anyone who heard him not understand the moral and political necessity of accepting the minority plank, which would signal that our nominee could look for an end to the war? However, when the Connecticut delegates voted in that caucus room, only ten of us went for the compromise plank – we nine McCarthyites and Ella. She broke ranks, a brave political action and one that immediately brought her scorn and ridicule from her fellow regulars. The delegate I was asked to watch didn't break ranks but did break his promise to his daughter. It was that kind of year.

The vote of the convention was 1567 for the original plank and 1041 for the minority version, 200 more than peace delegates expected. Still, the loss represented a final failure of the process to accommodate itself to the needs and demands of the times. To express our dismay, many of us put on black armbands and marched two by two around a room while the folk singer Theodore Bikel led us in "We shall overcome." I found myself paired with John Kenneth Galbraith, so tall I couldn't make eye contact and had to nurse my sorrow unconsoled.

As we rode back to the hotel on the bus provided the Connecticut delegation, passing the protesters in the park, I heard one of the delegates, a mayor of a small town, say "Scum of the earth." Hey! Those are our children! They care! You can imagine I didn't have much sympathy for that man when, several years later, he was convicted of some political chicanery. Scum indeed!

THE WASHINGTON POST   Friday, Aug. 30, 1968   A 21

Rowland Evans and Robert Novak

Bowing to Dixie Demands Cost HHH Chance of Making Peace With Doves

CHICAGO—Vice President Humphrey's failure to reconcile the Democratic Party's doves and its roots not only in the White House but in outnumbered Southern delegations who cleverly exerted maximum influence at the convention.

The tip-off, almost unnoticed in the convention hubbub, came Monday when Sen. George Smathers of Florida announced he would withdraw as a favorite son and support Humphrey. What he did not announce was a private conversation that day with Humphrey, who pledged he would not disown the LBJ war policy.

Smathers was the key that unlocked five other Southern favorite son delegations for Humphrey. Vouching for Humphrey's reliability on the war, Smathers personally convinced Gov. Buford Ellington of Tennessee that he too should release his delegates for Humphrey.

But to make sure Humphrey was not wavering, Smathers kept contact with him—following his Monday conversation with talks on Tuesday and Wednesday. The threat was unspoken but clear.

Actually, the risk of losing those 359 Southern votes was not as great as it seemed. When the Vietnam vote came on Wednesday, Sen. Eugene McCarthy's campaign had collapsed and the movement to draft Sen. Edward M. Kennedy had aborted.

Thus, Humphrey forces were informed Wednesday that his advocacy of the bombing-halt plank would win him 80 to 100 additional votes out of California (with

Novak   **Evans**

fort at compromise. He also collaborated with educator Clark Kerr and labor leader Walter Reuther in an effort to reach a middle-ground Vietnam plank.

The Kerr-Reuther scheme, which called for a bombing halt in "expectation" of reciprocal response from Hanoi, was embraced by the Humphreyite Michigan delegation and sponsored by its Chairman Sen. Philip Hart. But this was vetoed by the

Humphrey high command.

The short-run and long-run implications for Humphrey are doleful. In the short run, the relatively hard-line Vietnam plank passed Wednesday afternoon coupled with police head-smashing against the yippies, produced a nasty mood on the convention floor that night as Hubert Humphrey was being nominated.

For the long run, Humphrey confronts a herculean task in attracting Party workers in California and New York—States whose support he desperately needs against Richard M. Nixon. In those six Southern favorite-son States well satisfied with his Vietnam stance, however, few Party leaders give him much chance to win (in Florida, he is running a poor third).

© 1968, Publishers-Hall Syndicate

CHAPTER 34

DEMOCRACY UNDER SIEGE

Few people mention the violence inside the convention hall, but it was there as well as on the streets. Our delegation was comparatively safe because we were National Chairman John Bailey's people. It was the New York delegation, other McCarthy delegates, and newsmen describing convention events who were harassed – physically assaulted by the "security forces," intimidated, and generally mistreated. Any viewpoint conflicting with President Johnson's was suppressed. Just a minor example – McCarthy signs and banners had been banished from the hall, a whole bunch of them sprayed with mace and made unusable, but Humphrey signs and signs saying "I LOVE MAYOR DALEY" and "THANKS TO THE CHICAGO POLICE" were allowed and on the last night blanketed the hall. It was almost impossible for us McCarthy delegates to get visitor passes that week, but I got two for Thursday night when Humphrey and Muskie (Vice Presidential nominee) gave their acceptance speeches. Kate and her friend went with us on the Connecticut bus and were walking through the corridor of the hall when they saw the signs for Daley and the police. Kate pointed to them and said "Ha" and felt a sharp blow on her elbow. It was from a billy club, wielded by a nearby policeman she hadn't noticed.

But it was on the streets of Chicago that people could see what a totalitarian regime could be. Daley loosed his police and

photos LIFE Magazine, 9/6, 1968, p.28 ff

Mayor Daley in his element

the National Guard on spectators, news-men, Yippies, McCarthy "Clean-for-Gene" young campaigners, whoever wandered into the park across the street from our hotel, or was just out walking with a friend. An official study that was released several weeks later called the violence a "police riot." The police went berserk, said an English reporter. Kate saw a woman drive up to the park to collect her children, only to have her tires punctured by a police bayonet. One evening Kate and her friend were heading back to our hotel to find some safety when six white men jumped out of a passing car, knocked over, beat, and kicked a Black spectator as police nearby just watched.

This is Daley's Chicago—

Daley had created problems by denying permits for any marches or for staying overnight in the parks. There was one permit for a rally in Grant Park, and the protesters could use Lincoln Park during the day, but with those exceptions there was no agreed-upon channel for expressing dissent. Dan tells about standing with Bud and Kate across the street from the hotel when a phalanx of police in gas masks charged the crowd in front of them. The crowd sat down as they had been trained, but the police continued on, spraying tear gas and flailing their billy clubs. A club swung down on a head right beside Dan. Another club was aimed at Kate, but Bud pointed his camera at the policeman and he veered off. Not that cameramen were exempt from attacks. Kate remembers motorcyclists lending their helmets to cameramen because so many were being assaulted.

The street violence and the delegates came together Wednesday night during the climax of the convention when the nominating speeches were being made and the roll was called. Word had been coming in to the news people at the convention hall and to the various candidates' headquarters there that the Chicago police had become frenzied with rage. They were using mace indiscriminately. Someone called the police action a sadistic romp. "Someone must stop them!" "Someone please help!"

*Grant Park,
1968 Democratic
Convention*

Much of the country watching the news on their TV's knew what was happening, The whole world was watching, as the young people in the park were chanting, except for most of us delegates in the convention hall. However, some of the peace delegates were getting an inkling of the violence and moved for adjournment. Little Carl Albert, the chairman of the convention that evening, ruled that motion out of order. It took Senator Ribicoff, who had agreed

to nominate McGovern for the Kennedy delegates, to galvanize the Mayor, the one man who could curb his police. Part way through his nominating speech, Ribicoff looked at Daley, sitting less than 20 feet away, and said, "With George McGovern president, we wouldn't have gestapo tactics on the streets of Chicago."

The seating arrangements at the convention favored our delegation. We had seats front right just across the aisle from Daley's Illinois contingent which, as host delegation, sat center front. I had been asked to be liaison for the nine of us McCarthy delegates, counting and reporting votes, for instance, and consulting with Bill Ratchford, the Connecticut Senate majority leader who was my counterpart for the regulars. That gave me an excuse to wander, and at the moment of Ribicoff's memorable statement,

■ With his hand cupped to his mouth, Chicago Mayor Richard J. Daley shouts at Abraham Ribicoff, left, at the tumultuous 1968 Democratic National Convention in Chicago.

The Hartford Courant, April 21, 1996

I was standing on the floor facing our delegation just below Ribicoff, and thus had a bird's eye view of what happened next. It's true Mayor Daley turned purple and shouted an obscenity. And then almost immediately, the security guards, who were nominally there to protect all of us, surrounded the Illinois delegation, closing off all contact with the mayor. As we suspected, the security people were Daley's men, too, and were there to protect him and his interests with whatever means they deemed necessary.

The balloting for the nomination continued until about midnight Wednesday, and as expected Humphrey won with 1760 ¼ votes. Nothing we had said or done had changed that outcome one iota. Some tear gas wafted up to the Humphrey headquarters on the 25th floor of the Hilton Hotel, enough to cause Hubert to take a shower, and two floors below, a shocked McCarthy and his aides watched the police mayhem out their windows. But Humphrey was watching the delegate count and jumped with glee when he was sure of the nomination. He even kissed the TV screen when his wife Muriel was interviewed a short time afterwards. He exclaimed to Lyndon Johnson, who called with congratulations, "Bless your heart, Mr. President. Thank you." Whatever political stature he had once had, by the

The New York Times, August 30, 1968

time he had been nominated as our candidate that August night, he was a hollow man.

The night wasn't over yet. Some of us got out our armbands again and were supplied with candles for a "funeral march" back to the hotels and the park where those battered protesters were waiting. We marched with Theodore Bikel's voice leading once more, and as we got nearer to the young people still demostrating, others began to join us. One who walked beside me was a youth from Chicago's south side who told of the intimidation which kept most of the city's

LIFE Magazine, p. 32A

Winners and Losers ~ Dick Gregory and Eugene McCarthy at Grant Park; Humphries and Muskies

Strife-Torn Democrats Limp Home

Gannett News Service

CHICAGO—The Democratic Party limped home from the most turbulent national political convention in decades today, shocked by the violence that stained the city's streets and uncertain of its prospects in the presidential election campaign ahead.

The convention closed on the traditional tableau of the party's nominees for president and vice president, Hubert H. Humphrey and Edmund S. Muskie, acknowledging the party's applause from the brightly-lit, gaily decorated podium in the International Amphitheatre.

But behind the tableau lay the most serious divisions in the party in 20 years —

Inside Pages

The Hartford Times, 8/30/68

Blacks from participating in the protests although they had wanted to. Only celebrities like Dick Gregory dared defy the mayor. Another who walked with me was a young Vietnam veteran whose eyes looked as if he had seen too much. And there was my family waiting for us with the others.

The police kept up their intermittent harassment with one last outburst at four o'clock Friday morning. A National

The Rev. Ralph Abernathy rides in Chicago in a Poor Peoples Campaign mule wagon being led by Hosea Williams (at right with beard)

Democrats Awake to a Party in Ruin

DEMOCRATS, From A1

Richard M. Nixon or Wallace in their states.

A Texas delegate said of Humphrey's prospects in that State: "He might finish second."

Liberals Bolting

Meanwhile, the anti-administration, anti-war liberals, who were defeated on both the platform and nomination fights, were streaming out of Chicago with the declared

These men have two objectives: to save themselves from the expected ruin, and to position themselves for the power struggle that would follow the Democrats' ouster from office in Washington next November.

Many of them are, cynically or realistically, more interested in controlling the wreckage than in repairing it.

The best defense they offer for their attitude is

sion-making to gain a share of influence.

But outside the convention hall — in that assemblage of dissidents encamped across the street from the Conrad Hilton Hotel — the demand for reform was heard loud and clear.

In that "second convention," held under the gaze of rifle-carrying National Guardsmen during the predawn hours today, a New York delegate declared:

—pieces in a museum, you understand me."

Richard Goodwin, who moves in all political worlds, came to the "second convention" at 4 a.m. to report his view of the status of the intra-aParty struggle.

"We didn't make it last night," Goodwin said, in a feat, "but we came a long way in eight months. And in another two years we will take the Country away from the Connallys, the Meanys and the Daleys."

Party—was the man candle-bearing dele down Michigan Aven ment early today.

It was the first real ing of the two conven and in the darkness, on egate tried to bridge generation gap with that seemed singular propriate:

"You oung people, said, "who have been enemies of the Estal

The Washington Post, August 30, 1968

Guardsman pointed out to the police that something had been thrown from one of the rooms on the 15th floor where McCarthy's staff was staying. The police raided the whole floor, lined everybody up, even those who were already asleep, and beat them.

Our plane left Friday afternoon, so we had time to have a buffet breakfast with the rest of the Connecticut delegation and lunch at a low-priced eatery, where a dozen or so grieving college students told us their horror stories of the past few days. At breakfast, I was about to speak to Senator Ribicoff when another delegate dashed in front of me. "You creep!" he shouted, with venom in his voice. "You ought to be maced!" Our flight home was not a hilarious one. We were grieving for ourselves to be sure, but also for our country and for democracy.

CHAPTER 35

WE SHALL NOT BE MOVED

The following winter, Kate spent six months in Kenya. Her letters described in vivid detail the adventures she experienced. On the streets of Nairobi, she wrote, for the first time in her life she was not color conscious. It was styles of clothes, or lack of them that was noteworthy. She met Dr. Leakey and, about once a week, Jane Goodall brought Kate and classmates up to date on her chimpanzees' social lives. For a while during that semester Kate lived in a small village called Banana Hills at a well-baby clinic, helping some University of Nairobi medical students take a census.

She kept records of housing and plumbing arrangements, and counted parasites in stool samples from villagers. How much closer to reality can you get than that? Toward the end of her African stay, Kate had another memorable adventure when she went off to another village to write her journal. There she lived in an adobe house with an eastern style outdoor toilet and a warthog that seemed to linger every night between her and the outhouse. The rains came at the end of that week, but she was rescued before the water rose over her bed where she had piled her journal and other worldly goods.

In spite of, or because of all this, Kate remembers Africa with affection and enthusiasm: the hilltop where you can see Mt. Kenya in one direction and Mt. Kilimanjaro in the other; the moving sticks their Jeep's headlights caught one night in a game preserve that turned into giraffes; the wonderful space. But she was still in love with Fernando. She returned to Mexico in the spring and lived with his family for several months, then they both spent the summer with us. In September, since they were still bent on getting married, we had a simple wedding in our back yard with some relatives and

Kate & Fernando's wedding in the Sunset Farm back yard, Sept., 1969

friends. There would be a church ceremony in Morelia when they got back to Mexico. We watched the Valdezes head off in their second-hand VW Beetle for Guadalajara, where they would live for the next fourteen years. Although they were still young, 20 and 21, they at least knew a little more about each other and the families they were joining. They would be very far away, for much of the time in a small village that lacked even a telephone. They spent most summers in New England, often finding temporary jobs, and we usually spent about a week of each Christmas vacation with them in Mexico, but as of that September of 1969, we had no more apron strings attached to Kate, our youngest child and only daughter.

Dan had been told by his draft board to hang around until they could re-hear his appeal for CO status and he did, month after miserable month, waiting to get a notice of his second hearing. He did a little work for the American Friends Service Committee, found some temporary jobs, stayed up late and slept late, hung around with others who were hanging around, used Bud's tools and forgot to put them away, until suddenly he and a friend took off for Spain. They spent months on the island of Ibeza, eking out a hippy existence, and then just as suddenly Dan reappeared in the spring of 1970, only three days before his hearing notice arrived. For once, the Fates were with him. The draft board granted him CO status this time, but his usual antic nature had turned sullen. No more coop-eration with the government.

Kate and I with Fernando on Kate's left, with the Valdez family

He took off for New Hampshire and spent several spring months at Squam alone, neither the first nor the last of our family to seek solace in that simple cabin life, working hard on wood piles, exploring the woods, climbing, canoeing, finding ways of healing his spirit before he reentered society.

Dan still didn't know what he wanted to do. Any job for him would have to be unconnected with government or big corporations. He

Scheherazada, Kate, Fernando holding Eliott, and Natasha in 1979

wouldn't be "part of the system." What kind of work was left? Fortunately, in the fall of 1970, a friend in Burlington, Vermont, called and read Dan a help-wanted ad for a puppeteer's assistant. That must have sounded safe enough. He got the job, learned a good many skills and some years later started his own company. Now he makes his own marionettes, experiments with all forms of puppetry, teaches in schools from Alaska to Maine, puts on shows in Hong Kong, California, North Carolina, and points north, and in June of 2005 was given a Pell Award for contributions to the arts, along with Ruby Dee and Ozzie Davis, posthumously. Good company!

Bud and I went back to the comparative sanity of our respective schools. I had announced to Chaffee in the spring of 1968 that I would leave teaching in June of the next year. I was getting too involved in political action. I had loved teaching, especially the last eight years, but it was time to concentrate on politics.

Kate & Fernando looking happy – maybe late 1980's?

CHAPTER 36

BECOMING OLD PROS

Meanwhile, the war grew as did antagonism to it. Despite the blow to our hopes in Chicago, we plunged into even more vigorous political activity that fall. We still believed our political system was susceptible to citizen action. First we took over the Ribicoff senate campaign, helping him win the state by a large margin and pulling Humphrey along on his coattails. Humphrey may have been hollow, as I have said, but he was more honest than his opponent, Nixon, who claimed he had a secret plan to end the war. Why secret? We knew he had no more to offer than his predecessors when he declared he had no intention of presiding over an American defeat, yet he was not striving for a victory over North Vietnam. This was the same old recipe for disaster. It wasn't for frivolous reasons that Nixon was called "Tricky Dick." Humphrey never de-

Mims after seconding Abe Ribicoff's nomination at the Hartford Convention

~226~

veloped enough independence from Johnson to win the presidency, giving Nixon at least four years to make his "plan" work.

Our VW bus, Bud's contribution to Joe Duffy's

Thus, we started an organization called the Caucus of Connecticut Democrats, a progressive reform movement within the party. A big crowd of VIPs, Democratic regulars, McCarthy and Kennedy people showed up at our December 1968 founding conference: Jack Newfield of *The Village Voice*, Arthur Miller, United States Attorney Jon Newman, Bert Corona from Cezar Chavez's California Farm Workers, Secretary of State Ella Grasso, and Channing Phillips from Washington. There were speeches and workshops, twelve of them, whose purpose was to "explore…social issues and to consider which merit a long term commitment…" In the call for the conference, we claimed we "shared a common belief that men [sic] are capable of creating an increasingly humane world."

During the next several decades, many of us

around the state served on town committees, ran for higher offices, lobbied the legislature for such things as a state income tax, and even elected one of our people, Mary Sullivan, to the Democratic National Committee. She lasted almost to the end of the '80s, protecting the gains we had made, providing an alternate voice. In 1970, Joseph Duffey challenged the party nominee, a millionaire zipper manufacturer and a big donor to the party. Duffey won the primary but lost the election to Republican Lowell Wieker in a three-way race.

In 1974, when George McGovern became the Democratic candidate for president, I came close to being one of the regulars myself, in charge of organizing Connecticut's 6th District for the Party. One of the complaints many of the regulars made against us was that we were sunshine warriors, acting only when interested in some issue but not there for the day-to-day running of the party – licking envelopes, getting out the vote, etc. I suspect they soon wished we would fit their description of us.

CHAPTER 37

AND DISSENT GROWS

We know from his tapes that Nixon, too, wished we and other protesters would go away. Instead, we organized in our home town, persuading rabbis and ministers as well as mayors and town councilors from both parties to speak at rallies on West Hartford's Goodman Green. In November, we chartered as many buses as we could, and people from all over the state poured into Washington, along with thousands from the rest of the country, still trying to put pressure on congress and the president to stop the war. Nixon's response was to announce a gradual reduction of our armed forces in Vietnam, while escalating the bombing, as he attempted to bolster the Vietnamese army, "Vietnamizing the war." Since such attempts had already been tried, by the French as well as by the U.S. and had been proved counter-productive, we imagined that path would lead to our defeat, if Nixon held to his timetable, but only after many more deaths and much senseless destruction.

Mims & Bud with Cliff Leonart talking strategy with George McGovern in 1974

We now know that Nixon's further reaction to protesters was to hunt for a conspiracy, sending the "plumbers" to steal Daniel Ellsberg's psychiatric records and to bug Democratic headquarters, hoping to find, among other things, connections between the organizers of the march and the Democratic Party. This shows a fundamental misreading of the nature and depth of the protest – and its pervasiveness. We just put ads in the paper and people came. Those Washington rallies were highly emotional. We who were middle-aged were surprised to feel not just accepted but actually loved, certainly almost reverently taken care of by a whole sea of young strangers, young people packed closely together on the mall, as we sang "Let the Sunshine In." We must have provided a welcomed contradiction to young activists' belief that anyone over thirty was out to get them, a belief reinforced by the killings at Jackson and Kent State in 1970. As a result of those murders, college students left their campuses in protest, and a large number came to help Joe Duffey, one of the few strongly anti-war candidates running. Finding homes for those serious but high-spirited students and providing enough food for their lunches and snacks at the Duffey headquarters was a campaign in itself, but in the process our lives were lit up by a host of concerned and capable young people. Some of them became our good friends.

Others we became fond of at that time were students at the Hartford branch of the University of Connecticut. For about two and a half years, four or five of them spent weekends during school sessions, putting out a small newspaper from our house. They typed it, mimeographed several hundred copies on an old machine in our cellar, collated it on our living room floor, and gave it away on Mondays to their classmates. It was anti-war, discussed ways to extricate ourselves from Vietnam, described our bombing escalation and our invasion into neutral Cambodia, and included reprints of articles analyzing our foreign policies.

In 1970 Irving Stolberg, a fellow delegate to the 1968 Chicago Convention, became a legislator from New Haven and soon introduced a bill that declared the Vietnam War unconstitutional and empowered Connecticut's Attorney General to represent any Connecticut draftee who refused to serve in Vietnam. The bill was similar to one proposed in Massachusetts and several other states. I volunteered to be Irv's legislative aide, and we got some impressive people to come to Connecticut for a hearing. Of course, the bill didn't pass, but many of our actions those days were intended to raise issues and force debate, and we accomplished that.

In March of 1971, I went to the peace talks in Paris with a group sponsored by the American Friends Service Committee, the Fellowship of Reconciliation, and Clergy and Laity Concerned, but that deserves a separate chapter.

CHAPTER 38

PARIS PEACE TALKS

In March of 1971, 170 of us from 41 states, a "people's delegation," flew out of New York on Icelandic Airlines for the peace talks in Paris, participating in a Citizens' Conference on ending the war in Indochina. The cost for the week was $336, which included $161 for a round trip ticket and $110 for seven days of rooms and meals. We didn't stay at the Metropole. I went representing the American Friends Service Committee. We were housewives, doctors, nuns, rabbis and priests, educators, Vietnam veterans, members of the League of Women Voters, journalists, attorneys, nurses, engineers, business men, social activists, an aide to the mayor of Newark, New Jersey, a mysterious state representative from Wisconsin, a poet, and Judy Collins. A few of us had worked in Laos, Cambodia, or Vietnam in various programs such as A.I.D. and International Volunteer Services, and many had made an in-depth study of Southeast Asia and the war. But most of us had lots of questions to clear up before we would feel knowledgeable enough to speak authoritatively against the war on our return.

We had one thing in common, however. All of us felt the war was tearing our society apart and must be ended. We all wanted to find whether the negotiations in Paris held any promise of reaching a solution, and, if not, what we as United States citizens could do to get things moving. We spent the first two days listening to and discussing negotiating positions with Xuan Thuy and other members of the Democratic Republic of Vietnam (North Vietnam to us) and with Madame Binh and other members of the Provisional Revolutionary Government, the political arm of the Viet Cong. On the third day, we heard and questioned non-aligned groups: Buddhists, Catholics, French newsmen and historians, and some international journalists including Mary

McCarthy. On the fourth day, we spent several hours listening and questioning the Saigon delegation, and three hours in conference with the second tier of our U.S. delegation. One evening we met with Laotian students studying in France and on another with a Cambodian representative of Sihanouk's government in exile. There were also small luncheons and daily meetings between special interest groups. The Catholic clergy in our People's Delegation, for example, met with Vietnamese Catholics, some of whom had left the North in 1954 but were now against the continuing U.S. presence in Vietnam. Although we didn't all get to each of these meetings, we briefed each other often, and by the end of the week we thought we had a pretty complete picture of the situation.

Running through almost all the meetings were conflicting versions of Vietnamese history and the origins of the Indo-Chinese conflict. Was it aggression from the North or are North and South Vietnam one country, separated temporarily after a case-fire agreement with the French in 1954? Is the Thieu-Ky government a puppet of the U.S. with a narrow political base, or is it a legitimate government of a viable country? Eighteen months earlier, the U.S. had expanded the war into neutral Cambodia, installing Lon Nol as president, and, as we spoke, was helping the South Vietnamese soldiers fight in Laos. Had the war become a neo-colonial one between a large majority of Southeast Asians and an imperial power? Both the U.S. and Saigon delegations refused to discuss the past. "To get a historical understanding would take too much time." "If you don't accept our (aggression from the North) concept of history, nothing we say will make sense." Everyone else we talked with saw North and South Vietnam as one country, and the fight against the United States and its client state a continuation of the fight which had started years before against the Japanese and the French.

One other persistent theme, the U.S. demand for the immediate release of our prisoners of war, seemed suspect to me. Nixon had declared our troops would stay until our prisoners were returned. The North Vietnamese said they would return them when we withdrew our troops as stipulated in the Geneva Conventions. Stalemate! A convenient and emotional excuse for breaking off fruitful negotiations? The topic surfaced again at a reception given to our group by the DRV the night before we came home. I had just been asked by a North Vietnamese named Wuang if I felt any optimism after our week in Paris when that mysterious state representative from Wisconsin joined us. By that time he was not so mysterious. We had discovered he intended to deliver a batch of letters from his constituents to the North Vietnamese, demanding the release of the prisoners of war, and here was his chance to make that demand.. He could exploit this moment back home in his next election. A look of bafflement came over Mr Wuang's face. "We Vietnamese don't understand you Americans," he said in his answer to Wisconsin's request. "How can you be so concerned about a few hundred imprisoned men who have been incessantly dropping bombs on us when you are killing thousands of our people everyday?" The letters didn't come out of Wisconsin's pocket that night.

Here are a few more significant moments of that week. Some jubilant Laotian students reported what Nixon had said in a press conference two days after our departure for Paris and compared it to what they said was really happening. On March 5th, Nixon reported, "What has been accomplished in Laos has insured even more the plan for the withdrawal of American troops. The disruption of the supply lines of the enemy through Laos…has very seriously damaged the enemy's ability to wage effective action. Now in southern Laos and also in Cambodia, the South Vietnamese on the ground by themselves are taking on the very best units that the North Vietnamese can put in the field… General Abrams tells me the South Vietnamese can give an even better account of themselves than the North Vietnamese units…" The Laotian students described an entirely different situation, a devastating South Vietnamese and U.S. defeat in a major attack on Laos most of us hadn't heard about before and a desperate retreat of those still alive, piling into and hanging on to the U.S. helicopters sent to the rescue.

A conversation with Philip Habib, the behind-the-scenes U.S. delegation chief, was reported to us by Lee Rayson, a doctor from Illinois. Habib had agreed to see only two of our group, people with special letters of introduction from mutual friends, so we depended on them for that key interview.

Lee: "Was going into Cambodia a blunder?"

Habib: "That was a political decision, not military. Lon Nol was about to fall. Never lose a country to Communism before an election. No Mea Culpa. Forget about blunders. We could annihilate them in two weeks. Don't talk about history. War crimes?" (Habib smiling.) "Don't worry. We'll win.

The only possible outcomes are Vietnamization or negotiations on our terms."

Lee: "I think we're losing our national heritage, and I for one no longer want to be a good German."

Habib (mad): "We've been right all along. Never done anything wrong."

Lee: "Why can't we leave?"

Habib: "We're not going to let down our Saigon friends!"

As it turned out, the Laotian students were right and Nixon and Habib were wrong.

In answer to Mr. Wuang, no. I didn't see any hope for the negotiations to succeed. The U.S. had no intentions at that time of stopping the bombing or of agreeing to a neutral administration in the South that would hold internationally monitored elections, giving us a justification to exit from that quagmire. And the DRV and the PRG showed little sign of giving up their struggle for independence. The dropping of napalm and agent orange, the herding of villagers into "Strategic Hamlets," the destruction of land and countries, the killing of thousands and thousands, and the lying to the American people in an attempt to maintain support for this criminal folly would continue. And it did for four more years until our troops and advisors were finally ignominiously forced out.

INTERIM: WHAT'S FUN ABOUT IT?

At this point in my "mulling over and summing up," I find myself asking two questions: Why have I devoted so much of my life to working on causes whose outcomes are sure to be ambiguous at best, causes guaranteed to give rise to frustration and disappointments? And why have I had such a good time doing so? Curiosity is my quick answer. What really is going on? Why do different people think the way they do? Getting an insight into people's motives or having a revelation of a historical trend is almost as exciting to me as hearing the first spring peepers or a loon's wild call. As Bud used to say, whenever we experience something especially baffling or even reprehensible, "It's all a part of the grand pageantry of life." And life is pretty grand in all its sordidness and glory.

Another explanation comes from Socrates, who said we never truly live unless we participate in the affairs of the polis.

A third reason is friends. There is a rare richness in the relationships you have with people you work closely with on issues you mutually care deeply about. This applied first of all to Bud. We already had an unusual number of ties that bound us together: joint experiences, bringing up children together, long running arguments on *What is Art?* and *Are there any Absolutes?* In addition, we agreed politically. Bud wrote pithy letters to the editor, helped organize marches, spoke at rallies, and served on the local board of the American Friends Service Committee at a time when many young men needed draft counseling.

Once Bud was visited by an FBI agent, a funny little fellow with a big briefcase – holding a tape recorder! Igor Sikorski, a lawyer with the Connecticut Civil Liberties Union, was with Bud and pulled out *his* tape recorder. The FBI visit had been triggered by a sizable contribution Bud had sent to an organization headed by Corliss Lamont for a full page ad in *The New York Times*. The little man asked a few questions and left, but he wrote a letter urging Bud to stay away from Lamont, who was a dangerous person, probably even a Communist. Bud wrote back, thanking him for the warning and said he would happily contribute elsewhere if the FBI man would tell him the name of a "safer" organization that was as effective in opposing the war. He didn't get an answer.

And mutual friends! In the decades of the '50s, '60s and '70s, our story intertwined with that of Mary Jane and Jim Carpenter. Jim and Bud

Mims, Jim, Mary Jane Carpenter in Nova Scotia ca. 1968

were friends from childhood through college. I met Mary Jane when she and Jim were married in 1941, and we soon recognized we were kindred spirits. In the late '50s, they built a house in our community, about three minutes through the woods. From then on, we could meet half way for walks in the reservoir or join our meals for a spur-of-the-moment dinner together. Our families made merry together at birthdays and any other event we could celebrate, and both families cherish memories of the Carpenter's annual winter greening parties and the Butterworths' Christmas vacation potluck suppers and square dances.

Kate and Mike promenade

We four turned out to be good traveling companions, and we made many trips together – to Nova Scotia, Italy (with Elder Hostel), France, the Isle of Mull, and along the Norwegian coast. In the fall of Bud's 1970/71 sabbatical year, we kicked up our collective heels and left for a six-week European trip, right in the middle of the Duffey campaign. We wandered through the *Haute Savoie* sections of France, revisiting some of the places where our family had lived in the mid-'50s, then into Switzerland, after which we dipped into Yugoslavia, where we smelled the pervasive coal dust in Ljubljana's air and gloried in the beauty of Lake Bled.

Bud, Mary Jane and Jim Carpenter in Switzerland

We ended up in London, staying at a somewhat gloomy Quaker hostelry called the Penn House, located near the British Museum and within walking distance of the theatre district. There were some interesting characters at the Penn House. One was a wandering kleptomaniac older woman whose husband tried to return each night the things she had pilfered during the day. Two men from Vietnam were also staying there. Their money was running out, but they were on their way to the Paris Peace Talks, with a plan to end the war. One was an earnest Englishman accompanying a Professor Nhon, headmaster of a prominent Christian secondary school in Saigon. They believed all the delegations in Paris were negotiating in good faith, that they all wanted peace but just hadn't come up with the right formula. Our Penn House pilgrims had worked hard with others in Vietnam and thought they had found the magic recipe. I cringed at the thought of

Jim, Mary Jane and Bud in France

their coming disappointment. It seemed all too obvious to us by that time that one side, our side, was not looking for a way out but was stalling, still hoping for victory.

In early 1975, I was offered a state job by my old classmate, Governor Ella Grasso. It became obvious my time would be fully occupied and, before I was sworn in that fall, Mary Jane made us a proposal. She would like to be part of my new venture and offered to provide our weekday dinners while I was working. And she did! She cooked twice the amount she would have made for the two of them and we had gourmet meals for almost four years. Of course we paid, but very little – not a great deal more than costs, it seemed to me. Mary Jane was housewife for us all.

CHAPTER 39

SO THAT'S HOW THE WORLD WORKS

Rate structures, energy needs, fuel adjustment clauses, nuclear plant decommissioning! A phone call in the spring of 1975 from Governor Grasso, my old classmate Ella, thrust me on to new ground – a long way from the history, political, or civic fields I had been plowing. I had just finished a stint as chair of the state Caucus of Connecticut Democrats and had decided it was time to play my grandmotherly role and perhaps to clean out our attic.

"How would you like to be a commissioner on the Public Utilities Control Authority?" Ella asked me. "It's time to do some real work." I said yes almost immediately without needing any persuasion and without knowing what I was agreeing to. I soon learned that a commissioner's job was more than full time and was highly paid, all news to me. In her campaign for governor, Ella had talked a good deal about the need for regulation reform and had pushed through a progressive regulatory law during her first legislative session, but I had paid little attention. Now I would be functioning under that law. I got a copy of Public Act No. 75-486 and picked up books and articles that would give me some understanding of the decision-making I would soon be called upon to perform.

For several years I had been a board member of a Nader-style consumer organization called Connecticut Citizens' Action Group (CCAG) and knew they had worked on energy and regulatory issues. I looked through their files and found helpful basic information on utility regulation and references to more advanced material. Later, during the summer of 1976, after some experience on the Commission, I spent some weeks studying Utility Regulation in an excellent summer course given by the University of Michigan in East

Lansing. Except for these experiences, my understanding came from on-the-job training. In the early months of our work, Al Kleban, chair of Ella's new commission, wisely assigned two of us newcomers to any simple case that came in, with old pro Jerry McCann heading the panels. We sat mainly on small water company cases, and it was there I gradually learned how a quasi-judicial process such as ours should be conducted.

I had time the summer before being sworn in as Commissioner to wonder why Ella had chosen me. As the first woman governor elected on her own merits, I think she was hoping to make strides for women in her administration. The feminist movement was at its height in those years and both she and I were beneficiaries. I was the first woman appointed a utility-regulating commissioner in Connecticut. It was a small window of opportunity. Ella may have thought of me because she knew I was interested in economics. During the previous two years, as chair of the CCD, I had organized an ad hoc Committee for Economic Alternatives and three conferences: one on economic conversion (from dependence on military production) in general; one on Economic Alternatives for Connecticut; and a Forum on Multinational Corporations. We were concerned with Connecticut's overwhelming dependence on the defense industry for jobs and standard of living. This concentration on essentially one industry meant and still means an economy and state vulnerable and therefore resistant to peace, averse to a reduction in the defense budget. It also meant and means today that anyone we elect to represent us in Washington is reluctant to vote against any weapon system, whether needed or useful or even workable – an unhealthy political situation. I had been talking about the need for jobs in a peaceful society and, of course, my affiliation with the CCAG indicated my interest in the welfare of ordinary citizens. Ella must have seen me as both concerned about economic development and pro-consumer, as did I.

A more important question I asked myself that summer had to do with the process itself. We were beginning our work just when the movement for deregulation was coming into full flower. I came trailing assumptions and experiences from the '20s and '30s, when business excesses and bankruptcies, cutthroat competition and cartels, led to the big Depression and then gave way in the '40s to what seemed essential anti-trust laws and the burgeoning of regulatory bodies, "the fourth branch of government." I didn't believe the nature of free marketers had changed. The paramount value of the bottom line, the self-interested decisions that were supposed to produce the perfect economic equilibrium, had failed in the '30s and certainly couldn't achieve the universal utility services we had come to identify with a civilized society. Also, health, safety, and environmental issues were gaining significance, and I decided an unregulated market couldn't solve problems in those areas either.

The '70s saw a strong movement toward consumer-owned utilities. Municipalities around the country were developing their own power companies or talking about it. I have a large packet in my files from environmental groups with headlines reading: "PUBLIC POWER PUSH IN MASS," "REVOLT IN VERMONT," and "TURNING PRIVATELY CONTROLLED U.S. ENERGY INTO SOCIALIZED REGIONAL AND LOCAL NETWORK."

Gov. Ella Grasso swearing in the Public Utilities Control Authority commissioners Jerry McCann, Dick Jones, Mims Butterworth, Tom Standish and Al Kleban (Chair)

However, there was no such movement in Connecticut, and I doubted our country would go in that direction.

So regulation it would be, but I was aware of pitfalls there too. Regulators could and often did become too cozy with the industry they were supposed to judge. If we were to be trusted by the public, we would have to keep the companies at arm's length. People were amused when I insisted on paying for my sandwich and salad at the telephone company's cafeteria while being shown their up-to-date, recently equipped premises. And when I became chair, I always left my door open, and my assistant sat in on any conference involving a company we regulated. And for our decisions to seem fair and credible to the companies we regulated, we had to fend off political interference with our decisions too. In fact, the political hands-off mandate was a part of the law that applied to us. The integrity of our actions would determine the credibility of our decisions. Ella probably counted on me to deflect the common complaint that regulators are always coopted by the companies they are supposed to regulate. That would not be a problem, I was sure – too confident by far.

CHAPTER 40

A VERY EXCELLENT JOB

I am grateful to Ella for that job. Show me another that would have expanded my horizons so much. To begin with, the range of industries we regulated was amazingly comprehensive: all of the privately owned gas, electric, telephone, water, trucking and busing, and cable TV companies in Connecticut. There were five of us commissioners: two hold-overs from the pre-Ella commission: a Democrat, Al Kleban, who became chair, and a Republican, Jerry McCann. Of the three new-comers, Dick Jones from New Haven (who didn't stay long) and I were complete novices. The other, Tom Standish, had been a consultant in the field of utilities for a few years so had a head start in understanding the process. We had a staff of about one hundred: engineers, accountants, rates and management analysts, and consumer assistants, among others. Also there was a separate and independent Consumer Counsel whose job was to represent consumer interests in cases brought before us. A good deal of our effectiveness would depend on competent staff and the Consumer Counsel, at least until we neophytes knew what we were doing.

Title 16 of the General Statutes, the law under which we operated, described our duties. We were to see that the companies we regulated were "fully competent to provide efficient and adequate services to the public," that they "perform all of their responsibilities…so as to promote economic development within the state with consideration for energy conservation and the prudent management of the natural environment." We were charged with being sure the level and structure of rates were sufficient to cover companies' operating costs and capital costs, to attract needed capital, and to maintain their financial integrity; and we had to "determine whether existing or future rate structures place(d) an undue burden upon those persons of poverty status." We also had to implement rate principles "without being unfair or discriminatory or unduly burdensome or disruptive to any group or class of customers" as long as such implementation is "capable of yielding the required revenues." A tall order! Several of our mandates could conflict, and all of them would be subject to different interpretations and individual judgement. What constitutes "adequate service," for instance, and what level of rates is really sufficient to allow companies to attract needed capital?

I met with Al Kleban the summer before we were sworn in, looking for advice, and was surprised to be asked to become vice-chair when our term began. So from the start, I worked closely with Al and his able assistant, Ray McGannan. Ray knew more about utilities and the working of the commission than anyone else around. He became my assistant when, several years later, I took Al's place as chair. With Al as mentor, a wise, honest, humane

MIRIAM B. BUTTERWORTH
VICE CHAIRPERSON

and savvy model, and Ray as experienced and discerning secretary, who answered our correspondence in articulate and judicious prose, I think we did a credible job in spite of the extraordinary pressures surrounding utility regulation in general during the fermenting years of the '70s and some special tensions in our Commission in particular.

Energy was a hot topic in those years. The OPEC boycott, concerns about nuclear plant safety, worry about fossil fuel pollution, and above all rising rates caused a lot of dissatisfaction. Despite Connecticut's reliance on nuclear plants for almost half its electric power, rates were rising. Wasn't nuclear power supposed to make electricity practically too cheap to meter? Expecting to see lower rates the more electricity they used, people were suddenly told to conserve. Turn down that thermostat! Turn off those lights! They became uncertain. Would they be able to pay their bills, light their houses, keep their families warm in the future? Who was to blame for this insecurity, the utility companies who had planned badly and still made money, or the regulators who set the rates consumers had to pay? Or was it the

Arabs who made oil scarce and costly? Or did the *federal* regulators, whose concern over nuclear safety added so much to the cost of producing nuclear power, betray the promise of cheap electricity from that source?

Whatever the explanation given for consumer frustration and antagonism, we could feel it every day. There are several ways to respond to public anger. You can lend a sympathetic ear and do what is possible to ameliorate the burdens on those hardest hit. We could and did craft rate structures and took other actions for that purpose. We could and did make changes that would have some long-term benefits. One other reaction to public hostility is to exploit it for one's own advantage and some of us did that too.

CHAPTER 41

TOO CHEAP TO METER?

Some of the most complicated issues we dealt with revolved around nuclear power. Leland Sillin, president of Northeast Utilities, Connecticut's main provider of electricity, was a gung-ho nuclear power advocate, so by the mid-seventies, over 50% of that company's electrical output came from its three nuclear plants: Connecticut Yankee (500 kws) on the Connecticut river and Millstone I and II (both over 1000 kws) in Watertown on Long Island Sound. A third Millstone 1000kw plant was already in the works, slated to be on line in 1982. NU even had plans to build three more large nuclear facilities in Montague, Massachusetts – ambitious projects that were cancelled soon after we took office. At the first meeting we had with NU, we discovered they already had much excess capacity – 65% in fact. Industries and other consumers had responded to the rise in energy prices by conserving and demand had fallen substantially. Even the third Millstone probably wasn't needed, certainly not at the time it was due to be finished. Millstone III and the controversial Seabrook facility in Vermont would be the last to be built in New England for a long time. Reality was abruptly puncturing engineering dreams of cheap energy in those crisis years of the '70s.

Nuclear power advocates had made several big miscalculations having to do with the cost of those huge capital-intensive plants that take as long as a decade to build. One of the regulatory principles I agreed with is that construction work in progress (CWIP) should not be added to the rate base until a plant is on line. The idea is that consumers should pay only for the plants which are producing the energy they are using. It is assumed that the delay in payment for the construction of a new plant will force the companies to be sure they need a new facility. Gas, oil, or water-powered plants can be built with modest amounts of funding in three or four years, so the return on borrowed money begins to flow into the company fairly soon after loans are made. However, with nuclear facilities, large amounts of money must be borrowed and interest paid before consumers begin to pay rates that include the cost of the new construction.

To be consistent, consumers of nuclear energy should pay the *entire* cost of the facilities whose energy they use. That includes not just the construction of power plants but their dismantling too. Why should future generations pay for decommissioning plants whose energy they never used? This was an issue being debated across the country and in September of 1977, I was asked by the U.S. Nuclear Regulatory Commission to chair a national workshop on "Decommissioning of Nuclear Facilities." We were provided with reports from consultants and one from the U.S. Comptroller General to Congress entitled "Cleaning Up The Remains of Nuclear Facilities – A Multibillion Dollar Problem." That report went on to say, "The solution doubtless will be expensive, but the expense should be known so the responsible parties can plan for the inevitable costs. A strategy to clean up these private and federally owned nuclear facilities...cannot be developed until basic questions on the magnitude of the problem, such as costs, radioactivity, and timing have been answered." The assumptions our Connecticut commission made as a result of that workshop was that future regulators, faced with the final decisions when a plant's usefulness was over, would choose some variation on the safer and less costly "Safe Storage with Deferred Dismantlement" method instead of "Immediate Dismantlement," but nobody knew what new techniques would be available at the time of decommissioning or what snags would be found in the process we began to provide for. We and everyone else were flying blind. However, in the next NU case, we ordered the company to include in their rates dismantling costs that we calculated from the NRC reports, apportioning them over the presumed life of NU's facilities. We had little confidence in NRC's projections of costs or of their safety assumptions, but at least we made a start and forced a recognition of a future problem.

Miscalculations about safety issues are a paramount factor in the increased costs of nuclear power and its rejection as an acceptable energy source. In my early days as regulator, there was a well-respected scientist named Lapp who went around the country debating Ralph Nader on the safety of nuclear facilities. He touted the Rasmussen Report, supposedly the last word in a scientific study, which "proved" that the complicated plants with so many built-in fail-safe features were essentially infallible. I think Rasmussen asserted there was one chance in about 12000 there could be a serious nuclear plant accident. Chernobyl and Three Mile Island settled that debate. The responsibility for nuclear plant safety lay with the NRC, but it would be our plants and our citizens who would suffer from any negligence or mistakes. We received from NU almost daily reports of "incidents" at their facilities, but no one on our staff could tell us which incidents were serious and which called for only run-of-the-mill repairs. If you have nuclear plants in your state, there should be a nuclear physicist somewhere in state government to keep a concerned eye on them. For the time being (in the 1990s), a rejuvenated NRC seems an alert watch dog. NU has been fined for poor management, and their nuclear plants have been shut down as unsafe, but they must have become that way under NRC's earlier careless oversight.

For safety and other reasons, NU's nuclear facilities turned out to be less reliable than the company and we had forecasted. In a 1977 rate case, NU estimated their nuclear plants would perform in the coming year at 68.8% of capacity. Once those costly facilities are built they can produce electricity very cheaply – in 1977 at an average of 2.94 mills per kilowatt hour. In that same year, a kilowatt hour produced by oil cost an average of 23.37 mills. However, when in the next year both millstone plants had to be shut down for extended unscheduled periods, the consumers had to pay for the expensive construction costs of those plants *plus* the expensive cost of the substituted oil. The economies of scale had backfired. The reliability factor is a continuing factor and the hopes of cheap energy from nuclear power are long gone.

CHAPTER 42

CONFLICTS ON THE COMMISSION

While we were deep into rate cases, discussing incentives to encourage conservation, balancing consumer and company needs, we began to find Tom, our fellow commissioner, mystifying. During our first big case, a request from United Illuminating, which provides electricity to many downstate customers, for a rate increase, Al, Tom, and I made up the panel and we heard all the witnesses, read the material, listened to staff and the Consumer Counsel's recommendations and came to conclusions. At that point, Tom dissented, although I for one couldn't determine what part of our decision he objected to. Since the panel had broken down, the other two commissioners joined the case, read the material, discussed, and agreed with the decision Al and I had proposed. Connecticut law dictates the number of days after a request is filed in which the PUCA must issue a decision. If the deadline is missed, the company can put into effect the full amount of rates it has requested. Our decision went out to the company at the very last minute, without Tom's objections. To my knowledge, Tom signed only one rate decision for a big company, Connecticut Natural Gas, in a case I had assigned him to chair. In other big cases he was on, he distributed something he called "Tom Standish's Findings" after the decisions went out.

At the end of 1977, three of us were nearing the end of testimony in a major NU rate case with Al Kleban chairing when a decision made by our predecessors in 1974 was declared erroneous by a judge named Bielich, who remanded the case to us for correction. The appeal of the 1974 decision to the Court of Common Pleas originally had been made by the City of Hartford through their corporation counsel, Alexander Goldfarb, and had been joined by CCAG, that consumer advocate group I had once been a part of. However, in the meantime, the City of Hartford had withdrawn from the case and had fired Goldfarb, because, I was told, he had not reported to the city, his client, an offer from NU to settle. Goldfarb continued to pursue the case through the court with just the CCAG as his client, and that's where we came in.

Although we knew nothing about the remanded case, Al thought we could handle both cases since we were already in the midst of exploring NU affairs and both we and staff already had the information necessary. He set up a modified hearing schedule for the 1974 case, expecting to correct any errors we could find at that time, and we then resumed deliberations on the 1978 case we were working on. Much to our surprise, before we could begin the new hearings on the remanded case, we found ourselves served with an order from Judge Bielich to answer why we shouldn't be found in contempt of court for not immediately changing the decision he had sent back to us. Without hearings or deliberations? Without knowing what to change it to? In spite of being fired by the City of Hartford, Attorney Goldfarb, who was an influential advisor to Governor Grasso had clout.

I urged us to stick to our guns, letting Judge Bielich cite us for contempt and then appealing that ruling to a higher court even if it meant spending a few days in jail. My two colleagues convinced me, however, that confidence in the regulatory process would be shattered more by a contempt conviction, even if subsequently overturned, than by complying somehow with Bielich's irrational order. Al explained, too, that as a lawyer he couldn't afford to be cited for contempt if he expected to go into private practice someday. He offered to get a lawyer friend of his to represent us, arguing that we needed a sophisticated professional to defend us against our wily opponent. So early one December Saturday morning, we met in Al's office at the State Office Building, with Jake Zeldes, a well-known criminal lawyer from Fairfield. A criminal lawyer, for Heaven's sakes! There we wrote a decision that nullified the whole decision of our predecessors and set NU rates for that period back to those granted in about 1972, rates that at that time had been declared by the PUCA panel inadequate. I insisted on writing a concurring opinion, explaining that I didn't know if our decision was correct since we hadn't had time for hearings, but I believed it was better for the credibility of the Commission for us to make a wrong decision than to go to jail for contempt and at least anyone who felt aggrieved could always appeal to a higher court. Then we set off to Bielich's court for a day of high drama.

We found the hearing room packed. Many of the lawyers in the court house knew Alex and were looking forward to his usual histrionics and they also were eager to see the famed Jake Zeldes in action. Bielich seemed proud to have the two in his court, too. After the preliminaries, Alex took the floor to urge Judge Bielich to put us in jail for contempt. I heard him say, "Just look at Mrs. Butterworth's concurring opinion, Judge. She is not repentant!" *Repentant!* What a hilarious word! This was the theater of the absurd! Al had to sober me down so the judge wouldn't think I was being disrespectful. Then it was Jake Zeldes' turn, and we went from the ridiculous to the sublime. "Your honor," he said very seriously, "I urge you not to go down the road Brother Goldfarb is urging you to take. That way lies conformity of thought…" and a good many more high-minded arguments. In the end, Judge Bielich dismissed Goldfarb's case against us, pointing out that we had already obeyed the order to change the rates, so the question was moot.

Had we won? Not exactly. We had been forced to issue an ill-considered decision with which the company would have to deal. NU could have appealed to a higher court as I had suggested but chose instead to make a direct agreement with Goldfarb. The deal they struck essentially invalidated the rates we had reluctantly approved that December morning before we were tried for contempt. *And* it netted Goldfarb and his consultant, Tom, and a few other assistants a great deal of money for legal and consulting fees from the City of Hartford and the CCAG. Receiving money in such a deal might well look like a conflict of interest in any other NU case. In an article I wrote for the March 1979 issue of *Greater Hartford Business Magazine,* I refer to the CCAG, which was claiming their efforts in the remanded case had achieved a great victory, "yet some months later agreed to allow the decision to be quietly nullified in a settlement…netting the residential customers nothing and enriching the parties involved by $495,000."

CHAPTER 43

IN CHARGE

In the spring of 1978, after our court experience, Al Kleban decided to get off our beleaguered commission and made plans to resume private practice. He left in June after I became chair and Jerry McCann vice-chair by a unanimous vote of the five of us.

For one hectic year, I was in charge of our turbulent agency, responsible for personnel matters, speaking for the Commission to a variety of groups, presiding over biweekly meetings of us five commissioners, distributing the case load among us as fairly as I could. As overseer of any staff needs or vacancies, I managed to promote several competent women by encouraging them to take tests when there were openings, and I hired some able minorities, not only because we had pledged to follow affirmative action guidelines but because there was plenty of evidence that there had previously been a good deal of affirmative action for white males. I had to reprimand one old-timer for selling Avon products during working hours, but on the whole, the earnestness and hard work of the state employees I came to know were impressive.

I did have two serious personnel problems during my tenure. In the process of filling a vacancy in the transportation section, the least competent part of our organization, I discovered the trucking industry had controlled the hiring and promotions in that department for years. They had been selecting the examiners who ranked all job applicants in the oral part of the exam that was given. The competent guys always came in last. No wonder the two who ran that department , a wonderfully bumbling Laurel and Hardy couple, seemed perpetually at sea.

Another problem was even more serious. We had established a separate section to specialize in the analysis of economics and finance, cost of money, and other research. Up to that time, this work had been done by the accounting and finance division which was overburdened, auditing and testifying on the financial records of the companies we regulated. To head up the new division, we hired a retired army man who had worked the previous five years for the Colorado Utility Commission. Sounds good, but I had reservations about him from the start. In our interview with him, he described his expertise with computers and declared that, if only the army had given him the go-ahead, he could have automated the Vietnam battlefields and won that war! Did we have a megalomaniac on our hands? I didn't say anything, however, because when we finally had a chance to talk with him, he was already hired. We were stuck with him.

By the time Al left, it was obvious that our new man was a disaster, causing fear and extreme turnover in his department to the substantial detriment of the Authority and its work, and it would be my job to handle the chaos he had created. With lots of advice from the State Personnel Department and our legal advisers, I first met with him to discuss problems in his division and several months later met again before putting in writing what I saw happening: "I am reluctantly forced to take necessary steps to protect the Authority from the threatened loss of valuable personnel who, although they may not be capable of adjusting to your supervisory 'style', are nevertheless fully qualified and competent and are assets to the Authority." I wrote, "... employees in your division have left state service in apparent despair.... An aura of fear, reprisals, punishments and threats of banishment appear to permeate the division...all appear to be working under the threat that, without a moment's notice, assignments will be taken away from them and placed elsewhere to their humiliation, without logical explanations." There was lots more discussion of the failure of his division to perform the functions he had insisted on taking from other divisions before he was ready to perform them. My letter stated, "...during much of your tenure, your relations with other division heads have been marked by divisiveness, disruption, and discord." The army man responded by hiring an attorney who, by the end of November had convinced him that "we have a basis for grievance..." The attorney he hired was Alexander Goldfarb! Perhaps they really weren't all that convinced, however, because, instead of taking the next step against me, Army Man stopped coming to work and disappeared.

My duties as spokesperson for our agency were often stimulating even though they sometimes gave me a case of anticipatory nerves. I testified at the state legislature on bills that affected us, wrote a few articles, and talked to various groups when they requested it. I have a copy of a speech I gave soon after I became chair before clients of Argus Research Corporation in New York City. I was trying to reassure investors we commissioners knew what we were doing. If investors saw utility companies as risky and demanded higher interest on their loans, the consumers would have to pay with higher rates. I assured them that "Mr Kleban was concerned, as I will be, about the appearance of politics or bias in assignments we make to the various panels that will be sitting on rate requests. We…will take into account any adversary positions any commissioner has taken when we make our assignments." This was, of course, a reference to Tom's work as a consultant for the City of Hartford and the CCAG against NU, and I considered my words a promise.

I had one funny experience when representing the PUCA at the annual meeting of the Association of Northeast Electric Companies. It was held at the men-only University Club in New York City, and the chairs of the regulatory commissions in the Northeast were invited. On entering the imposing doors of the club, I was ambushed by two club employees who asked what I was doing there. I explained I had been invited to the meeting on the fifth floor and they both saw me into the elevator as if I might escape and contaminate some other part of the premises. As I stepped off the elevator, I was rushed at again and wasn't left alone until I disappeared into the room where several hundred company officials and heads of state utility commissions were gathered. All eyes turned toward me, the lone woman invading those male precincts. We regulators were asked to make some statement and then lunch was served. By that time, the company officers had recovered from the shock, but not the waiters. The one assigned to my table came to me and asked, "Would you like something to drink, sir?" It was a man's world.

CHAPTER 44

MORE INTERNAL PUCA

It was a man's world on the Authority, too. All heads of departments were male as were all the CEOs of the companies we regulated. Sometimes we saw a bright young woman lawyer representing a company, but most of the consultants, officers, and staff who presented cases before us were men. I sensed some resentment of me as a woman when on rare occasions I had to give directives to a company official by myself, but most of the time our decisions were made by a panel of three, so at least two men were involved to soften the blow. All of my fellow commissioners were men, too, but I almost always felt treated by them as an equal. I was older than all of them and perhaps they all loved their mothers. Whatever the reasons, there was little female/male maneuvering, and I was surprised and felt exhilaratingly liberated.

Not that the conflicts we had when Al headed the Authority disappeared. In fact, they got worse. Paul, the University of Connecticut professor I had met earlier, was Ella's replacement for Al Kleban. Paul should have been a positive addition. He not only taught business regulation but had been on both Governor Meskill's and Ella's councils of economic advisors. He seemed surprisingly tentative at first, evidently looking for direction. I once heard him mutter, "I thought there would be a Democratic position on this." I can't believe Paul taught his students that decisions were made in conformity with political party stands. Did he see himself a political operative? I saw us as akin to judges, making decisions on the basis of evidence and law. Of course, we would each necessarily interpret these according to our various personalities and biases, but party interests would hardly be part of the equation.

Paul's thinking became more evident in a Southern New England Telephone case that had begun shortly before he arrived. He took Al Kleban's place on the panel and for months, he, Jerry McCann, and I listened as the company asked, in addition to other rate change requests, to be allowed to charge for Directory Assistance after three free calls a month for that service. SNETCO's evidence showed the company would have to buy much expensive new equipment and hire more operators unless they could discourage the burgeoning free use of those assistance calls. They pointed out that businesses used DA most and fewer than 5% of residential customers asked for company help for five or more calls per month. Since the costs were spread over all customers, businesses and others had little incentive to use the telephone book or to keep a record of the numbers they used most often. SNETCO asserted that the vast majority of customers would have lower bills if they didn't have to pay for the service they weren't using. Sounded like a good consumer issue to me.

By November, we had come to the end of testimony and were beginning to discuss with the company, in public sessions, of course, what conditions we might add to the proposed change. What would the savings be if people were allowed *five* free requests per month for Directory Assistance before the charges began? How were disabled people protected? Could the company make special arrangements at places like colleges where telephone books were often not available? Would the changes dampen political participation? How could the company guarantee that savings would go to the customers and not to the shareholders? And what protection could they give to employees whose jobs might be eliminated if people cut their use of DA service significantly?

All three of us were proceeding in sync, working out a modified plan, when on the last morning, Paul suddenly changed his tune. He began to argue that SNET had left open too many questions on the impact of the new charges and said the company "has not shown an iota of efficiency in this proposal." (Of course, efficiency was what it was all about!) We took a break and Jerry and I walked across Bushnell Park to lunch. "Someone has gotten to Paul," I said. "Looks that way," Jerry agreed. And if it looked that way to us, it certainly must have looked that way to the company representatives and anyone else in the room watching and listening to us that morning.

I suggested we make our modifications of the company's proposal so sweet for the customer that Paul would have a hard time turning it down. Then we could see what he would do. And that is what we did. For instance, we stipulated seven calls to DA before the charges would begin. Under those conditions, very few residential customers would be affected and their bills would still be lower. Paul looked uncertain and called for a recess. He was not a subtle man. As we walked back to our offices, I saw him lean down to his secretary and a few seconds later his phone line lit up. A few minutes later, he walked into my office, shut the door, and said, "Mims, the word has come down. Jay Jackson..." Jay was Governor Grasso's Corporation Counsel. Ella must have had some compelling political reason for putting such overt pressure on us, and through such a weak reed at that. I was extremely angry and before Paul could finish, I interrupted. "Paul, the word doesn't come down!" By this time, he was backing through the door away from my wrath. Soon his phone line lit up again – reporting my response, I assumed. We returned to the hearing room, where we took a vote. Two to one, and the case was turned over to the whole commission. Tom and Dave Harrigan voted with Paul and the proposal was dead for the time being.

I talked to Ella after that and tried to tell her how obvious her interference had been and how destructive of our credibility, but she was, of course, on the defensive. Also, we had lost Paul. From then on, he sided with Commissioner Standish who would give him all the direction he seemed to need.

CHAPTER 45

MORE PAUL

You might imagine, if you've read the previous chapter, that my days at the PUCA were grim. On the contrary, I found them exciting. I didn't take personally any differences I had with my fellow commissioners. Al Kleban had the same problems. And I was given a good deal of support. The staff seemed almost unanimously helpful, my secretary Ray McGannon particularly, and even fond of me. I was on friendly enough terms with Dave and really close to Jerry. Our friendship was a surprise because we came from very different political backgrounds and beliefs. However neither of us was an ideologue and I respected his abilities and integrity.

My greatest support came from Bud who did all sorts of things to encourage me. The morning of February 14th, I stopped at the Audit Department on the way to my office. "Was that your husband's valentine to you in this morning's paper?" one of the staff asked, showing me a sweet rhyme "to our favorite commissioner." What a lovely way to begin the day! Bud was eager to hear all the details of my work, entering into the complexities of the issues I was dealing with as if they were his own.

Usually Bud was a steadying influence in my rather feverish life, but once he seemed particularly irate. In late 1978, I had a call from a Mr. McGarity asking me to look into why he hadn't heard from Commissioner Weiner about a water company matter Paul had evidently promised to handle. Our agreed-upon procedure was for complaints to go through the Consumer Assistance Department or through the chair to be brought up at one of our scheduled commissioners' meetings where we would decide what action should be taken. Instead, unbeknownst to the rest of us, Paul had tried to solve the complaint on his own. Was there glory in it? He had asked one of our engineers to look into the problem, failed to get a satisfactory answer, filed the material he had on the subject in the bottom desk drawer, and neglected to get back to Mr. McGarity. Hoping the whole thing would go away?

Mr. McGarity was not a happy man. His call to me was the first I had heard about the matter and I promised to look into it. As Paul was out of his office, I asked his secretary if she knew about the case. She did and promptly pulled out the correspondence from Paul's bottom drawer. Neither she nor I thought of using stealth. No files, we commissioners had agreed, would be secret. They were to be open to staff, commissioners, and the public. Yet while I was trying to discover what Mr. McGarity was incensed about, Paul returned, found I had his McGarity file, and went off like a volcano. He had a very short fuse. A reporter, more interested in interpersonal friction than substantive issues, was roaming the PUCA halls at that moment, found a ranting Paul and got some juicy quotes. The next morning's Hartford Courant had a large front page headline: "BUTTERWORTH ACCUSED OF UNPROFESSIONAL CONDUCT." It was this headline that got Bud's goat. You'll have to answer that," he fumed. "You've got to write a letter to the editor, explaining," he kept urging. I finally calmed him down, reminding him that probably about fifty people in the state had read the headline and of those perhaps five would remember it by week's end, and that it would get wider attention if I responded. "Well, all right," he muttered, "but at least they could have said 'Mrs.'" Oh. That was it. "Who steals my purse steals trash..."

CHAPTER 46

MORE HURDLES

By the time Northeast Utilities filed its next rate cases for its two Connecticut corporations, Connecticut Light and Power and Hartford Electric Light Company, toward the end of 1978, Tom had pretty well secured a reputation in some vocal quarters for being *the* pro-consumer commissioner. All that fall and winter, he wrote memos to me on various subjects: "The action which you recommend…contravenes and is in violation of the compromise." "I recommend…that the present assignment of three commissioners be extended to five in order to avoid further destabilization of the regulatory process." "I recommend that a meeting be scheduled…that all commissioners be invited to attend such a meeting." "I…request of you a copy of any and all memoranda received by you from the Office of the Assistant Attorney General or any of its representatives over the period of the last four months." "I believe it is in the interest of this agency and the public to come to an early decision on wage/price guidelines. I asked that we meet today…and have heard no definite word in this regard. I urge that we hold a meeting to debate this issue as soon as possible as I regard it as a high priority item." "I urge that you take steps to insure that all possible evidence be brought into this case so that a fair decision can be made." "I recommend to you that duplicate copies be sent to all commissioners when scheduling of mail transfer might produce a situation…" And we were all still meeting on a regular basis where these items, if they were genuine concerns, could have been brought before us all and debated. And some of Tom's pro-consumer reputation rubbed off on Paul, who had become his shadow. Ella acknowledged that perception and added to it by publicly, in a press conference, asking me to appoint all five commissioners to hear the newly filed NU cases. I was well aware of the political quagmire I was in. I had two reasons not to appoint Tom to the panel: first, the perception that he had a conflict of interest, having received a substantial amount of money in a private agreement with the company after he became Commissioner; and second, the fact that Tom had often found reasons to delay decisions in big rate cases. Would we be able to finish the hearings, discuss the evidence, and come to a decision that was fair to all factions before the July 1st deadline, the very day our terms were over and the cast of commissioners might well be changed? If we didn't make that deadline, the company could by law institute the rates they had asked for with no modifications, a sure recipe for consumer overcharges. I felt sure we could find modifications that would allow us to establish rates significantly lower than those NU was asking for.

I had six weeks before I had to appoint the hearing panel, during which time I spoke to as many influential people as I could about my intention not to honor Ella's request and why. One friend, a federal judge, clarified my thinking best. When I suggested I might resign, he said, "Why? You only resign if you're forced to make a decision that is against your conscience. You're in the catbird's seat. Do what you think is right and let the chips fall where they may." And that's what I did. A few minutes before the deadline, I announced to the press the appointment of Dave Harrigan and Paul Weiner with me as lead commissioner, knowing that I for one would not be reappointed in June when Ella had another opportunity to appoint all five of the commissioners. I tried to soften the impact of my defiance by pointing out the unusual number of cases on our docket – 190, I counted – some of which were minor, some major. There was too much work to do for us all to sit on any one case. In addition, I had appointed Tom lead commissioner for a large Connecticut Natural Gas rate case whose deliberations in May would run concurrently with the NU hearings. He would have to direct much of his attention to testimony in that case to do justice to CNG rate payers. I also hoped putting Paul, with his semi pro-consumer reputation, on the NU panel would help. Nothing helped! The front page headline the next morning read, "BUTTERWORTH DEFIES GOVERNOR." Poor Bud. There goes his good name again.

CHAPTER 47

WINDING UP

The last six months of my regulatory career was fittingly climactic. We did have our hands overfull. We had no hearing officer at that time, so all five of us held the hearings on electric and gas regulations, co-generation, load control programs, pricing principles and rate structures. I tried to allot as fairly as I could the responsibility for the rest of the cases such as disputed bills, water company matters, Railroad Standard of Services, and a surprising number of Cable TV wrangles. But CNG's and Northeast Utilities' rate cases were the largest and of these, NU's the most politically charged.

In a March 18th article, a *New York Times* reporter wrote, "The Authority [PUCA] will begin hearings next month on the largest proposed rate increase in the state's history – a $131 million rise sought by Northeast Utilities. The action comes at a time when, through a quirk of state law, all five of the agency's commissioners are facing reappointment by the Governor, who has not been pleased with the way the body is handling the case." The reporter then cited "the difficult task of trying to balance the interests of people who pay the rates for electricity, natural gas, telephones and other essential services against the financial need of the companies that provide those services." It was a long, insightful article and was only one indication that we were being watched by more than our friends and relations,

At the end of April, Ella announced her new slate of commissioners to be sworn in July 1st and, of course, I was not one of them. Neither was Jerry McCann, honest, judicious, and the only one of us with extended regulatory experience. And to my great surprise – and to his, too – neither was Tom. I got some cherished fan mail in the next couple of months. A friend wrote,

"It isn't fair and it isn't wise and it makes me mad as a friend and citizen!" Another amused me: "PUCA's loss is the next guy's gain – that's all I got to say!" I saved another letter that said, "I hope knowledge that there are many who recognize the size and quality of your contribution will make up, at least a little, for the action of one who doesn't." The vice-president of Trinity College wrote, "I am terribly depressed by your departure from the Authority. The state was mighty lucky to have someone with your integrity and balanced point of view at the helm..." One that especially pleased me came in the form of a resolution passed at the end of May by the Hartford City Council. They knew well the cast of characters, had obviously been watching carefully, and believed we had been helpful to them and other consumers. After some laudatory "Whereases," they resolved "That the Hartford Court of Common Council hereby expresses its appreciation to Miriam Butterworth for her years of service to the residents of Connecticut as a member of the PUCA."

The letter that surprised me most came from the governor's residence and is undated and addressed only to Hon. Miriam Butterworth, Chair, PUCA. I think it arrived at my office on the 30th of June, my last day as commissioner and the day after the three of us, Dave, Paul, and I had triumphantly wrapped up the NU cases.

> *I don't know of any decision [not to reappoint me] that has saddened me as much.* [Isn't that what they all say, I thought.] *I am truly sorry that circumstances did not provide a better alternative. You have borne tremendous burdens with integrity, courage and fortitude,* [Well, I was beginning to like this. Maybe I had been too cynical.] *As Jay* [Jackson] *has indicated, I hope you won't be lost to state service and that we may have another chance to work together.*
>
> *Fondly, Ella*

The rumors I was hearing must have been true. Someone important had gotten to Ella and had described the Byzantine state of affairs in our agency. Within the year, Ella was in the hospital, dying of cancer. I wrote her feeling a good deal of love, bemoaning her condition and loss of a dream I had that we two would someday sit together in our rocking chairs, telling each other what had really been going on in our respective areas during those exciting days of the '70s.

That was the end of my regulatory career. I had learned a great deal about how state government works, about managing a big organization, about human character and, of course, about the importance and difficulties of various industries – energy in particular. I felt we had left a more efficient group of companies and had kept rates for these essential services as low and as fairly apportioned as possible, while keeping the companies healthy enough to provide those services. Though I would miss being in the midst of so much action, I was prepared to resume my grandmother role – and here was another chance to clean out our attic.

CHAPTER 48

ATTIC MUST WAIT

For one golden month, we relaxed at Squam, doing all those leisurely things that get you prepared for a long winter. Bud and I swam, picnicked on the lake islands, climbed with various friends and family members – not in any hurry because we had weeks ahead of us. For all the summers I had been on the PUCA, Bud had loyally driven four and a half hours from West Hartford to Center Sandwich, New Hampshire, every Friday evening, and had returned with me the next Sunday, even though I'd urged him (but not very hard) to stay at the lake during the week. Now at last we had time to recuperate.

But plans aft gang agley. At the end of July, I had a phone call from a member of the Hartford College Board of Trustees. "Don't you want to speak with Bud?" No. To my surprise, the call was for me, and the college was in trouble. The new, rather shy president had decided after a year's experience that she was not made to be head honcho. Mount Holyoke had offered her a job as assistant to their new president, and she felt she was more suited for that. Could Hartford College find an acting substitute while they searched for a more permanent president? and would I be that substitute – just for a year?

Hartford College had been Bud's bailiwick for three decades. It was so much a part of his life that sometimes I felt like a fifth wheel when I visited. And now I was to become his boss? My first reaction was that it wouldn't work. As I told him, we had developed a way of relating in our everyday lives that meant cooperative decision-making and deferences to the other. I had been able to function independently at the PUCA because the issues I was dealing with were outside Bud's ken. But Hartford College? There wasn't a corner of that institution that he didn't know. He called himself Dean of

Grounds, but he had been consulted on everything. To be sure, Miss Johnson, the heart and soul of the college, and the one who had depended so completely on Bud, was no longer there, but he was still an important cog in most of HCW's gears. If I should take the job, I would have to rely on my own judgement, consulting with *all* the members of the college community and then come to my own independent conclusions. Well, I eventually agreed to become acting president because Bud persuaded me he would stay out of my business. I would mainly administer and he would mainly stick to academic matters. So I became Bud's boss, and he was put on the search committee to find my replacement

HCW IS MINE NOW, TOO

My year as acting president of Hartford College was "a piece of cake" compared with chairing the PUCA. Everyone tried to make things easy for me, knowing I was filling in during an emergency. The faculty expressed in words and actions how much they cared for HCW. The staff, almost to a woman, had few petty antagonisms or jealousies. No one was trying to enhance his reputation by undermining the institution. It was an unmitigated pleasure to go to work every morning.

Mims as acting president of Hartford College

The school year started with a bang. Very soon after I took over, a tremendous storm of high winds and torrential rains swooped into our area. The eye of the storm was a bit north, in Windsor Locks, destroying a wide swath of Bradley Air Field. It was the rain that did us in. The backed-up storm sewers blocked all streets connccting us to West Hartford, an unprecedented situation. Fortunately, the college was on high enough ground to avoid direct damage from those sewers except for a lower commuter parking lot. Some drivers recognized the danger in time to move their cars to safer places, but by the time I went to investigate, some cars had only their roofs showing. About five were floating, bumping into each other like the bumper cars at fairs. One roaming Volkswagen Bug with a shorted wire went on honking for over an hour until it gave up and sank.

There's nothing like a destructive tornado to bring a community together, but not all took the disaster calmly. That was the day a new student arrived with her father from Calcutta. She was late because a devastating hurricane had closed the Calcutta airport for several weeks – nature acting up at both ends of their journey. Papa was not amused. At that time, Hartford College for Women appealed to many families from other countries who wanted their daughters to have some American education. New England seemed safely familiar and a small woman's college safe, too. HCW's academic reputation made them feel they would get their money's worth. These foreign students were often exceptionally talented and interesting. Another late student to arrive the year I was president landed at Bradley Field from Nigeria, wearing sandals and a flimsy dress, no coat, during Christmas vacation on the coldest day of the winter. She was a tall, rangy, strong-looking Ibo who, during the recent war in her country, had walked eight miles each morning to get

MIRIAM BUTTERWORTH

Woman To Head College

Miriam B. Butterworth, former chairwoman of the state's Public Utilities Control Authority, has been named acting president of the Hartford College for Women, the board of trustees announced.

Mrs. Butterworth will take office Sept. 3.

She will replace Joan B. Davis, who will become assistant to the president at Mount Holyoke College, South Hadley, Mass., in the fall.

The college expects to name a new president by July 1, 1980.

Mrs. Butterworth was an organizer of the 1971 Economic Conversion Conference, the 1973-74 Ad Hoc Committee for Economic Alternatives, the 1975 Forum on Economic Alternatives for Connecticut and the 1975 Forum on Multinational Corporations.

She also founded and chaired the Caucus of Connecticut Democrats and was a delegate to the Democratic National Convention in 1968. She was the first recipient of the caucus' public service award at its annual convention June 9 for her work with the public utilities authority.

Mrs. Butterworth received a bachelor's degree from Connecticut College and a masters' degree from Wesleyan University. She was a history teacher at the Ethel Walker and the Loomis Chaffee schools.

Hartford Courant 7/12, 1979

~267~

water for her large family. She acquired a variety of mittens, scarves, coats and boots, her sense of humor emerged, and you could see she was a survivor. She came to see me in my warm office soon after college resumed, sat down for a chat, and said, "You don't mind if I keep my mittens on, do you?"

A FEW BUMPS ON A SHORT ROAD

Hartford College was small and its financial situation often precarious. One of my responsibilities would be to keep on top of money matters. My predecessor had tried to bring the college's record-keeping into the modern age by ordering the long-time bookkeeper to stop keeping the records in the old-style account books as she had been doing for many years. Instead, she was to give all the accounts to the woman who knew everything about our rather elderly computer. Several months into my presidency, the woman who knew everything but who had an alcohol problem quit with no warning. For almost a month I had no idea what our cash flow was, what bills were due, and all the other financial matters vital to the running of an institution, nor was there anyone around who could help me. Not even the business schools I contacted could find someone who could work our computer. Several tried. One looked promising, but after a few weeks, by which time I surmised she had an abusive husband, she didn't show and we never saw her again. Finally, we persuaded the original computer expert to come back to train a new person. Also, we were given a new modern computer and I reinstated the old system of keeping books as a back-up. The next president could modernize all she wanted, and in the meantime whoever needed to know our financial status (me) could do so.

And there were students' concerns. Early in the school year, a delegation of resident students, with determined expressions on their faces, came to see me. They explained that one of their professors, who lived on the ground floor of a campus building, each year picked out some girl in his second year language class to be his pet student and sexual partner. It wasn't fair! It wasn't moral! Bad for the girl, bad for the class, bad for the college! I had been around educators long enough by that time to think there is a bit of seduction in much teaching, especially the most inspired, but this was going too far. I promised I would see what I could do. Several days later, the professor in question dropped by my office and said he wanted the college to provide some opaque curtains for the large, floor-length living room windows in his apartment. I explained that he would have to supply them himself, and I would tell him where he could find some material, but the college had already provided some adequate, rather gauzy, see-through curtains and couldn't afford to produce another pair. A few days after that, a letter came in my mail from a National Association of Student Governments, describing exactly our problem, which was obviously not unique. It included a joint resolution opposing such actions on the part of professors and describing why. How timely! I made enough copies to slip one into every professor's mail box, and we had no more student delegations about that particular difficulty.

There was one big problem that called for a solution that winter. More students wanted to live on campus than we had room for. I could see we would lose potential students unless we could provide more places for them to live. Thanks to a sympathetic and imaginative architectural firm, Smith and Edwards, and to some helpful trustees, especially Dorothy Goodwin, we created enough new residents' quarters to carry on. In the process, there was much upheaval. Some faculty had to move to new offices, the counseling center was consolidated into one renovated building, one resident faculty member lost some of her apartment, yet she and most people accepted the turmoil with good grace and understood its necessity

One happy event, the 40th anniversary of the college, fell in my year, and everyone wanted to celebrate that milestone. I asked Karen Petersen, who taught art classes at the college, if we could mount an exhibit of students' work in the entrance lobby of the science building. That space had been planned for a possible art gallery when the building was built some years before and even had some fixtures ready for track lighting to be installed, but some large cork bulletin boards with various scientific displays had been hung on the walls instead

Sculpture Unveiled

DROPICK PHOTO

Miriam Butterworth, acting president of Hartford College for Women, applauds and artist-in-residence Karen Petersen of West Hartford appears pleased as a sculpture constructed by Ms. Petersen is unveiled on the college campus Sunday. The unveiling was part of a celebration marking the college's 40th anniversary. The celebration also included the dedication of a new art gallery in honor of Mrs. Butterworth.

of art. One day Karen came to see me with an anxious but determined look on *her* face. Karen is now a well-known sculptor with the same integrity and know-how she was about to show me. "About that student art exhibit," she said. "If I hung some students' work in the science center lobby as it is now, I wouldn't be happy and you wouldn't be happy. But if you took down the bulletin boards, puttied up the remaining screw holes, painted the walls white, and bought some lights to go on the tracks, I think we could have a good gallery." She was talking my language. I could use a screw driver, putty up holes, and wield a paint brush myself if need be, but of course Mr. Jesse, our Maintenance Department, did the honors and soon we had a very adequate gallery. There have been a number of excellent exhibits shown in that renovated space since then, and I feel pleased that such a simple collaborative decision could have such a lasting effect.

Bud kept his word. He never interfered with decisions I had to make, though I talked things over with him, as I did with others. I eventually felt at home in the job, and Bud would come into my office for tea and an afternoon chat –

Mims & Bud with Karen Petersen who helped produce the Art Gallery (photo A. Dropick, 1980)

one more benefit to that year's work. He and his search committee found a very capable successor, and I no longer felt a stranger at HCW. It was now my bailiwick, too.

I really did retire that summer. The presidency of Hartford College for Women was my last paying job. But I was still young, 62, and energetic and found a whole political world waiting. Part IV of these memoirs will be a summing up of the next 20 plus years, not in as much detail, I promise.

* *

Before I close the year of 1980, I want to record a personal loss. Bud's father, Paul Butterworth, died at age 92. He was respected, even revered by a wide community, and by me. He could be highly critical of family members but turned out to be an easy father-in-law to live near, both on Sunset Farm in West Hartford and on Squaw Cove in the summer. He passed on to everyone around him his love of the outdoors and was good company on camping trips – to the Metabetchuan in Quebec, to Mount Katahdin and Lake Caucomgomoc in Maine, and to Squam in mid-winter. I remember a wonderful long weekend at Squam with our family in deep snow, when he shared his bunk bed one night with a squirrel. I liked him very much and admired him and cherish the many memories I have of him.

Uncle Paul on a winter trip to Squam ~ 1950's with Kate tunneling in snow on the roof.

PART IV

THE PAST IS PROLOGUE

INTRODUCTION

Here I am, starting Part IV of my memoirs in October of 2004, after a stint as town historian. Four of the years between writing Part III and working on Part IV I spent co-authoring a history of West Hartford called *Celebrate! West Hartford*. I still want to tell about the momentous things that happened in the '80s and '90s, hoping this will help make sense of the discouraging beginnings of this new millennium.

The two most important matters I was involved in during these years were the Nuclear Freeze movement and the low-intensity conflicts (LIC's) our country was waging in Central America. Working on both these problems, I gained an understanding of the growing U.S. militarism and today's wars, the ideological split in our country, and the assault on our democratic institutions. We have come full circle and are now facing the same dangers, intensified, that we faced twenty-five years ago: attacks on our civil liberties; determination to control other societies (as seen in the Iran-Contra "affair"); military spending skewing our economic priorities. And now a chilling new element has been added - the growing backlash in the rest of the world against our economic and military hegemony.

Personally, these were decades of rejoicing in a new generation and grieving for losses that one knows are inevitable but are nonetheless heart-wrenching. And perhaps I'll find time to describe coping with old age.

Well, here goes!

Mims and co-authors sign *Celebrate! West Hartford*

W. Hartford Town Council: (top) Mims, Chick Felsen, Joe O'Brien, Myron Congden, Bob Gross, Marge Anderson(below) Bill Brady, Chris Droney, Kevin Sullivan, Chuck Matties, Nan Glass (Town Clerk)

CHAPTER 49

THE TOWN R US

As my year at Hartford College wound down, I was approached by the West Hartford Democratic town committee chairman, who asked me to run for the Town Council. It would be a part time unpaid job and I agreed to file for the office. One of the town committee members heard about my candidacy and complained to the chairman because, he told him, I had gone to Vietnam to protest the war. Nine years earlier he had heard me describe the peace talks in Paris, and his memory had translated Paris into Hanoi. The chairman, a Vietnam veteran, said he answered, "What's good enough for me should be good enough for you." "That's the first time I've been mistaken for Jane Fonda," I joked, acknowledging the rumor, when we candidates sought endorsement of the town committee. I imagined then that the conflicts of the Vietnam era would soon be behind us, but the 2004 elections showed I was wrong. That Bush was a draft dodger gone AWOL and that Kerry did not deserve his ribbons were accusations that loomed large in that campaign.

The town was well run, I found, while serving two terms on the Town Council, and became even better run when we solved a feud between the town manager and the finance officer by eliminating one position and hiring a new, highly competent town

Mims Campaigning for Town Council

manager. I take pride in one other accomplishment. We broke a 15-year stalemate concerning the use of the old Hall High School. It was a substantial, solidly built structure, so tearing it down didn't make sense. Should it be made into office and commercial space or renovated for a new town hall? A Republican colleague, Chuck Matties, and I worked together, forming a majority to vote for the town hall option. The handsomely renovated building is now an integral part of town buildings surrounding the center green, and people using it look happy at being in beautiful, up-to-date surroundings.

Two other issues of general interest during my terms on the Council arose from outside local town affairs. The first had to do with FEMA which required every town to adopt emergency plans in case of a nuclear attack. FEMA had already decided what routes we would take north and which communities would take us in. We were told that if we didn't formally approve its escape policy, FEMA would not help us recover from a natural disaster should one occur in our town. After discussions, we unanimously agreed the FEMA plan wouldn't work, nor could we think of one that would. How could the receiving communities be prepared for the thousands of evacuees from the Hartford area? Think of the traffic jams that would be created by parents trying to find their children and all of us trying to get out of town at the same time! The message we sent to the federal government was that no amount of planning could help most of us survive a nuclear war. The only answer was to prevent one.

By my second term on the Council, the freeze movement was on the table. A resolution was submitted asking us to urge our representatives and President Reagan to negotiate with the Soviet Union a bilateral freeze on the production and deployment of nuclear weapons. Cities and states around the country were passing similar resolutions, showing a growing awareness of the dangers of the nuclear arms race. The Council held a town meeting and we had a crowd. Concerned clergy (Rabbi Kestler, quietly persuasive, I remember best); labor union leaders (passionate and articulate Lew Kiefer, for instance, of the International Association of Machinists and

Rabbi Kessler

Aerospace Workers, IAM); and business and citizen groups all took part in the debate. The Council voted and the resolution passed.

Since a town councilor's work is by no means full-time, most members have full time jobs but I, retired, was free to concentrate on civic issues wider than town concerns. In the early 1970s, I joined the national board of an organization called SANE as a representative from Connecticut. We met four or five times a year to discuss alternative and sane nuclear policies. SANE had been influential in achieving a ban on above-ground testing of nuclear weapons during the Kennedy administration. It renamed itself Peace Action in the 1980s and widened its issues to include the United States' involvement in the "low-intensity conflicts" being fought in a number of countries, particularly in Latin America. But before my visits to these trouble spots, I became involved in the problems of the nuclear arms race, a concern not only in our country, as could be seen in our Town Council hearings, but throughout the world.

In the fall of 1980, a friend, Roz Spier, asked me to co-chair a Forum on Military Spending and the Economy to be held in February of 1981 at the University of Connecticut Health Center in Farmington. Roz had already done much of the planning, so it was easy to agree to help where I could. The subject of military spending was familiar to me. As I have mentioned, I had organized conferences on Connecticut's economic dependence on military industries in the early 1970s for the Caucus of Connecticut Democrats. Because of that dependency, our congressional representatives felt they had to vote for every military spending bill proposed. Wasn't there some form of manufacturing to which our economy could convert that would thrive in peacetime? We had made little headway earlier but, by the 1980s, more of us knew about the increased possibilities of large scale nuclear destruction and our country's part in exacerbating that danger. The planned US deployment of nuclear weapons into Europe and the cost of producing ever more weapons of annihilation we believed would inevitably lead to war. The threat was not just to the U.S. and the USSR but also to Europe, which was becoming our first line of defense, and to the rest of the world, which would experience nuclear fallout in a nuclear war. The increased awareness of the possibility of annihilation added to the skewed economic priorities of outlandish military spending might give us another chance for change.

A CONFERENCE ON . . .

Military Spending and the Economy: Security or Disaster?

- **What are you paying for?**

- **Are you getting what you're paying for?**

- **Are there SAFE alternatives?**

FRIDAY & SATURDAY
FEBRUARY 27 & 28
at the
Keller Auditorium
UConn Health Center
Farmington, CT
FRIDAY 7 P.M. — 10 P.M.
SATURDAY 9 A.M. — 3 P.M.

"We've been turning out weapons since the Second World War. We're just continuing to make weapons on top of weapons on top of weapons"
— *Jim Daniels, Defense Worker*
Pratt & Whitney Aircraft

"The foundation of a nation's security beyond its military strength is its economic strength. We've seen some of our choices. In a democracy we are in charge here. We can be secure and cut back on the arms race."

— *Eli Wallach, narrator*
"Who's In Charge Here?"

SPONSORING GROUPS

- American Friends Service Committee
- Capitol Region Conference of Churches
- Caucus of Connecticut Democrats
- Citizens Lobby, Hartford
- Commission for Justice and Peace, Diocese of Bridgeport
- Committee for Peace, Connecticut Conference of the United Church of Christ
- Connecticut Federation of Teachers, AFL-CIO
- Connecticut Impact
- Council of Churches of Greater Bridgeport
- Episcopal Peace Fellowship, Connecticut Chapter
- Hartford Friends Meeting
- Hartford Peace Coalition

- Health Professionals for Social Responsibility, New Haven
- International Association of Machinists and Aerospace Workers, District 91
- Justice and Peace Commission, Diocese of Hartford
- National Association of Social Workers, Inc., Connecticut Chapter
- National Lawyers Guild, New Haven Chapter
- New England Health Care Employees Union, District 1199
- Peace Education and Action Center, New Haven
- Physicians for Social Responsibility, Hartford
- Promoting Enduring Peace
- Social Concerns Committee, Episcopal Diocese of Connecticut

- Social Issues Management Team, CHRISCON
- Storrs Peace Center
- The Service and Outreach Board of the First Church of Christ, Congregational, West Hartford
- Unitarian Church of Hartford
- Unitarian-Universalist Peace Fellowship
- United Auto Workers
- Urban League of Greater Hartford
- Women's International League for Peace and Freedom, New Haven Branch
- World Federalists Association, Mansfield Chapter

(List in formation)

CHAPTER 50

FIGHTING THE WAR IN CONNECTICUT

MILITARY SPENDING CONFERENCE

A little background: Connecticut's economy was, and maybe still is, the most defense-dependent in the union, two and a half times that of the next, California. In the '80s, the Soviet Union was the threat we were arming ourselves against, and both the Soviets and the U.S. were facing bankruptcy as well as becoming great threats to the rest of the world. How could we rouse people to say "STOP"? We would have to find a formula that would make people feel safe in both countries. There would have to be convincing verification of any agreement, and the pressure would have to be world-wide.

A conference on Military Spending and the Economy was Connecticut's contribution to that pressure. It started Friday Evening, February 27, with Herbert Scoville speaking first. He had once been the CIA Deputy Director as a Soviet specialist and was then president of the Arms Control Association. He talked about the U.S. defense posture and the Soviet threat. Randy Forsberg also spoke that night on *The Arms Race and Global Security.* She had co-authored *The Price of Defense* and was director of the Institute for Defense and Disarmament Studies in Massachusetts. We saw more of her later when we were working for the Freeze resolution formulated by Randy and her Institute.

On Saturday morning we heard Betty Lall, an economist at Cornell University and the author of *Prosperity without Guns.* I was particularly

Randall Fornsburg, Oliver Butterworth, Mary Elizabeth Nash, planning freeze action

impressed with the next speaker, Mel King, a large and dynamic man and a member of the Massachusetts House of Representatives. He described the impact of large defense budgets on cities, Boston in particular. We had one more session to go. Dick Greenwood of the IAM spoke of making economic conversion work. Congressman Toby Moffett, who chaired the U.S. House Subcommittee on Environment, Energy, and Natural Resources, wrapped up the conference by talking about the need for citizen action. Bill Moyers offered to make a video of the conference and showed it on his program several weeks later – the icing on the cake!

I've written in some detail about that conference because it was the start in Connecticut of a decade of efforts to change the militaristic direction our society was taking, and people saw it as the beginning of something important. The printer of our flyers and programs donated his services, and all the speakers and responders waived their fees, as did the moderator, Don Noel, senior correspondent at TV Channel 3 and a member of a sponsoring group, the American Friends Service Committee. Close to 500 people gave up their February weekend to do something to relieve their increasing anxiety. It filled a hunger for action in many worried people, and suddenly we had volunteers from across the state wanting to join us.

The success of the convention showed these were ideas whose time had come. We had over thirty sponsors who, when they signed up, pledged to give money if they could, but more importantly, to notify their constituencies about the conference and the issues. They promised to organize a group to which one of us would speak, and/or show a film entitled *Who's in Charge Here?* In addition, they agreed to follow up the conference by forming a group to create a regional "impact statement" on military spending and social needs, or to make a slide show themselves, and to sign up people who wished to meet with their congressmen, locally or in Washington, to lobby against the growing militarization of our society. This was not a half-hearted effort.

WE FREEZE

After our conference on military spending, we concentrated on a specific portion of military spending, the most dangerous part, the billions going into the nuclear arms race. As I have mentioned, Randy Forsberg and her Massachusetts-based Institute formulated the concept of "an immediate, mutual freeze on all further testing, production and deployment of nuclear weapons and of missiles, and new aircraft designed primarily to deliver nuclear weapons." We set out to show that a nuclear war would destroy more than could possibly be justified by any conceivable objective. We explained that the 50,000 nuclear weapons already in existence could obliterate our enemy and us many times over, and the planned increases of 20,000 along with new delivery systems would not make us safer but would make a nuclear war more probable. We had to show that a freeze could be verified and that only if the U.S. and USSR agreed on a nuclear moratorium would other nations feel safe enough to stop working on their nuclear programs, making non-proliferation possible.

Pat Wass, at The Freeze Office

Our allies, the Physicians for Social Responsibility, made charts showing who would be killed and who would be made sick if a bomb were dropped on Boston or Electric Boat in Groton. Environmentalists showed what would happen to the environment and the climate in such a war. This educational process was happening across the country and indeed around the world. I think that by the end of the decade, almost everybody understood the impossibility of any side really winning a nuclear war. Nuclear weapons were only useful as a deterrent, a system of mutual assured destruction, MAD. The world wide outcry did achieve a comprehensive test ban treaty and other treaties that incorporated the freeze concept, but by the time I am writing this, early in the 21st Century, our present leaders have forgotten the lessons learned in the '80s. They have canceled treaties negotiated with much care and are planning a new generation of "more usable" and more lethal nuclear weapons as well as the militarization of space. Protesters' work, like women's, is never done.

TECHNIQUES FOR SURVIVAL

In July of 1983, Bruce Martin and Marta Daniels, heads of the Connecticut Chapter of AFSC, became co-executive secretaries of The Freeze and opened an office in the Colt building in Hartford. A Board was formed as were many local affiliated groups around the state. From then until the end of the decade, we worked for a bilateral nuclear weapons freeze and persuaded many individuals and groups to join us - churches, scientists, labor unions, physicians, women, business people, educators.

We hosted experts at teach-ins, and even became experts ourselves, learning the characteristics of weapons: what Trident I and Trident II were and their Soviet ICBM counterparts, for instance. We knew "mirving" meant turning bombs into multiple reentry vehicles, making the arms race

The Freeze Lobbies Congress

more dangerous to both sides, and became familiar with the latest technology in verification methods. Fortunately, some well-known experts with unassailable credentials joined our board and speakers bureau. I've mentioned Herbert "Pete" Scoville, formerly a Soviet Union specialist in the CIA, a professor at MIT and vehemently opposed to the MX missile. Harold Nash, the former director of the Groton, CT Underwater Systems Laboratory, also joined us and in addition funded a staff person in our office. Another addition was Bill Yates, a former commander of a nuclear submarine, one of the people prepared to push a button that would have started World War III. Bill used to describe the day he quit the Navy and joined the Freeze. He was watching with a cheering crowd the launching of a new nuclear submarine and suddenly realized that, contrary to the speeches he was hearing, that new sub would not increase the safety of the American people one iota.

We worked with the mayor of Norwalk, the deputy mayor of Hartford, Congressman Toby Moffett, and State Representative Irving Stolberg; with various organizations such as the Urban League and the National Lawyers Guild; and with health professionals as well as social workers. But our most essential support came from ordinary housewives, retirees, flex time artists, and the like, all of whom found they had previously untapped organizing, public relations, and management skills.

THINK GLOBALLY, ACT LOCALLY

The local Freeze group I was most familiar and active with was West Hartford's, organized mainly by Martha Vinick, who also had been inspired by the Military Spending Conference. The West Hartford Freeze group was particularly good at getting media attention. Martha sent a form letter to newspapers around the state. It went like this:

Dear News Director;

It must be almost impossible for those in the media to be fully informed on all the stories they must report on. Realizing this, the Connecticut Freeze Campaign believes it is important that you receive periodic information and updates on Freeze positions concerning the nuclear arms race and administration and congressional actions....

She didn't ask; she just assumed they would want to be informed. She scoured newspapers around the state, thanked all who wrote letters-to-the-editor on our subject, then copied the letters and sent them out as samples to friends, encouraging them to write their own versions to their local publications. We established Writing Wednesdays when people got together to write to their congressmen, the President, and anyone we felt should be hearing from us. And at noon on the first Friday of every month a number of us met at the library and marched to the post office where we mailed those letters. Each month we featured a different support group. One Friday the clergy joined us. Another Friday it was businessmen, lawyers and doctors, another it was mayors, council members, and members of boards of education, and then people in the arts. The *West Hartford News* was especially ready to report our actions and to print our letters to the editor, and we were grateful.

We did polls to find out what people knew about nuclear weapons. We had popcorn and cider evenings to show films and to talk about the arms race and what we could do about it. We signed petitions and presented them to congressmen. We even raised money to give a peace scholarship to a West Hartford High School senior who had "made important contributions 'thinking globally and acting locally' about the nuclear arms race and other challenges to peace."

In the meantime, the state office, staff, and board were planning state projects. One organization we worked with,

Members of the Hartford Symphony and friends invite you to support

Symphony for Peace

A Benefit Concert
Sunday
March 31, 1985
8 o'clock p.m.
at
Bushnell Memorial Hall
Hartford, Connecticut

"It would take a very strong voice, indeed a powerful chorus of voices, to say to the decision makers of the two superpowers what should be said to them:

For the love of God, of your children, and of the civilization to which you belong, cease this madness."

George Kennan
Former Ambassador to
the Soviet Union

Musicians Against Nuclear Arms, helped us put on a benefit concert in 1985: "A Symphony for Peace." That evening was a highlight of our Freeze efforts and one of the top musical experiences of our lives. Arthur Winograd, conductor of the Hartford Symphony, directed an orchestra made up of members of Musicians Against Nuclear Arms. Benita Valente came from Philadelphia and sang Mozart's *Exultate Jubilate*, and trumpeter Philip Smith came up from Manhattan. Pete Scovill, substituting for Gen. Noel Gaylor, who had to cancel at the last minute, gave a short but ardent speech at intermission. Robert J. Lurtsema, Boston-based host of NPR's *Morning Pro Musica,* hosted the evening.

Pat Wass from Winsted was overall chairman of the event, and her description of the many moments of suspense in the planning process was hair-curling. Could Sally d'Alessandro, a Farmington housewife and chair of the state Freeze committee at the time, sell enough tickets to fill the Bushnell auditorium? She did! Who could find an alternative place for the pre-concert banquet we had planned for our distinguished guests when the restaurant we had hired closed that very day because of a flood in the basement? Well, Flo Woodiel negotiated with the state for the use of the nearby armory, and we carried on. In conjunction with many others, our efforts were successful. By the end of the decade there was a worldwide consensus that no one could win

The Freeze Ladies Today

Witness for Peace Newsletter

Vol. 3, No. 2   April/May 1986

Rev. William Sloane Coffin speaks against U.S. aid to the contras as participants in WFP national conference launch *Crosses of Sorrow and Hope* campaign on March 4 by forming human cross on steps of Capitol in Washington, DC. (photo by Rick Reinhard)

In this Issue

a nuclear war. Some weapons were never deployed, treaties were negotiated, and we celebrated.

The Freeze movement closed up shop when the Berlin wall came down and the Cold War ended. We had won the battle, but had lost the war to restrain military spending. Today, the US spends about as much on its military as the rest of the world combined. And what about nuclear weapons? Many of us in the U.S. understand the danger of nuclear proliferation on the part of other countries, but not so many see that our country's military might and nuclear threat must also be curbed. We've always been the good guys, haven't we? Why should anyone be afraid of us?

CHAPTER 51

ENEMIES GALORE

While our country was rattling its nuclear swords at the Soviet Union, it was expanding its military presence closer to home. Central America, the Middle East of the '80s, was in turmoil, and the U.S. was blaming Communism and its proponents, Russia and Cuba. Others were pointing to deteriorating economic conditions – low prices for commodities such as coffee, growing government repression and the squelching of attempts by poor people to find ways to subsist. Because I had taught U.S. History with emphasis on foreign policy, especially as it related to Latin America, I was particularly concerned about ominous developments in that area.

The U.S. was supporting all of the governments in Central America against uprisings except for Nicaragua, where in 1979 the Sandinista revolutionaries had ousted dictator Gen. Anastasio Somoza and his brutal National Guards. Reagan and his administration labeled the new Nicaraguan government Communist, called its new president, Daniel Ortega, a dictator, and threatened to invade with our military forces or with surrogates, the Contras, a group of former Somosan National Guards, organized, armed, trained and funded by the United States. Reagan called these Contras, who were burning farms and destroying fuel depots across the Honduran/Nicaraguan border, "freedom fighters."

In November of 1984, I joined 16 other members of SANE as an official observer of the first elections to be held in Nicaragua since the Sandinista revolutionaries took power. Reagan, campaigning for a second term, was working hard to discredit those elections. He and Vice-president Bush, in their campaign debates that year, called El Salvador, ruled by a repressive and brutal military, a democratic country and praised its recent elections, which foreign observers had declared fraudulent. At the same time, the Reagan/Bush team called Nicaragua evil, and their coming elections, yet to be held, "seriously flawed." We also heard the U.S. had mined Nicaragua's harbors – an act of war. I was eager to have the chance to see for myself what was happening "in our backyard."

In Managua's airport, waiting for the bus to our hotel, we watched the lounge TV which was broadcasting live a campaign rally for Daniel Ortega and the FSLN, the Sandinista slate. I kept an eye on the Nicaraguans in the room. They were listening attentively with what seemed approval and pride. Even the children stood up straight and stopped their roughhousing when Ortega spoke. The Somoza family, in the 44 years of its greedy rule, had antagonized almost every segment of Nicaraguan society except for the National Guard. That is probably why, of all the countries which had attempted to oust dictators and create more just and equal societies in that region, only Nicaragua was successful. It is also probably why the Nicaraguan revolution

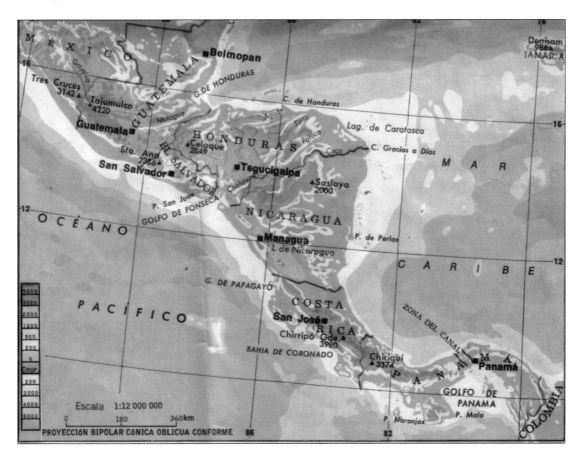

was so moderate. The Sandinista leaders espoused three principles: pluralism, a mixed economy, and non-alignment. For the next five days, we would be looking for evidence of compliance with these promises made by the revolutionary government.

IMPRESSIONS OF A REVOLUTION

An exciting time to visit a country is soon after it has achieved a revolution – at least a revolution which most of the population has supported. We found everywhere an atmosphere of a communal emotional high. The second night we were there, the government hosted a magnificent spread, a barbecue in Managua's Hotel International for all of us foreign observers. Many hundreds of us from all over the world mingled with official Sandinistas, big and small. I talked to the ambassador from Iceland, a towering, red-bearded Norseman with a booming voice. He was particularly happy because the host assigned to him was Nora Astoriega, a heroine of the revolution – about half his size and very beautiful. In 1979, she had finally agreed under pressure from her revolutionary comrades to entertain in her bedroom a persistently ardent pro-Samozan CIA operative. In the struggle with her Sandinista friends waiting for him, he was killed. In the late '80s, when appointed Nicaraguan ambassador to the UN, she was refused entry to our country because of that episode.

We ate dinner with Lord Kenny who boasted "I almost was Virginia Woolf's son" because his father had proposed to Virginia. Bianca Jaeger was there and we met Fr. Miguel D'Escoto, a Maryknoll priest and Nicaragua's foreign minister. Everywhere you could sense idealism and hope, pride in what had been accomplished: the literacy campaign, cooperative coffee harvesting, the beginnings of an improved health care system, progress in reforming the judicial system, and, of course, pride in the election process we were in the midst of observing.

I wrote an article for the Caucus of Connecticut Democrats when I returned in the middle of November and, at the risk of repeating what I have written above, I'll reproduce excerpts of it:

REPORT TO THE CAUCUS OF CONNECTICUT DEMOCRATS

One thing to be grateful for this holiday season is that we don't live in a small country in a superpower's "backyard" . . . .

We have learned from the U.S. press over the past few months that our CIA is funding and participating in attacks on Nicaragua by mining their harbors, destroying fuel depots, and training the Contras in Honduras to attack Nicaraguan villages near the Honduran border . . . .

We also read that long before the details of the Nicaraguan election process had been worked out, and certainly months before Nicaragua's election day, our government was branding their November 4th elections a 'farce'. Why were the Nicaraguan elections so important to both the Nicaraguans *and* the United States? Were they a farce, or were they fair and open, and what did it matter either way?

Our itinerary was planned by a Washington-based organization, the Nicaragua-Honduras Education Project, which arranged almost continuous meetings with V.I.Ps in these countries. In Nicaragua, we had long discussions with both pro and anti-Sandinista party officials, with a representative of the U.S. embassy, and with Dr. Mariano Fiallos, the head of the Supreme Electoral Council, which organized and carried out the voter registration and the November 4th elections. We also met with some of Nicaragua's leaders who were not specifically involved with the election process. Among the latter were: Dr. Orguello, the chief justice of their supreme court; the anti-Sandinista bishop, Obando y Bravo; Sister Mary Hartman, the Maryknoll nun who is head of the Sandinista Human Rights Commission; Father Gorostiego (a Panamanian) who runs a research institute; and the editor of one of the three daily newspapers which, although there have been some instances of censorship, print widely divergent opinions on Nicaraguan events.

As far as we could judge, Nicaragua is pluralistic, both as a society and in its economic system. What was a surprise was the large amount of Christian thought that was mixed in with Nicaragua's revolutionary concepts. As for the economy, we were told that 60% of the gross national production is in private hands. Even Mike Joyce, the U.S, Embassy representative we talked with, said that Nicaragua is *not* a Marxist-Leninist society *yet*, nor is the Nicaraguan economy modeled on the Cuban or Soviet models, but he saw a potential for that. What our government is looking for is stability, he said, and the Sandinista government can't provide that. Besides, he told us, the Sandinista government isn't good for the Nicaraguan people. That brings us to democracy and the elections.

It is hard for us North Americans to understand the tremendous effort it took to organize elections (the first in 44 years) that were held throughout a country under attack. Lacking even the most essential resources, the Nicaraguans were given such things as ink from Finland and paper to print the ballots on by Sweden. Forty thousand people were chosen and

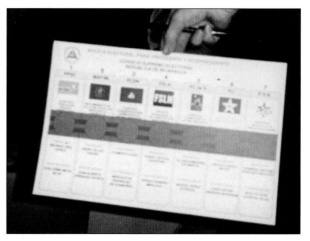

Presidential Ballot, with 7 parties, in Estelé. FSLN in middle.

Lecture by Dr. Mariano Friallos, Pres. Supreme Electoral Council

Debbie McCarthy, City Council of Atlanta, Mims, Father Xaurey Gorostiego, authority on Panamanian

trained to run the elections. The vote was not compulsory, and it was really secret. The seven registered parties, some to the left and some to the right of the Sandinista party, were given $300,000 each to start the election process, 30 minutes a week on radio, and 5 minutes a day for TV advertising (free).

The Sandinistas reaped substantial benefits from their election. They had the chance to campaign door-to-door to gain support for their policies, the chance to rouse patriotic fervor in order to hold popular support during the U.S. attacks they anticipated, and (above all) the chance to legitimize their government in the eyes of the world. We observed inside and outside a number of polling places throughout Nicaragua on election day, and nowhere did we see any intimidation or election fraud. These Nicaraaguan elections seemed much closer to our ideal of democracy than any other Central American elections in modern history (and maybe our own).

Why then did our government try to discredit them before they started? Why did Bush in the vice-presidential debates praise the elections in El Salvador, where most opposition leaders had been assassinated or exiled, while he attacked the Nicaraguan elections as a complete fraud? We pressed this point with Mike Joyce at our embassy. His

PSC Headquarters. Marie-Ellis translating for Susanna F., Director of International Relations, and Adam Flentes, Vice-Presidential Candidate with A. Cruz, member of CTN labor union

answer was that we have no obligation to measure our friends and our enemies by the same yardstick!

[And no obligation to tell the truth to us, the American people.]

A democratic election and a legitimate government [in Nicaragua] would make it more difficult to get Congress and the American people to support increased aid to the Contras, and to get our approval for a sustained policy of overthrowing the Sandinistas. If the Reagan administration is to continue destabilizing the Nicaraguan government, it needs most of all the acquiescence of its own citizens.

Our aims in Nicaragua are to reestablish the control we had when Samoza was in power. This is no longer easy to do, nor does it work for long. Some of our influence in the world is based on moral principles, on our reputed respect for law, justice and true democracy. Are we jeopardizing "the good opinion of mankind" by our actions in Central America? With travel and communications now so easy and with covert actions becoming overt so quickly, will the American people be willing for long to support our government's actions there? A policy which creates divisiveness within our own society and loss of respect from other nations seems the height of folly.

U.S. GETS TOUGH

The things I didn't stress enough in the above report were the extreme efforts the U.S. used to try to de-legitimize the Nicaraguan 1984 elections: the successful move to get Arturo Cruz, the head of the Social Christian Party, which some called the international front of counter revolution, to boycott the elections; the unsuccessful pressure to get Godoy, head of the PLI, a "liberal" party, to do the same; the false rumors of the imminent arrival of Russian MIGs to convince the American people that Nicaragua was becoming a staging area for communist expansion in our hemisphere; the months-long joint maneuvers with the Honduras military to convince Nicaragua a U.S. invasion was at hand; the trade sanctions and the mining of Nicaragua's harbors so no one, not Cuba or the Soviet Union or the rest of the world, could ship

CPDN Headquarters
(Permanent Committee on Human Rights)

in essential supplies; and the sonic booms over Managua causing sleepless nights and further worries about invasion. Otto Reich, a Miami Cuban who has reappeared in the Bush II administration, was hired by the Reagan administration to head an office of disinformation, institutionalizing the President's attempts to mislead the American people. Reagan wanted above all to rid our country of the "Vietnam syndrome" so his administration could carry out his threatened invasion if our surrogates failed to oust the Sandinistas, the FSLM party. At least he hoped to persuade Congress to rescind the Boland Amendment of 1981 which banned funds to the Contras. The FSLN hoped to gain the independence they had fought for if it stayed neutral in the Cold War. But neutrality and independence for the Reagan people were unacceptable. This was a second Cuba and all too good an example. "Anyone not with us is against us."

However, Nicaragua was geographically too near to cover up what our government was really doing and what Nicaragua was really like. Many idealistic young Americans, reminiscent of the '60s civil rights movement, traveled south to work for the Sandinista social reforms or to help with the coffee harvest, and they told their families back home what was happening.

Of course, Reagan wasn't happy with opposition to his policies. When Congress cut off funding for the Contras, his administration continued to raise money from private sources and diverted federal funds from other projects. So we were treated to the clandestine Iran/Contra affair when Colonel Oliver North and a White House advisor delivered a cake, a Bible signed by President Reagan, and some missiles to the Iranian government in exchange for money for the Contras. About the same time, the savage CIA manual advocating torture and assassinations used in training our proxy army in Honduras surfaced. If we remembered these actions in Central America, we would not be so surprised at the Abu Graib and Guantanamo torture scandals of today.

Nor should we be surprised at the claims of Bush II that he as Commander-in-chief is above the law. The International Court in the Hague eventually ruled in a case brought by the newly installed Nicaraguan government that the mining of Nicaragua's harbors was a violation of international law, but before the decision was rendered, Washington declared that the court had no juris-

Kay Stubbs, translator, with Dr. Arguello, Chief Supreme Court Justice

diction over the U.S. So much for a government of laws! Colonel North had his staff shred classified papers that pertained to the Iran/Contra transactions, and he defied the congressional oversight committee questioning him. Otto Reich was judged to have broken laws by misleading the American people through planted articles of misinformation, but he was never punished. And Reagan (the "Teflon President") escaped impeachment although he had violated laws and treaties and lied to the American people while pleading ignorance with his sly, endearing grin. If a government can violate so many laws and moral standards with impunity, there was bound to be more of that kind of corruption in the future. And sure enough, twenty years later we have the same problems intensified under another Bush administration

BACK TO ELECTIONS

Karen Paget (Mims' roommate) and Obando y Bravo, Anti-Sandinista Arch-Bishop

The FSLN won by a substantial margin in an election widely regarded as exceptionally honest. One British observer said it was "extremely well thought out and a little bit superior to what we do in Britain." We could certainly have said the same. An older Nicaraguan woman told us she had voted before but this was her first free election.

The National Lawyers Guild delegation wrote in their report:

> *The Reagan administration's…criticisms of the electoral process are based on incomplete or false information and innuendo…. Because of this disregard for facts, it is apparent the administration's target is not the elections or the electoral process, but rather the very existence of an independent Nicaragua. To the administration, unless the FSLN loses, no electoral process in Nicaragua can be characterized as "fair." If the Reagan administration were truly concerned with the promotion of democracy in Nicaragua, it would abandon its promotion of the abstentionists and abandon its campaign to discredit the first democratic elections in Nicaragua's history.*

The fall-back position of the Reagans was to ratchet up the pain of low intensity warfare through the Contras, isolate Nicaragua further by screwing the sanctions tighter, and escalate ever more convincing threats of invasion. These military threats caused the Nicaraguan government to divert scarce resources from its social programs to its military to repulse the Contra incursions and the expected full-scale war. Health clinics, literacy programs, land reclamation, essential harvesting plans – all had to wait. The FSLN, again playing fair, lost the next election (Nicaraguans crying "uncle?") in 1990, but it had put a structure in place that allowed it to survive as a party and again today in 2005 seem a viable option in the face of renewed and growing inequalities and corruption.

NEGROPONTE'S HONDURAS

November 6 was election day in the U.S., and it was clear that Reagan would be reelected to a second term. Our itinerary now took us to Honduras. We arrived in Tegucigalpa in time to talk with several people before we were expected at an embassy reception celebrating the Republicans' electoral triumph. Ian Cherrette, the director of HIVAS, a Dutch development group, had been working in Honduras for 12 years and gave us a brief history of that large rural land, almost all of which was privatized – a banana economy with no real oligarchy. The only institution with power, he explained, was the military, which was independent of the government. M. Cherrette told us there had been much disintegration since 1981 and the arrival of Ambassador Negroponte, "the source of all evil."

Another European, who directed the Honduran Catholic Relief Service told us of the many refugees then in Honduras, most from Guatemala and El Salvador, and of his conviction that the U.S. was about to invade Nicaragua. "What will become of all the refugees on the border if a U.S, invasion comes?" he told us he had asked a U.S. embassy friend. "That's why we've got to move them out," was the answer, and in a few days 12000 people were moved miles away from the border. This made space for continual U.S. joint maneuvers with Honduras, Big Pine I and II, Grenadera I, etc., openly billed as practice invasions into Nicaragua.

We had an appointment with Gen. Walter Lopez, who had replaced the notorious Gen. Alverez, ousted by young army officers earlier in the year for being "too heavy-handed." Honduran generals didn't mean much to American forces. During joint maneuvers, U.S. sergeants ordered them around, insulting the officers' sense of sovereignty. We asked General Lopez how much our government was helping his army, and he slapped his boots. "Everything! From boots on up," he said, thinking we would be pleased.

Our visit with Ambassador Negreponte himself shook us. We asked about the kidnappings, disappearances, and torture we had heard about. "Those cases are just a little mole on a white democratic body," was his particularly offensive response. We knew democracy had no hold on Honduras, the only country I have seen where soldiers in camouflage uniforms rode through the city streets in the back of pick-up trucks with machine guns

youth and young men. They can show them an unloaded rifle so that they will learn to load it and unload it; their use, and aiming at imaginary targets since they are potential recruits for our forces.

The guerrillas should always be prepared with simple slogans in order to explain to the people, whether in an intentional form or by chance, the reason for the weapons.

"The weapons will be for winning freedom; they are for you."

"With weapons we can impose demands such as hospitals, schools, better roads, and social services for the people, for you."

"Our weapons are, in truth, the weapons of the people, yours."

"With weapons we can change the Sandino-Communist regime and return to the people a true democracy so that we will all have economic opportunities."

All of this should be designed to create an identification of the people with the weapons and the guerrillas who carry them. Finally, we should make the people feel that we are thinking of them and that the weapons are the people's, in order to help them and protect them from a Communist, totalitarian, imperialist regime, indifferent to the needs of the population.

3 - Implicit and Explicit Terror

A guerrilla armed force always involves implicit terror because the population, without saying it aloud, feels terror that the weapons may be used against them. However, if the terror does not become explicit, positive results can be expected.

In a revolution, the individual lives under a constant threat of physical damage. If the government police cannot put an end to the guerrilla activities, the population will lose confidence in the government, which has the inherent mission of guaranteeing the safety of citizens. However, the guerrillas should be careful not to become an explicit terror, because this would result in a loss of popular support.

In the words of a leader of the HUK guerrilla movement of the Philippine Islands:

"The population is always impressed by weapons, not by the terror that they cause, but rather by a sensation of strength/force. We must appear before ..., the people, giving them support with our weapons, that will give them the message of the struggle."

This is then, in few words, the essence of armed propaganda.

- The spontaneous hostility that the majority of the population feels toward the target.

- Use rejection or potential hatred by the majority of the population affected toward the target, stirring up the population and making them see all the negative and hostile actions of the individual against the people.

- If the majority give their support or backing to the target or subject, do not try to change these sentiments through provocation.

- Relative difficulty of controlling the person who will replace the target.

- The person who will replace the target should be chosen carefully, based on:

  - Degree of violence necessary to carry out the change.

  - Degree of violence acceptable to the population affected.

  - Degree of violence possible without causing damage or danger to other individuals in the area of the target.

  - Degree of reprisal predictable by the enemy on the population affected or other individuals in the area of the target.

- The mission to replace the individual should be followed by:

  - Extensive explanation within the population affected of the reason why it was necessary for the good of the people.

- Explain that Sandinista retaliation is unjust, indiscriminate, and above all ., a justification for the execution of this mission.

- Carefully test the reaction of the people toward the mission, as well as control this reaction making sure that the population's reaction is beneficial towards the Freedom Commandos.

6 - Conclusions

Armed propaganda includes all acts executed and the impact achieved by an armed force, which as a result produces positive attitudes in the population toward this force, and it does not include forced indoctrination. However, armed propaganda is the most effective available instrument of a guerrilla force.

Congressional Research Service
The Library of Congress
/Translation - Spanish/

Washington, D.C. 20540

PSYCHOLOGICAL OPERATIONS IN GUERRILLA WARFARE

by Tayacan

PREFACE

Guerrilla warfare is essentially a political war. Therefore, its area of operations exceeds the territorial limits of conventional war-fare, to penetrate the political entity itself: the "political animal" that Aristotle defined.

In effect, the human being should be considered the priority objective in a political war. And conceived as the military target of guerrilla war, the human being has his most critical point in his mind. Once his mind has been reached, the "political animal" has been defeated, without necessarily receiving bullets.

Guerrilla warfare is born and grows in the political environment; in the constant combat to dominate that area of political mentality that is inherent to all human beings and which collectively constitutes the "environment" in which guerrilla warfare moves, and which is where precisely its victory or failure is defined.

This conception of guerrilla warfare as political war turns Psychological Operations into the decisive factor of the results. The target, then, is the minds of the population, all the population: our troops, the enemy troops and the civilian population.

This book is a manual for the training of guerrillas in psychological operations, and its application to the concrete case of the Christian and democratic crusade being waged in Nicaragua by the Freedom Commandos.

Welcome!

- The force of weapons is a necessity caused by the oppressive system, and will cease to exist when the "Forces of Justice" of our movement assume control.

If, for example, it should be necessary for one of the advanced posts to have to fire on an citizen who was trying to leave the town or city in which the guerrillas were carrying out a mission and propaganda or political proselitism, the following is recommended:

- Explain that if that citizen had managed to escape, he would have alerted the enemy that is near the town or city, and they would carry out acts of reprisal such as rapes, pillage, destruction, captures, given attention and hospitalities to the inhabitants of the place for having given attention and hospitalities to the guerrillas of the town.

- If a guerrilla fires at an individual, make the town see that he was an enemy of the people, and that they shot him because the guerrillas recognized as their first duty the protection of citizens.

- The commando tried to detain the informant without firing be-cause he, like all Christian guerrillas, espouses nonviolence. Having fired at the Sandinista informant, although it is against his own will, was necessary to prevent the repression of the Sandinista government against innocent people.

- Make the population see that it was the repressive system of the regime that was the cause of this situation, what really killed the informer, and that the weapon fired was one recovered in combat against the Sandinista regime.

- Make the population see that if the Sandinista regime ends the repression, the corruption backed by foreign/powers, etc., the freedom commandos would not have had /sic/ to brandish arms against brother Nicaraguans, which goes against our Christian sentiments. If the informant hadn't tried to escape he would be enjoying life together with the rest of the population, because he would not have tried to inform the enemy. This death would have been avoided, if justice and freedom existed in Nicaragua, which is exactly the objective of the democratic guerrilla.

5 - Selective Use of Violence for Propagandistic Effects

It is possible to neutralize carefully selected and planned targets, such as court judges, mesta /¿/ judges, police and State Security officials, CDS chiefs, etc. For psychological purposes it is necessary to take extreme precautions, and it is absolutely necessary to gather together the population affected, so that they will be present, take part in the act, and formulate accusations against the oppressor.

The target or person should be chosen on the basis of:

OPERACIONES SICOLOGICAS EN GUERRA DE GUERRILLAS

ENGLISH TRANSLATION

CIA warfare manual

Selections from Psychological Operations in Guerrilla War-fare, by "Tayacan", translated by the Congressional Research Service, Oct. 15, 1984, distrib-uted by NYC SHAD Alliance, NY, NY.

aimed at sidewalk passersby. The military was a law unto itself, not under the control of the civilian government.

It was our talk with Oscar Anibal, head of the Honduran Human Rights Commission, that confirmed our impression of a U.S. foreign policy gone mad. He told us that the first kidnapping was in 1981, coinciding with Negreponte's arrival as ambassador. Since then, a group of Honduran soldiers called the Cobras had carried out both psychological and physical torture, with complete impunity. Senor Anibal had worked for a European-funded economic development organization until 1982 when another employee, his close friend, was kidnapped in open daylight, held thirty days, and then dumped back on the city street. "He was completely destroyed, sub-human," reported Anibal, who immediately left his job and committed himself to human rights. "This is a monster let loose," he said with a visible shudder, "and it can't be contained."

That night my roommate and I skipped the embassy party celebrating Reagan's reelection. We knew what that meant to the people we had been talking with – more "low-intensity conflict," more illegal breaking of laws, more CIA training manuals, more destruction of people's attempts to better their lives. We knew we couldn't fake a celebratory mood. It was time for disabling headaches.

HISTORY DOES NOT EQUAL PROGRESS

My experiences in Central America reminded me as a woman to be grateful I live in the United States in the 20th and 21st centuries. Women in the U.S., through struggles, have gained the right to own property, to vote, to share equal rights with our husbands, to divorce, and to be guardians of our children. We have the right to testify in courts, the right and the means to take part in decisions about family planning, and equality in access to sports and other programs. This progress has made more life-enhancing experiences possible for me and many others. However, my natural optimism has faded during the last twenty-five years. A good many gains for women, minorities, and the disadvantaged are again up for grabs, and even the intricate, invaluable structure of our democracy is under assault. What I observed on my five trips to Central America added to my pessimism.

I blame two trends for our retrogression: first a growing militarism and the demands of what is perceived to be national security; and second, an unfettered capitalism. The first has engendered hate and fear, distorted our values and claimed more and more of our resources. The second, with its worship of the bottom line, the belief that "government is part of the problem, not the solution," and that the "free market" can solve all economic and social problems, rewards greed and gives rise to a callous disregard for fellow earthlings (and the earth itself). Jack Nelson-Pallmeyer, who was our guide in 1991 on another Central American trip, called the resulting attack on the weak in developing countries and within our own "The War Against the Poor."

This brings me back to Central America and the next time I traveled there in 1988 with the American Friends Service Committee. Bud and I had contributed money annually to that organization, and when they announced a trip, a kind of seminar, "to help participants understand the root causes of current characteristics and consequences of the crisis in Central America," to hunt for potential solutions, and to observe the various projects the AFSC was supporting in that area, I signed up, eager to get back to countries whose plight continued to haunt me all through the '80s and '90s.

CHAPTER 52

CENTRAL AMERICA AND THE FRIENDS

On January 9, 1988, I flew to Miami, where I was met by four Florida-based AFSC staff, our two guides, Angie Berryman and Bob Snyder, and the six other tour participants. More staff would join us in the countries we were about to visit. The next morning we drove to Homestead, Florida, past the Krome prison where the AFSC staff worked with undocumented immigrant inmates, and to the housing projects where farm workers, grouped according to nationality, lived. Then through acres and acres of farm land, where again the workers were separated by country of origin: Mexicans were picking the tomato crop, and Guatemalans (mainly *Indígenos*) were picking beans, etc. These workers sent what money they could scrape together to their families left behind in the countries we were about to visit.

AFSC trip-mates

AFSC
PERSPECTIVES
ON
NONVIOLENCE

in relation to groups
struggling for social justice

● Approved by the Board of Directors
of the American Friends Service Committee
January 24, 1981

The next morning we flew into Guatemala City. Don't go out alone after dark, we were warned. Kidnappings and suspicions of foreigners were prevalent. Angie Berryman, a former Maryknoll nun, seemed nervous and we discovered why. A decade earlier, she was living in Guatemala City with her husband, a former Maryknoll priest, and their two young children. They were working for the AFSC trying to find ways of improving the lives of Guatemalan peasants whose miserable lives were getting more miserable through loss of land, military repression and meager income. (2% of Guatemalans owned 70% of the land, over 1 million owned less than 2 acres, not enough to sustain a family, and half a million had no land at all.) In 1973, some coffee pickers, among them Vincente Menchu, a Preacher of the Word and the father of Rigoberto Menchu, a future Nobel Peace Prize winner,

stayed overnight at Angie's house before occupying the Spanish embassy. They were hoping to stir the plantation owners' consciences by notifying the world of their plight. Instead, the government of Guatemala burned down the embassy, killing all except the Spanish ambassador and one Guatemalan employee. Angie's

Will NAFTA create a level playing field?
The burdens continue.

husband, Phillip, was away and when word of the massacre reached Angie, pregnant with her third baby, she grabbed her passports and the children, drove to the airport, and boarded the first plane she could get herself and children on. It didn't matter to her, she said, where it was going. She knew the ruthless character of the Guatemalan regime, a government our government was and is providing with arms and other support.

There had been nine years of reform and hope in the late 1940s and '50s, but in 1954 democratically elected Jacobo Arbenz was ousted in a coup organized by the CIA. What were Arbenz's crimes? He had carried through a genuine land reform program that included expropriation with compensation of some of the vast holdings belonging to the United Fruit Company and had persuaded his congress to pass legislation that would guarantee the right of labor to organize, bargain collectively and strike, all proof that Arbenz was a "Communist." Guatemala reverted to a dictatorship, most of the land

and labor reforms were lost and, as Angie discovered, by the 1970s the country was riddled with death squads, militias fighting a guerrilla movement, and citizens expecting arbitrary violence from all sides. This hadn't changed much by 1988. The U.S. was supporting the government and the military with a good deal of American taxpayers' money.

On our first full day in Guatemala we drove west into the mountains to Lake Atitlan, territory of *Indíginos*. I had thought I had seen the two most beautiful lakes in the world, Potscuara in Michoacan in Mexico and Squam Lake in New Hampshire, but Atitlan, surrounded with volcanos, was starkly breathtaking, stunning, but there was no gentleness to it.

We were briefed by Roberto Wilson Grau, a researcher and journalist with Infor Press. He gave us many statistics – 32,000 *Indígenos* slaughtered by the military, 8 out of 10 Guatemalans living below the poverty line, 5 out of 10 starving, inflation 35% per year, 80% of taxes from sales taxes and 20% from wealth and income, and other dismal information. He said land owner-

Lake Atitlan

ship in Guatemala was the most inequitable in the hemisphere, and elections in that country were by no means indications of democracy. He described a cycle of repression, then a let-up when reformers gained space for organizing, and then another shut-down when repressive screws were applied once more. At the moment, he claimed, there was space for action. Organizers like the AFSC were trying to be more low-key so the ownership class would feel less threatened. I wondered who would be fooled if people really began to achieve some power over their own lives. In the days that followed, we would discover what an opening for organizing meant in Central America and what possibilities there might be for any lasting reform.

THE FRIENDS' PROJECTS

The methods the AFSC has developed after working for many decades to help change the lives of the poor involve organizing communities to find their own solutions. At Guatemala City we were met by a young AFSC field representative, Drew McKinley. It was he who had planned our itinerary, making appointments with community leaders and other AFSC regional representatives.

We spent some time in Sojugma, a slum section of the capital city, a crowded ramshackle area made up of thousands of rural refugees hoping to find jobs and anonymity in the city. Such poverty! People were arriving every day carrying a few meager goods on their backs and herding whatever animals they could salvage. Pigs and chickens were every-

Barrio Sojugma, and a guitar maker

where. Yet there was much hope and good will. Several years before our visit, organizers had gathered some of the refugees together to decide what was most needed.

Refugees from the same village were kept together as much as possible to maintain a sense of continuity and neighborly commitment. Roofs and siding for new housing were scrounged from dumps or wherever cast-offs could be found. Cement privies were being erected to mitigate the danger-ously unsanitary conditions. Health workers had been trained and a clinic, very inadequately supplied to be sure, had been built. Some were taking classes on Home Economics and others were learning carpentry and house building, sewing, weaving and basket making There was even a very modest "factory" for making guitars. However, few of the children we saw attend-ed school. In all of Guatemala, only 54% of children attended elementary school, and of these 3 out of 10 finished 6th grade and 1 out of 1000 reached the university.

We talked with a new arrival, a young mother, reluctant to give us her name or tell where she had come from, afraid of the authorities. We had lunch in a large communal dining and assembly room, discussing the two things they needed most, clean water and many more sanitary facilities.

SAN JOSÉ

We went on to a more stable community of about 7,000, which had been started three years earlier than Sojugma. In its beginning, about 80% of the peasants fleeing the poverty of the countryside suffered from malnu-trition, mainly from lack of protein. Two of the AFSC projects in San José were aimed at overcoming these nutritional problems. Some people worked in market gardening; another group was growing herbs and other healing, disease-preventing plants and had a thriving mail order business. Some in San José were becoming midwives, and some were chosen to work in the local hospital.

LA BRIGADA

A jolly, plump little man, Mario, sponsored by his Episcopal church and the AFSC, drove with us to another community called La Brigada. There we sat in on a biweekly class for mothers taught by volunteer health promoters from San José. We watched these health promoters train twelve volunteer La Brigada women to become health promoters themselves. The twelve young women had committed themselves to an eighteen-month program. The La Brigada twelve were to find 20 families they could help and to whom they could pass on the knowledge they were getting – about hygiene, treatments for diarrhea, small cuts, etc. They were taught how to get cooperation from their twenty families and eventually, with experience in their very primitive clinic, they would learn how to take blood pressure, keep track of children's weight, and even set bones. One large part of their training was in pharmacy basics. All of this sounds so positive, one would think encouragement would be the reaction all around.

I was standing next to Angie when I heard her say quietly to Mario, "I understand you were kidnapped a little while ago." Suddenly Mario's veneer of jollity cracked. "Yes," he answered, obviously shaken by the memory. The previous October, two and a half months earlier, he, another staff member, and a visiting Norwegean had been picked up by the military and driven around for hours over rough terrain with machine guns at their heads. Their captors threatened them, called them Communists, and warned them they would be watched in the future. Mario believed they would have been killed if the Norwegian hadn't been there. His captors undoubtedly feared an international embarrassment for the government if the foreigner disappeared. Mario and staff were still very scared and had stopped going from one community to the other except with European or North American witnesses like us. He pointed out several soldiers hanging around, keeping the communities under surveillance. And these were the good years of the cycle of repression!

GUATEMALA CITY

On January 13th, we talked with a one-legged leader of an independent labor coalition. There were also government-sponsored unions, essentially company unions, and workers who didn't join the government unions were labeled undemocratic and Communist. But except for the independent unions, there was no restraint on companies which paid whatever wages and charged whatever prices they wanted. The Coalition had successfully pressured the electric company to lower its rates, price controls had been reinstated, and there had been a slight increase in the minimum wage. The man we talked with had lost his leg, shot by the Guatemala military during an earlier march while demonstrating for the right to organize unemployed workers. He and his fellow workers were busy making signs and preparing for another demonstration to be held the following day, a march to better their living conditions. How did he know he wouldn't be shot again? Well, solidarity with other unions was greater, the methods being used were more grassroots and

*Independent labor unions organize
a protest march, Guatemala City*

had reached up to mid-level workers. The land co-operative movement was reviving and the peasant movement, which had been shattered by the massacre in the Spanish embassy, was gathering strength again. The peasants planned to join the demonstration, although they had been threatened with arrest if they participated. Besides, the new union leadership had been less confrontational, had taken a more back-seat advisory role. Still, they seemed to me exceptionally brave, but I have never been in a situation when I and my family were dying little by little through malnutrition and ghetto conditions. Perhaps trying to make life bearable is more important than mere survival.

That afternoon, some of our group flew with Angie to El Salvador while three of us chose to ride with Drew and his handsome, pregnant Salvadoran wife, Anna, in their jeep. We drove over mountains, down to the plains where we saw horses and cowboy hats, and up to a check point and customs station at the border. As we approached customs, we saw a surprising number of army jeeps and a cluster of military men in uniform. Drew and Anna suddenly seemed very nervous. I heard them wondering what the military was watching for at the border and if this meant trouble for us. Drew took a few sheets of paper out of his bag and slipped them into a newspaper he carried under his arm. We were told we could walk around if we wished but not to get out of sight while he and Anna conducted the customs business with our passports and theirs. When we were given a signal, we were to get back to the jeep immediately so we could leave as soon as possible. The signal was given, we sauntered back to the jeep, and Drew drove with no appearance of haste over the border.

What a sigh of relief from Drew and Anna! Tension dissolved. Singing and happy chatter were once more the order of the day. What did our drivers fear the soldiers would find? What was on those sheets of paper Drew had shifted to the newspaper under his arm? Names of those who had been killed or disappeared since the last visit from someone from the network of people trying to shine light on Guatemalan crimes!

We turned off the main road at Santa Ana into a calm residential neighborhood. Dusk had already turned into night, and we were hungry. We parked at the end of a street and walked back about a block to join a group of people eating at a large table on the sidewalk spilling out into the roadway. The five of us were greeted with hospitable hugs by Anna's family: her mother and father, a few brothers, an aunt and uncle or two, and some cousins. More chairs were brought and tacos produced. Our new friends exchanged news in a quiet, cheerful chatter, and we relaxed until, shortly after we were served, there was a loud bang and the street lights went out. A transformer we had walked under to reach our dinner companions had been blown up. Our hosts showed no surprise, maybe even some amusement. They brought out candles and we went on with our meal. While dining al fresco that night, we were relieved that our friends (and we) were not targets.

Dinner with Anna's family in Santa Ana, El Salvador

SAN SALVADOR

Later that evening, Drew and Anna deposited the three of us at the hotel in San Salvador where our group was staying. They turned us over to a new guide, Jim Stevens, another AFSC field staff member. Unrest in the entire Central American region had boiled over during the 1970s, '80s and '90s, we were told in a briefing. The rebels in each country had achieved different levels of success, meaning land reform, a change in the distribution of political power, and a more equal sharing of their country's resources. But only in Nicaragua had the Sandinista rebels become the legitimate government. They had held a genuine election, carried out significant land reform, raised the literacy rate, instituted health clinics, overhauled the justice and prison systems (more about this later), and instituted new health standards. Guatemala was still tentatively probing openings for social change, as we had seen. What about El Salvador?

El Salvador's 20th Century history, like that of the other Central American countries, was a bloody one. In the early 1930s, during a worldwide collapse of coffee and other commodity prices, there was much unrest and demand for land reform and higher wages. Land and power were in the hands of a small group of large landholders, and rural workers' status was essentially feudal. The army and private paramilitary groups were in the pay of the oligarchy and reacted to pressure for reform by slaughtering as many as 30,000 peasants in a country with a population of less than 5 million. I've seen a documentary showing some of the land owners proudly referring to *La Matanza*, the massacre of 1932, reminding their people fifty years later how they dealt with "Communist" groups.

In the 1970s, as an answer to another attempt at reform, the oligarchy struck again with cruel repression. This time the government was getting more effective support from the United States, but the rebels benefitted by closer world scrutiny, the Cold War rivalry, the successes of the Nicaragua revolution, and a split in the Catholic church. Pope John XXIII's Vatican II declaration of the option toward the poor, which led to the Liberation Theology movement, had a profound effect on opinion across the world, particularly in Latin America. The next trip I took to Central America was with a group studying Liberation Theology. I'll write about that trip in another chapter.

By 1988 the opposing forces in El Salvador had reached a stalemate, with approximately half the country in guerrilla hands and half in the hands of the government, which was supported with vast amounts of U.S. taxpayers' money. Jim, our new AFSC contact, was gloomy. He saw no end to the eight-year war as long as the U.S. continued to supply arms and money to the government and military with its death squads, kidnappings and disappearances, and as long as the rebels held the trust of those living in their section of control. I thought Jim needed a vacation and a less stressful job. We would soon gain an even fuller understanding of his pessimism and the daily tension he was experiencing.

Unlike Jim, Peter Schmeelk, the human rights officer at the United States Embassy, was optimistic and surprisingly candid. Although he didn't think the military could take over the whole country, the U.S. was making progress in promoting democracy. He described the recent Salvadoran elections as "reasonably fair," even though the U.S. contributed billions of dollars to El Salvador and to its military, but he realized there was more to democracy than elections. A free press, for instance. The real problem in El Salvador, he thought, was a bad judicial system. Since the massacres in 1979, over a thousand military people had been dismissed but few convicted. The accused had been held in prison a long time before being given a trial, but only 15% were ever convicted. Juries and judges were all intimidated. Unfortunately, Duarte, the leader the U.S. backed, seemed to be losing power because the oligarchy despised him for his attempts at land reform (in 1978, 5% of the people owned 95% of the land), and the military supported the oligarchy. Where is the cause for optimism?

We heard more about land reform – that all land confiscated involved compensation but that the peasants who received the redistributed land often sold it (under duress?) once they got deeds, and were almost back where they had started. The peace talks among the five Central American presidents had broken down, and Peter thought the war would go on another 20 to 30 years, but he still saw progress. Not long ago there were about 800 political deaths per month and now there were only about 200. In fact criminal deaths had surpassed political ones during the past month. Colonel Lopez, connected with the most brutal of the political deaths, had been kicked upstairs and sent off to a consulate in West Germany, and D'Aubusson, Duarte's main opponent, was un-electable because of his involvement with death squads. We asked Peter how he got his information. He didn't speak Spanish, he said, and didn't get out to talk to ordinary citizens because it was too dangerous, but he was well briefed by the government's Human Rights Commission. No, he didn't find the Archbishop's Human Rights group helpful. (Some things you don't want to hear). Peter told us that Nicaragua was the number one threat to security and that El Salvador would have fallen to the Communists if the U.S. hadn't been there. This was the crux of the matter. In our government's view, the upheaval in the Americas was not caused by desperate economic inequalities and repression but by aggression from Russia and Cuba.

We met with Salvadoran labor and peasant church groups and visited an AFSC-supported health promoter training program. The factory and plantation workers were facing "the worst crisis of Salvadoran history," we were told. Owners didn't respect minimum wages, which were "wages of hunger." Seventy-eight percent of the workers did not have secure jobs and unemployment was growing. Health care was miserable. The government didn't think it was its job to provide health care for the non-military population, so civilian hospitals lacked proper equipment and medicine while military hospitals had a surfeit of both, and of course the continuing war diverted money needed for social purposes.

There was some hope among the peasants, who were reorganizing, struggling for new laws to protect a resurgent cooperative movement. However, over the last year repression of the cooperatives had increased. In short, many we talked with could only see continuing deterioration with more acts of rebellion leading to more government repression: a bleak future unless ordinary Salvadorans could stop the war and gain enough power to have some say over their own lives.

SANTA MARTA

You may wonder how the ordinary Salvadoran could keep up hope. On Friday, we visited a community of campesinos recently returned from a refugee camp in Honduras. It was in the countryside not far from San Salvador and we saw hope in motion. One of the most devastating government actions in the early '80s was the wiping out of whole villages, trying to "dry up the sea to kill off the fish." This was similar to the Phoenix program in Vietnam. In December of 1981, news of a massacre in the farming village of El Mozote, where over 500 men, women and children were tortured and killed and their houses burned leaked to a shocked world. In other cases, villagers fled to the cities or to other countries, mainly Honduras, seeking safety from the approach of marauding soldiers. The refugees who are pertinent to

Saw pit for new homes, Santa Marta

my story escaped from soldiers attacking their villages in May, 1980 and crossed the Sumpul River that forms part of the border between El Salvador and Honduras. As they were crossing the river on logs, they were strafed by

Salvadoran helicopters and by Salvadoran troops and paramilitary groups shooting from the river banks. At least 600 were killed. The ones who survived joined other Salvadoran refugees in Honduras. UN and other international relief agencies tried to provide food and shelter and safety for the estimated 50,000 to 70,000 refugees in Honduras for the next seven years. During that time, the refugees suffered from

Kids helping with temporary housing, Santa Marta

malnutrition and sickness, raids from Salvadoran military over the border, and harassment from the Honduran military.

The villagers stayed together in the Honduran refugee camp, tight-knit groups of neighbors helping each other and planning their futures, which they

Washing in stream, Santa Marta

determined would be back in the places they had come from. Finally, when threatened with further dangers from the Honduran army who wanted them gone and in defiance of the Salvador government who didn't want them back, they announced to the world press that they were returning to El Salvador and described their route, destination and timing. They had learned that if they returned singly or in small family groups, they were disappeared, so they moved in large groups that included many widows, orphans, and elderly. It was to one of these villages of returnees, Santa Marta, that we drove on January 15th.

We rode in two four-wheel-drive jeeps for perhaps half an hour till we came to a check point. Jim had asked us to be quiet while he did the talking. Asked where we were going, he said we were going to talk with a campesino Co-op member who gave technical assistance in animal husbandry, and we did that. We picked him up and drove on over rutted dirt roads to a place that was alive with activity. This was Santa Marta, a settlement of 255 families, about 1500 people who, with the help of the Catholic and Lutheran churches and others, had bought 600 acres for their new village. When they finally reached their land on October 14, 1987 they found mainly weeds, but three months later we found a functioning town. Men were grinding maize and sawing logs into boards for permanent housing. Women were busy bathing their children and washing their clothes in the river that flowed through the

Santa Marta returnees in new homes

town. We were offered radishes, the first produce from their garden. We crossed the river and climbed a mild rise where the permanent village was being built. There were already 56 permanent houses, and 125 more two-family houses were planned. We continued on into the woods to an open space with a circle of logs to sit on. The 4-year-old son of Louis, the village spokesman, climbed all over his imperturbable father and then snuggled into his arms as we were told of Santa Marta's plans. The community had formed a coordinating committee with a treasurer, health promoter, and production and construction managers. They planned to raise rabbits and already had a number of pigs. We could hear them making a sort of hum in the woods. In February a school would be opened and planting season would begin at the end of April.

One significant characteristic of Santa Marta was their religion. They were people of the Word, devout catholics who had formed themselves into a Christian-based community, a part of the Liberation Theology movement. This movement was especially strong in Latin America, where groups of lay Catholics read the Bible together and tried to apply its messages to their present-day lives and, in the process, "began to recognize their obligation to themselves and their communities."

In the midst of this briefing, Louis paused, stood up, pointed to Jim Stevens, who was translating for us, and said, "Two years ago, in Honduras, you saved my life!" They threw their arms around each other, and the rest of us, realizing that something dramatic was happening, waited eagerly to get filled in. Here's the story. Two years before, just as Jim and Bianca Jagger, on an inspection tour for an international organization, drove into a Honduran refugee camp, they saw a string of about 50 men, roped together at their necks, with thumbs tied together, being driven along by some Salvadoran soldiers. One of the men – it was Louis – managed to reach Jim's car, put his tied hands over the mirror and cry, "Help us, Help us. We're

Louis and Jim recognize each other at Meeting, Santa Marta

about to be killed!" Jim and Bianca (the story would have been dramatic enough without such a celebrity in it) drove after the group shouting to the soldiers, "Let them go! Let them go! We have cameras and we'll tell the world what you are doing!" When the soldiers turned their captives off the road into a dry gully, Jim and Bianca got out of their car and ran shouting after them. Finally the 50 refugees were abandoned and returned to their encampment with their rescuers. There was much rejoicing, of course, until a woman from an outlying building, hysterically weeping, burst in. The Salvadoran soldiers, having lost their original quarries, had broken into her house and hacked her husband and children to death. How can one understand such blood-lust?

Back in El Salvador, the Santa Martans still worried about the Salvadoran military, which often patrolled threateningly near the camp. However, they were watched over. We had met their guardian watchman when we first arrived: a tall, young American Mennonite, standing a bit apart from the construction activity. He was one of a remarkable volunteer band of people who try to hold off violence by witnessing and reporting to the world what is being done to these most vulnerable people.

CALLE REAL

On Saturday we went to the Catholic diocesan headquarters to meet with Monsignor Urioste, the Social Secretary of the Diocese. He had been Archbishop Romero's right hand man and was very much involved with the returnees. While waiting for our appointment with Msgr. Urioste, we talked with Reverend Hennesey, a Maryknoll priest from Iowa who had been stationed for many years in a small mountain village in Guatemala. He told of an attack by the Guatemala military on the village; they had burned houses and killed the people and their animals. Could you ever get numb to these stories?

When we did get to meet with Msgr. Urioste, he welcomed us and apologized for keeping us waiting. He had been at a high-level meeting with the Archbishop to decide how to react if Calle Real, a repatriated community like Santa Marta that the diocese was protecting, needed help. (The Calle Real community of 3,300 people had returned from Honduras the previous October in defiance of the Salvadoran government's orders.) A hundred soldiers had invaded the day before but had been removed when the Archbishop complained. Today, however, the soldiers were back. Urioste said he would gladly talk with us but might have to leave quickly if sent word of an attack. We asked about the attitude of the Church toward the struggle and were told that part of the bishopric, now sympathetic to the returnees, was being given to a conservative bishop, but Urioste and the present archbishop saw themselves as giving voice to the voiceless. They felt the Church should always show a "preferential option for the poor." "We used to think *we* were the teachers but now they are teaching *us*." He told us of one woman whose brother, husband and whole family were killed while fleeing across the river into Honduras seven years before. She gave birth very soon after reaching the Honduran river bank. The baby was hungry and was given some water and sugar, and now is a healthy seven-year-old. "Father, isn't that a miracle!" Urioste urged us to look at the country not through political eyes but with human eyes, with Christian eyes. He approved the campesino lay groups who were interpreting biblical stories in reference to their own lives. The interpretations were not always right, but many important questions were discussed. "What would Jesus say if he returned to this country at the Last Judgement?

'How did you treat the poor?'" At this point, an aide came in quickly and bent down to Urioste's ear. Urioste excused himself and hurried off because there was an emergency at Calle Real.

We were further briefed by Roberto Codas, another AFSC representative whose job was to analyze the situation in the Central American countries, to give background reports, and to talk with government people, people in power. He tried to understand U.S. policies and to fashion responses to them. He called our low intensity warfare program "a bankrupt failure." The U.S. was giving more money to the Salvadoran military than the whole Salvadoran national budget. Also, we were giving about 300 million dollars per year to the business sector, bolstering the ruling class. Fifteen percent of our aid was earmarked for development, but of the 400 farm cooperatives created in the reform period of 1980, only 10 or 12 were still working. Roberto saw Salvador heading toward a much worse crisis.

That same afternoon, we picked up Alberto, a psychologist, who took us to El Limon to show us some health care projects. The emphasis again was teaching self-help techniques. Health-givers from the community learned to give talks about boiling water and keeping animals out of houses, and they talked about hygiene with first graders and about alcoholism with older students. Three women had been trained as midwives, and anti-bacterial soaps and medicine for coughs were made at a clinic they had built. We saw a garden where indigenous plants to make natural medicines were grown. "The committee" that ran the clinic promoted adult literacy and also put on dances and plays. One aim of this organization was to build solidarity, but that might be going too far. Certainly a local priest thought so. When "the committee" started its work, it was given space in the local church until the priest kicked them out. They were getting too independent!

NICARAGUA

Early Sunday morning, we flew to Nicaragua and drove to Leon, where we met with AFSC staff member Tony Esqualia, who described the economics of Nicaragua's agricultural sector. Then we were taken to a cotton plantation to observe the devastating pollution problems that came from much spraying of pesticides to eliminate the boll weevil. A young American,

Bob McConnell, was there studying the toxicity of these pesticides and experimenting with alternatives in a program supported by the AFSC and with the full encouragement of the Nicaraguan government. Bob reported that the poison was beginning to reach the drinking water, and this was just one plantation in that country, 60% of whose income came from coffee.

That night when we turned on the lights at our motel room, we saw bigger cockroaches than I ever knew existed. They scurried out of sight, and we inspected bed clothes before we turned in. The next morning we again inspected shoes, etc. before dressing. We had slept some and we had survived, but I yearned for a bit of that poison.

The next morning, before visiting a health clinic, we talked about the damage done in the section of the country we were in by the U.S.-supported Contras. The Contras had destroyed 146 schools and 56 health clinics in the past eight years. The war had exacted a terrible price on the whole society, a society that seemed even poorer than the other Central American countries. Tony Esqualia's wife and a Nicaraguan nurse ran the clinic. A dentist came to work there once a week but with no doctor, the caregivers made life-and-death decisions by consulting their medical books. What kind of diarrhea does that child have? The "staff" gave sputum tests when TB was suspected. If the test proved positive, the rest of the family had to be tested, taught how to give injections, and persuaded to keep the infected person's dishes separate. Several midwives worked with the clinic. One couldn't read but was wise and had delivered about 800 babies in the past eight years. Another, now age 36, had been a midwife since she was 16.

Anyone with half a heart could see that Nicaragua was near the bottom of the ladder economically. I marveled at the young people, a good many of them Americans, who were helping to dig latrines, install water pumps, harvest the coffee crop, and volunteer in the clinics. The Sandinista government was a bona fide democracy. Its election had been clean, and its constitution written and adopted with a great deal of citizen-participation. It even had a functioning and fair judicial branch. There was no aura of repression and no curfew such as we had experienced in other Central American countries. The government had carried out an effective land reform and had helped agricultural cooperatives get seeds and fertilizers. And no international inspection team ever found any evidence of arms-smuggling. Yet the Reagan administration was an adamant adversary, insisting that Nicaragua was the greatest threat in the western hemisphere.

That night, instead of returning to the El Europa Motel in Leon, we were taken to Selva Negro, a hospitality house in a quiet woods, reminding me of our primitive Squam Lake cabin. We talked over the experiences we had had and the plans for the next day. The calm of the country made for good sleeping – and there were no cockroaches.

SANDINISTA PRISONS

On Tuesday, we went to the sixth district prison outside Matagalpa. We had visited a prisoner, Herb Brown, for eight years and I was serving on the board of the Connecticut Prison Association, so this was of particular interest to me. We met with the warden, Carlos Leiton from Leon, who worked for the Minister of The Interior, Tomas Borge, one of the five leaders of the 1979 revolution. He told us there had been no real prisons during Somosa's reign except for a torture center. Otherwise, the guard posts of the National Guard functioned as warehouses for prisoners. The first Sandinista jails were in private homes until they could build real ones. By 1988, there were six prisons, one in each zone of the country. "Now everyone has a bed, health services, sport and work programs." After traveling to other countries to study penal systems, the Sandinistas, in their revolutionary idealism, decided to comply with United Nations standards. That meant no death penalty; a maximum sentence of 30 years; and an emphasis on learning to read, free food, shoes, and jobs where prisoners could earn money they could keep. Anyone under 16 could not be charged with a crime but would be turned over to the welfare department. The aim was rehabilitation and reintegration back into society.

As we approached the 6th District prison, on a wall near the entrance we saw a big sign which announced "Learning to read can make you free." The guards didn't wear guns inside the prison. They consciously tried to act with moral superiority in front of the prisoners. "We can teach that way. We don't attack the person. We try to change negative habits."

I liked the idea of incentives for prisoners being rehabilitated. During the first 10% of their sentence, a period of adaptation, they could have overnight visitors every 45 days. The next period, they could have a 48-hour home

Sandanista Prison

pass every three months, etc. At the next Connecticut Prison Association meeting, I tried to report on the Nicaraguan system. Wouldn't some incentives that prisoners could count on and a regime that kept prisoners productively busy and profitable be something our organization should explore and encourage? Our present system results in high recidivism, much overcrowding, and often deadly riots. I heard some snickers and felt a pat on the head.

In Managua we met with Julio Arevlo from the North American Section of Nicaragua's foreign ministry. He claimed the United States aimed to destroy the revolution. Contra terrorism was scaring people away from helping in clinics and agricultural coops, and 20 to 30 young Nicaraguans were being killed every day.. He pinned some hope on the Escapulis Peace Plan then being negotiated. He sounded tired.

We also met Joe Mulligan at the Centro Historico. He was a journalist with ENVIO and UPDATE, two publications I subscribed to for many years. Joe, too, described the need for and the possible road-blocks to the Escapulas Peace Plan. He defended the Sandinista government, pointing out that Nicaragua had no curfews and no aura of repression. He described the conflict with the church and the split within it. Two Jesuit priests were members of the Nicaraguan cabinet: Father d'Escoto, Minister of the Interior and Father Cardinal, Minister of Education. However, the Vatican had given the two priests a choice – leave the Sandinista government or leave the priesthood. Obando Y Bravo was appointed cardinal by the Vatican, although many of the lay Catholics in his district thought him corrupt and self-serving. But he was against the Nicaraguan revolution and Liberation Theology. Again we were hearing about that fermenting new theological concept. In 1991 I would grab a chance to travel to Central America with a group studying Liberation

Theology, but our American Friends Service Committee trip was over. We flew home early the next morning. Most of the projects we had seen were supported by the AFSC – by our contributions to that organization – and I approved. The insistence on grass-roots participation in planning and carrying out these projects made them more viable. and the types of projects we saw as well as the processes for implementing them promised positive consequences for the future. The journey had not diminished my enthusiasm for the AFSC – nor our future contributions.

Cardinal Obando y Bravo,
Prince of the Church

CHAPTER 53

ANOTHER NICARAGUAN ELECTION

1990 was presidential election year again in Nicaragua, a decade after the revolution and six years after the first Sandinistan elections. The vote was set for February 25, but this time Peace Action planned a trip for January 27 to February 6 in the midst of the campaign, and it included some days in Costa Rica. I was anxious to join the trip, having kept up with events in Central America through magazines and at several seminars on Central America in this country.

Three recent events seemed bound to influence the 1990 elections. In August of 1989, the four Central American presidents and the U.S. agreed among other things to a cease-fire in Nicaragua: the Contras were to be demobilized and disbanded by December 5 and the U.S. embargo removed. However, in September, the U.S. Congress released thirty million dollars in "non-lethal aid" to the Contras, which helped them continue their infiltrations into Nicaragua to disrupt the elections. In October the U.S. resumed the embargo and sent nine million dollars to the Sandinista's main oppo-

Cora Weiss, Jane Milikin and Peter Weiss in a pre-election trip to Nicaragua in 1990

One of four Contras returning to Managua from Miami

nent: UNO, a coalition of 14 parties (all of this in violation of the August accords)

In November, a Salvadoran death squad brutally murdered six Jesuit priests at the university they operated, as well as their housekeeper and her daughter. In December, the United States invaded Panama and, having failed in a coup attempt the previous month, kidnapped its head of state and Commander-in-chief, Manuel Noriega, and tried him for drug-running, sentencing him to 45 years in prison. The drug charges were suspect. Noriega's real crime was refusing to cooperate with the U.S. and the Contras against Nicaragua and opposing the presence on Panamanian soil of the School of the Americas, where the U.S. trained Central American military such as the Salvadoran death squads. Also, the Panama treaties arranged under President Carter, which would return sovereignty to the Panamanians, were about to go into effect. Regime-change would allow the U.S. to maintain control of the territory surrounding the canal.

Cora Weiss, Peter Merchatti, Mims, Fr. Gorstiaga and Peter Weiss at Jesuit House

There were only eight of us on this preelection trip. We had interesting company on the flight from Miami to Managua: Marion Piatroni, the new secretary to Jack Leonard, the U.S. Ambassador to Nicaragua; Jim, an aide to Robert White, who had been Ambassador to El Salvador at the time the three nuns and lay church woman were murdered by the Salvadoran military; and five exiled Contra comandantes, given a raucous farewell in Miami and welcomed by a CIA operative in Managua – all eager to meddle, for better or worse, in the coming elections.

Jesuit House: Fr. Cardinal's 55th birthday

Our organizers, Cora and Peter Weiss and the N.Y. Riverside Church iconoclast, Rev. William Sloan Coffin, were well-known peace and civil rights leaders, and as a result we had entree to the two Jesuit priests in the revolutionary administration, We talked with them about the decision they were forced to make by the Vatican: dismissal from the Jesuit order or ceasing participation in the Sandinista government. We know Fr. Cardinal's answer: "In our formation as Jesuits…we knew that love…was the way to express our Christian faith. I realized that to love the poorest in any effective way meant revolution…. It was pure fantasy…to say that one loves the poorest while doing nothing…to liberate them from the structures of oppression which were killing them."

He couldn't obey the order to leave government service. That would have meant "a betrayal of the people precisely at a time when our country was being attacked." He would be "sinning against love for the people." He was a passionate conscientious objector.

The election process was similar to the one in 1984. This time there were three prominent observer teams, one from the UN, another from the OAS, Organization of American States,

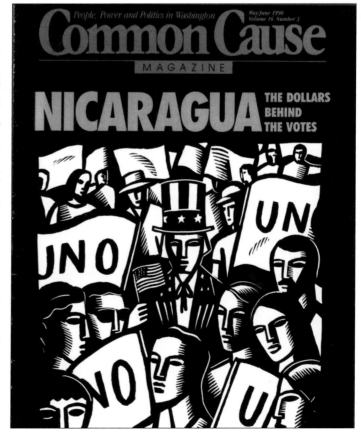

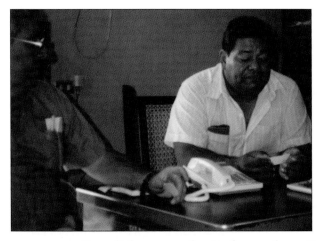

Candidates at the Independant Producers Party Headquarters

and the third an international group led by former President Jimmy Carter. The first two of these had been at work since the previous July. We came across them in Managua, Matagalpa and Leon, and had lunch one day with one of the UN observers.

The U.S. had helped form the main opposition group, UNO, out of fourteen very diverse parties, had chosen Violeta Chamorro and Virgilio Godoy to be the candidates, had given that unity party 23 million for the campaign, and had promised Violeta that if she won the election, the U.S. would lift the sanctions and stop the war.

We visited the headquarters of some minor candidates representing the cooperatives, the private producers, the middle class, etc. but the action was with UNO and FSLN We had meetings with Violeta's campaign manager, Daniel Lacayo, and heard their platform: no army (privatized militia?), freedom to produce (no taxes or regulations?), and work.

Uno Party Headquarters, funded by the US

And we talked with Bayard Arce, one of the 9 directorates of FSLN, which was running on the present government's record. We also met with the FSLN mayor of Sandinista Barrio and some youth

FSLN candidates Bayardo Arce, Directorate of 9; Patricia Elvira,
International Relations Ministry & Chair of Campaign;
Marta Medina, Vice-Minister of Health

workers there. He showed us an art exhibit at the youth center in that town, and we saw a home-grown play (a bit like Social Realism propaganda or the skits put on by West Hartford's *The Bridge*). The mayor described the difficulties in keeping restless young people productively occupied in his poor barrio that had once been a slum.

There were other types of contacts we made, but the political situation was always uppermost. We had lunch with a group from the World Council of Churches, met with a young woman who had just been appointed Minis-

Sandinista political theatre and barrio headquarters

Sandinista slogans: Let's win, everything will be better

ter of Health, and were briefed by an old acquaintance, Panamanian Xavier Gorostiega, an expert on regional issues. One day we went to the Ben Linder House, a new visitors' center in Managua, named after a young American killed by the Contras while installing a much-needed water pump in a small village near the Honduran border. I was delighted to find the center was being run by Jenny Howe, the daughter of friends in New Hampshire, and even more delighted and surprised to find our friends there too. We sat with them while listening to an Episcopal minister, a specialist on Panama, talk about

the recent invasion. Panama again! Many we talked to thought that the invasion, with the kidnapping of Manuel Noriega, had been a turning point, that the Nicaraguans who had not made up their minds about the coming elections had decided then and there against the U.S. and its candidate, Violeta.

One day we drove to Corinto, one of four ports in Nicaragua that the U.S. had mined. It was impressive – deep water, clean docks, space for many merchant ships and a bustling trade. And it was empty!

Almost all those with whom we talked believed the FSLM would win, but they were wrong. Violeta's UNO party won, and the issues the revolution tried to address had to wait for another day.

Casa Ben Linder

COSTA RICA

On February 3 we flew to Costa Rica, where we had several briefings; first by a professor of sociology at the National University, then by a spokesman at the U.S. Embassy, and later by a TV commentator, a former ambassador to the U.S. and a one-time aide to Costa Rican President Arias. One saw a new conservative triangle emerging in the region, with new leaders in Costa Rica, Guatemala and Honduras, and predicted more drugs, more pro-U.S. policies, and less pressure for peace. One said that the Salvadoran rebels, the FMLN, despite their strength, would have to negotiate with the government, and they were both right.

Too much hospitality: a whole fish

We had a grand day walking in the national rain forest and later wandering through the Museum of Pre-Columbian Gold, but the most memorable time in Costa Rica was spent with friends of the Weisses and Bill Coffin, a couple named Tony Avirgan and Martha Honey. The Avirgan/Honey household was memorable, offering a warm welcome to anyone who dropped in and an extra dinner plate for any who cared to stay. I remember two young women, just back from El Salvador, who described watching U.S. planes in a "saturation bombing run" pulverize an area the size of a football field. The women had been visiting friends in a nearby village, and no one knew if there were any farmers or rebel soldiers in the way.

We made an eager audience as our hosts told of their recent court case defending themselves against an accusation of libel. Tony and Martha

Grupa Mujer

Hosts and journalists Martha Honey & Tony Avirgen

were both journalists, covering the consequential events in Central America during the 1980s. During a press conference at La Penca in May of 1984, called by Eden Pastora, an anti-Sandinista General who refused to meld his "army" with the National Guard Contras, a bomb was detonated, killing three journalists and five guerrillas. It was obviously intended for Pastora, who was wounded, as were Tony Avirgon and dozens of others gathered to hear the General.

No one was apprehended, so three press organizations asked Tony and Martha to investigate the episode to discover who was responsible. In October of 1985, Tony and Martha made public a report that, among other things, claimed an American, John Hull, who owned a ranch in Costa Rica near the Nicaragua border, worked for the CIA, received money from the U.S. National Security Council and helped to insert a group of Miami Cubans into Pastora's ranks, was a part of the La Penca bombing and of a later plot to kill Pastora. The report also revealed that Hull had been under investigation for drug-trafficking. Hull called these assertions libelous and filed a suit against the two journalists shortly after the report became public. One other assertion in the report – that Hull had plotted with others to bomb the U.S. Embassy, kill the U.S. ambassador, and blame these actions on the Sandinistas to provide an excuse for direct U.S. invasion of Nicaragua – was not made a part of Hull's libel suit. The story Tony told was about assassinations of witnesses, death threats, and other intrigues and intimidations. I often felt I was a minor character in the midst of a mystery novel on those trips to Central America. Tony and Martha won the libel suit, Pastora quit his war against the Sandinistas a month before the trial, and Hull was exiled from Costa Rica.

Central America was the Middle East of the '80s and '90s, and if we remembered more about that period we might be less surprised by the news of today. Our foreign policy had little to do with democracy, physical threats to our country, or concern over living conditions and human rights. And the outcome in the long run was not what our policy-makers had in mind. A *New York Times* February 2006 headline read "LATIN AMERICA HEADS LEFT."

.

Rev. William Sloane Coffin, Maggie Riggs and U.S. Ambassador to Costa Rica, Jack Hamilton

CHAPTER 54

A SEMINAR IN LIBERATION THEOLOGY

In November of 1989, shortly after the six Jesuit priests and their housekeeper and her daughter were murdered at their Catholic University by the Salvadoran Atlacatl Battalion, a group of us made an appointment with our senator, Chris Dodd. There were about ten of us, mainly clergy including Catholic Bishop Whelan and his counterpart in the Episcopal Church, a labor leader, Jerry Springer, and me. Dodd was Catholic, had lived for some time in Central America, and had expressed empathy for its people. We had hopes he would vote against any further support for the Salvadoran military and would work to close down the School of the Americas in Panama, where the U.S. had trained the Atlacatl Battalion and other brutal military in the region.

We had agreed to meet for breakfast before the meeting to decide how best to approach the senator. One of us, a priest (I swear his name was Bernie Bush) was late and rushed in looking distraught. "Do you mind praying before we begin? I'm so angry and I want to talk with Dodd with love in my heart," he explained. So we all said a silent prayer and sure enough, the mood was remarkably altered. We decided we'd do the same when we got to Dodd's office, thus preventing him from monopolizing the conversation from the beginning as he tended to do, and perhaps help him to better hear our concerns. He did that and was sympathetic, but U.S. policy remained the same.

But why had Archbishop Romero, three nuns and a church woman, six Jesuits, and quite a few priests been killed in a Catholic country like El Salvador? Why was the Church split in Nicaragua between Archbishop Obando y Bravo and the Sandinista priests? Why was the Vatican taking action to silence its most beloved priests? In my mail came an advertisement from the Center of Global Education at Augsburg College in Minneapolis for a travel seminar from January 10–24, 1991 in El Salvador, Costa Rica, and Nicaragua. It was sponsored by Harvard Divinity School and would be studying Liberation Theology. I signed up.

Two Dollars

envío

Instituto Histórico Centroamericano   Managua, Nicaragua
Volume 9   Number 102a   January 1990

Special Issue

Hommage to Six Jesuits:

New Martyrs of El Salvador

Envío: The Monthly Magazine of Analysis on Nicaragua

EL SALVADOR

There were eighteen of us, counting Jack Nelson-Pallmeyer, the staff member who would be our guide for the next two weeks. Most of us were connected to a church, one worked in a small psychiatric hospital in a Mennonite community, and another, a retired clergyman from Oregon, had read about the seminar in *Sojourners* magazine. My roommate, Cheryl, a recent graduate of Yale Divinity School, was a minister in a small Tennessee town. When she had graduated several years earlier, the only job offered her was from a Memphis church that had a congregation of eight women who claimed to be a coven of witches. Cheryl recounted with amusement hearing one of her

Cheryl & Mims

congregants say, at a Memphis parade, "Sisters! Synchronize your cauldrons!" By the time we met in El Salvador, her congregation had more than doubled, and the witch element had been somewhat diluted. I had worried there would be too much esoteric church discussion, but the group was so diverse that I was immediately comfortable with my new friends and never felt overwhelmed with arguments about how many angels could dance on the head of a pin.

Before talking with Liberation Theology advocates, we were exposed to a variety of opinions about the Salvadoran situation in general. The U.S. Undersecretary at our embassy described the danger posed by the FMLN, the rebels who controlled almost half of the country. They were Communists, and if successful would turn El Salvador into another Sandinista state, another Cuba. He stressed the crime of the recent shooting down of a helicopter flying over the rebel-controlled area and the killing of the two captured army pilots. Colonel Varga Ponce, Salvadoran Army Chief of Staff, also decried the downed helicopter. He admitted that the military must reform so it would serve all Salvadorans, not just certain elites. We asked how the U.S. helped El Salvador. "Boots, uniforms, helicopters, Coast Guard vessels, spare parts, vehicles, education at Forts Benning and Leavenworth." Another question: How did he feel about fighting other Salvadorans – a question Archbishop Romero was asking in 1980 at the time he was killed. The colonel explained that he and the military regretted that, but they had to defend their principles and values.

We had a wrenching time with three women who were running the headquarters of COMAFAC (Christian Committee of Mothers and Family Members of Disappeared and Assassinated). These women held demonstrations, using bull horns to denounce the military, held press conferences, displayed posters of missing relatives in the market, and accompanied family members on hunts for the Disappeared. Twice, their office had been ransacked, their equipment stolen, records and papers scattered. They had been tear-gassed and were being watched and threatened. Yet they persisted. They hoped to gain the release of political prisoners, get news of the whereabouts of the Disappeared, bring about punishment of the guilty, and end the impunity of the armed forces. We discovered that COMAFAC had been formed by twenty members of a Christian Base Community, motivated by the community and the Gospels. Here was Liberation Theology in action.

LIBERATION THEOLOGY

Here's a short and therefore inadequate description of Liberation Theology as we came to know it. My sources are my own experiences and several books on Liberation Theology that I read at the time of our seminar. Of these, the most helpful has been *Liberation Theology, The Essential Facts about the Revolutionary Movement in Latin America and Beyond*, by Phillip Berryman, a former Maryknoll priest and Angie's husband.

The Catholic Church historically has been conservative and closely connected with civil authorities. It was part of the conquest and colonization of Latin America, but even in those early years of Spanish and Portuguese occupation, some Benedictine priests clashed with their superiors and tried to defend the *Indígenos*. During the wars of independence, the bishops sided with the Spanish Crown, but the clerics supported the struggle for independence.

Before Pope John XXIII convened Vatican Council II, most Catholics had been taught the main business in life was to remain in a "state of grace" in order to get into heaven. I remembered the Lutheran preachers I heard in Germany in 1938. Don't get involved in worldly matters. It's the next life you should worry about. By the 1960's, however, even the bishops, worried about the spread of Protestantism, Communism and secularism, began to see the connection between the deepening poverty, increasing gap between the rich and the poor, and world-wide upheaval of that decade. (President Kennedy was concerned about the economic crisis, too, and established the Alliance for Progress with Latin American countries, a program that combined aid for development with the upgrading of armies and police.)

In 1968, Latin American Bishops got together at Medellin to discuss how to apply the understandings of Vatican II to their region and called for Christians to be involved in the transformation of society. The church should conduct its mission with "a preferential option for the poor." The bishops declared that an authoritarian society makes Christian love impossible and that the most basic right is the right to life and consequently the right to the means of life – employment and land.

The first action, the bishops agreed, was to defend human rights and to carry out a "consciousness raising evangelization." They agreed people must become agents of their own advancement, which meant a sharing of power. Only then could there be genuine development. One way to achieve this goal was through education. A Brazilian priest, Paulo Friere, designed a teaching technique that dealt with real issues in people's lives, and he was so successful that his methods spread throughout Latin America. Many illiterate peasants and workers learned to read in several months.

The Medellin bishops took on the economic system, too, At Vatican II, the Council declared that "authentic socialism is Christianity lived to the fullest, in basic equality and with a fair distribution of goods." Did this mean leveling the hierarchy of the church too? Later Liberation Theologians called on Christians "to engage in the ideological struggle by identifying and unmasking the manipulation of Christianity to justify capitalism." This was going too far, and the Vatican, under the new pope, John Paul II, pulled back, gradually silencing the most effective of the Liberation theorists.

One characteristic of Latin America was a lack of priests. Local priests realized they were mainly serving the privileged in cities, teaching at schools for children whose families could pay tuition. They visited outlying villages only at intervals of several weeks and then mainly to perform rituals like baptism and marriage. Out of this situation grew the Christian Base Communities, small lay groups in which the Bible and church doctrines could be interpreted "out of the experiences of the poor." The Bible, the Liberation theorists claimed, understands poverty as an evil involving the oppression of some people by others. Poverty dehumanizes human beings and is an offense against God. In the Base Communities, the poor learn to read Scripture in a way that affirms their dignity and self-worth and their right to struggle together for a more decent life. The emphasis is on this life, not on death and resurrection, a religious point of view close to the Methodist concepts I was brought up with. The ideas of Liberation Theology had caught on with the Latin American Protestant churches as well as among Catholics, and our seminar would speak with members of those communities too.

Critics saw Liberation Theology as "an exotic brew of Marxism and Christianity." And the Base Communities had a political potential, "preparing the soil for grass-roots organizing and revolutionary struggle." If, as the critics believed, Liberation priests were Communists, they deserved to be eliminated. So Bishop Romero, the nuns, the six Jesuits, and a number of other priests were killed, and the murderers paid no price for their deeds. The Church, like society as a whole, was split between those who joined the world-wide movement for human emancipation and the hierarchy that hoped change would come, if at all, through consensus, through the conversion of the privileged and powerful.

BACK TO THE SEMINAR

In San Salvador, we had dinner with a group of Mennonite church workers, visited the Lutheran University, talked with an opposition party leader who represented the Popular Social Christian Movement, worshipped with Father Daniel Sanchez in a marginal community, and had an emotional ex-

Mass at Christian Base Community of Adolfo Reyes

perience at the Catholic University where the Jesuit priests had been murdered (more about this later). In Costa Rica we sat in on a Bible study session to get a sense of how the Base Communities worked. We were learning that out-

side the Catholic Church, other denominations were also adopting Liberation Theology. A member of the Ecumenical Department at the University of Costa Rica, a minister of the United Church of Canada, an Episcopal minister, and one from the Baptist Church of Faith filled us in on the growth of Liberation Theology in their Protestant denominations. In Nicaragua, on Sunday we went to mass *twice*, once with a Christian Base Community in Adolfo Reyes.

I want to describe in more detail two memorable experiences we had in El Salvador. We had an appointment with Jon Sobrino at the Catholic University where his colleagues, the six Jesuit priests, their cook and her daughter were murdered. Father Sobrino, one of the leading proponents of the new movement, was spared because he was out of the country at the time of the assault. He summed up the situation in El Salvador as he saw it and discussed the possibility for peace through the negotiations then being held. As

*Fr. Jon Sobrino,
death squad survivor*

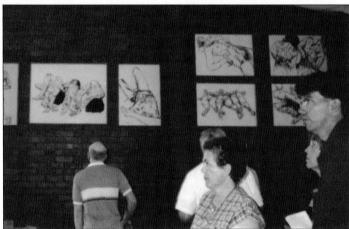

we left, he said with a voice full of passion, "A person can't claim to be human today unless stopping repression is central to his life." His voice along with the emotional cry of the Honduran describing torture as "a monster let loose" echoes in my memory.

Jack, our guide, had arranged an over-night trip to a rather well established community of returnees called La Gualcho, where we lived for a short time in a Christian Base Community. To get to La Gualcho we went from the government-controlled west El Salvador, passed a check point, crossed the Jerusalem River on a Bailey Bridge, and entered the FMLN east. As we crossed the makeshift bridge, we could see the skeleton of a twisted bombed bridge a short way upstream. On the FMLN side we passed the wreckage of the army helicopter we'd been told about. The rebels predicted that the U.S. would use the helicopter episode as an excuse to reinstate money for the military, money that had been withheld to force the Salvadoran government to take action against the death

Bailey Bridge and hydro plant

Welcome to Nuevo Gualcho

squad that had murdered the Jesuits. They were right.

The story of La Gualcho was similar to that of the village we had visited in 1988. The peasants had been hounded out of El Salvador into Honduras by the military. There, they had been helped by several NGOs to organize, to read and write, to become shoemakers, carpenters, farmers, and teachers, and eventually to demand the right to return to their homeland. La Gualcho, by 1991, was better organized and felt more secure than Santa Marta because they had bought land

La Gualcho town council

protected from the government by the guerrillas. Several bright-eyed young people were assigned to us as guides and we were shown the recently built health clinic, church, and child care center.

We went to mass performed by Father Daniel Sanchez and then talked with him about the hardships his parishioners had gone through: the repression and poverty, the orphaned children and aging widows, the dehydration and unemployment. And the harassment that was still going on. Two days earlier, a communique on the radio from death squads, emboldened by the furor caused by the helicopter crash, threatened

Father Daniel by name as well as "leaders of popular movements."

We discussed economics with Father Daniel and heard, not for the first time, strong criticisms of NAFTA and other trade agreements. The "free market system," he said, "helps the rich and hurts the poor." The debt inevitably resulting from the

Fr. Daniel at La Gualcho economic discussion

kind of investments and privatization the trade agreements encouraged led to certain "structural adjustments" serving to discourage governments from funding anything other than interest on their debt; and the military had to establish stability in order to hold down the unrest of the growing poor. Domestic programs improving health, education, or housing went by the board.

COSTA RICA

We spent five days in Costa Rica, talking again about Liberation Theology. Although all the Central American countries experienced somewhat similar economic problems, each had a different past which had brought about a different present. Costa Rica was the most stable and most peaceful of the five countries I visited. There had never been mass land holdings, so there was not a traditional land-owner oligarchy, and the farm owners worked their own land. The president of Costa Rica had to be a Catholic, but there was respect for other religions. Best of all, the ruling class didn't share power with an uncontrollable military. In fact, decades earlier the army had been abolished! Protection was provided by a police force, and there was money to spare for the social sector, so literacy was high and there was almost universal health coverage. It was a conservative country with a safety net.

Yet there was social tension and Liberation Theology was a growing movement in Protestant as well as Catholic churches. To summarize what we learned in Costa Rica: Liberation Theology developed out of injustice and great disparity in wealth. That led to repression, one of the greatest of sins. We heard a lot about sin. Structures of government can be sinful. If the Church condemns Liberation Theology, that is a sin against the Holy Spirit because it shows the Church doesn't believe in the presence of God in the people. If in order to pay debts, a society sacrifices its people by depriving them of the essentials for survival, that too is sinful. On the other hand, we were told the elite and the military, wherever it existed, thought the impeding of markets was a sin.

On the third day we had a welcome change of pace. We drove to a public beach at Limon on Costa Rica's Caribbean coast and expected to loll around in the waves and under the sun. The beach was part of a territory claimed by an independent community of Blacks who spoke English and had occupied the land for centuries. They were descendants of Africans who had escaped slavery from Jamaica or from slave ships, and they had brought their banana culture with them. Settled as they seemed, their future looked pretty tenuous to us. The Spanish-speaking Costa Ricans didn't consider them citizens, even though they had been born there. They had worked the land for centuries but were not considered landowners. They had their own school, but their education didn't correspond to that in the rest of the country and was therefore considered inferior. Some World Bank money was being invested in a big nearby resort that would bring tourists. The Caribbean Blacks were losing some of their land, they were being taught Spanish, and they would enter the modern world as waitresses, bus boys, and yard tenders at the new hotels and condominiums.

Our attention to our new acquaintances was suddenly interrupted when we heard on a radio an announcement that the U.S. had bombed Baghdad. It was the beginning of the Gulf War. I recorded the reactions of Costa Ricans seemingly so remote from the events on the other side of the world: "If it gets over in ten days, Bush (number I) will be a hero." "It won't be a quick war. Even if this phase is over fast, there will be counterinsurgency." "It will be a technology war – who has the right to do that much damage?" "Will it get out of hand?" "What right has Bush to ruin so much?" "We won't be safe!"

I was surprised at the vehement response we encountered. The culture of developed countries, especially the USA, was criticized as consumerism, individualistic greed, a culture of death. It was pointed out that many laws in the U.S. as well as in Central American States defend oil, property, and contracts, not democracy and liberty. The Base Communities asked for an economy that satisfied basic needs. They talked about self-sufficiency, about finding the will of God in society, and believed Third World societies in the South could resist the aggression from the North not militarily but through the strength of their culture and religion. Twenty five years later they are still trying.

NICARAGUA

Back in Nicaragua, we were seeing that country about a year after the Sandinistas had lost an election to UNO, the party that represented business and large entrepreneurs. The Contra war had come to an end, and the economy was in a transition from a mixed economy to a neo-liberal model. However, because of the changes in the political structure under the Sandinistas, the executive power was balanced between UNO and the Sandinistas, and there had to be compromises. In exchange for promising not to strike for six months, UNO agreed that in the process of privatization, not many workers would lose their jobs and there would not be much cutting of health and education funding.

At a Christian Base Community we visited, a Moravian Church was running a very active soup kitchen, and we heard of attempts at reconciliation in the immediate wake of the war. It was Sunday and there was a special mass for the war dead. The priest turned it into a mass for peace. He talked of non-violence and declared that war was justified only as a last resort. The Gulf War, he said, didn't qualify. A second fundamental principle about war is that civilians should be safe. He talked about Vietnam, condemning saturation bombing and the destruction of towns. The third principle

Fr. Cesar Jerez, President of the University of Central America

involved the justice of the cause for going to war. Is war justified? Money for the military is wasteful, taking bread from the mouths of the poor. How painful to see the Arabs suffering too. I was startled at the pervasive awareness and passionate condemnation of U.S. foreign policies. Why are we surprised in 2006 to find the U.S. so universally disliked and distrusted?

At the Nicaraguan University of Central America, Liberation Theology was becoming more mature, more profound and spiritual, we were told, and the Church was relenting somewhat, asking for a meeting and reconciliation between the opposing factions.

Nicaragua's Planned Parenthood

At a women's center called IXCHEN after a Mayan fertility goddess, we found a group of doughty women who had established a laboratory and pharmacy. They were relieved the war with the Contras was over, but they told us the economic crisis was worse. All the more reason to continue advocating family planning and fighting off attempts by the new Nicaraguan government to cut out sex education and rescind the rights of women to divorce. They provided free service to victims of rape and abuse, supplied food to some desperate women and children, and were expanding legal services.

Tomb of Archbishop Romero, assassinated by a death squad

At a discussion with five Kairos (Liberation Theology) theologians, there was much analysis of the world situation. These ecclesiastics from the Third World saw First World countries as Fascist, racist exploiters of people without power, their actions based on raw ma-

Our guide Jack Nelson-Pallmeyer at the farewell discussion

terialism. Capitalism had triumphed. There was only one value: money, with no other alternative. No shade left. Poor countries needed some protection. The Persian Gulf War was another step in the growing hegemony of the U.S., and Central America was being integrated into the world economy through privatization, growing debt, and increasing austerity. They were gloomy! Their hope was that the U.S. would get bogged down in the Gulf, making it possible for Third World people to rise. Perhaps that is what is happening twenty-five years later. Again we heard, "You can't be a human being these days if stopping human oppression isn't the central purpose of your life."

The last night of our trip we asked our tour guide, Jack, his ideas about the Central American situation. Up to that point he had been fairly non-committal and had set up appointments with a variety of people with diverse opinions. In each country we had talked with someone in our embassy as well as representatives of opposing political parties. Now Jack suddenly became very passionate. He saw the conflicts in the world as a war against the poor. In fact he had written a book with that title and was to publish another in 1992 titled *The Brave New World Order*. He explained to us that night and wrote in his coming book that the Gulf War showed the "misery of the poor will continue to sustain the appetites of the rich." He saw the consequences as a continuing "transfer of wealth from the poor to the very wealthy (in our country as well) leading to the decay of our cities and increases in racial violence, drug abuse and crime." He hoped for the further spread of Liberation Theology and for a radical discipleship that worships the God of Life rather than the idols of power and wealth."

And thus ended our 1991 seminar.

structural adjustment in nicaragua

BITTER MEDICINE

A WITNESS FOR PEACE PUBLICATION

nicaragua in crisis

A lingering economic crisis batters Nicaragua.

And the US-influenced structural adjustment program, the measure the government has taken to alleviate the crisis, is not working.

In the stifling heat of Managua, expensive, air-conditioned four-wheel drive trucks whiz by, drivers and passengers insulated behind smoked glass

CHAPTER 55

CENTRAL AMERICA ADIOS

My fifth and last seminar trip to Central America, in 1998, was again planned and guided by the Center for Global Education at Augsburg College in Michigan. It was called BUILDING A JUST SOCIETY: THE HONDURAN CHALLENGE. There were only six of us plus two group leaders, and we stayed all ten days in Honduras. I was eager to see what changes I could find since my last visit to that country. One welcomed change was the lack of soldiers sitting in the backs of pickup trucks, aiming machine guns at civilians on the sidewalks.

The people whom we met talked about the "Lost Decade" of the 1980s. But there was still fear. The Commissioner of Human Rights had received so many death threats against himself and his family that he had sent his wife and children out of the country.

Honduran Commission of Human Rights

HOW TO MAKE A LIVING

We could see the country's extreme poverty when we visited barrios and observed children with extended stomachs, some living on what they could scavenge from dumps. Because farmers had lost land, there were only

Scavengers at the dump

two main sources of jobs — at the banana plantations and at the *maquilas*, factories making clothes, shoes, and other items under sweatshop conditions. There were about 65,000 workers working in the maquilas by 1998, which meant there had been a tremendous influx from the impoverished countryside into communi-

ties without enough housing, water, or even roads. The government subsidized these needs for the foreign company owners who were also given free land, paid no taxes, and had no bothersome regulations. Only a few of the maquilas were unionized. The workers worked 12 months a year suppos-edly for 44 hours a week, but the system of quotas

Chickens for sale

often meant they were paid for eight hours of an 18-hour day with no overtime and no child care. Most of the workers were young women tested to be sure they weren't pregnant before being hired.

We also traveled to some banana plantations in La Limon and again learned of poor working conditions for the harvesters, those who soaked the bunches in a solution to kill off diseases, and the packers. Ninety percent of the workers were single mothers earning just enough for one to subsist but not enough to feed their children.

*Banana growing uses
many chemicals*

Banana Packers Union Headquarters *Lidia at the school/church, St. Martin*

THE TOURIST TRAP

We talked with the president of the Honduran Private Enterprise Council who expected the maquilas to last only five or six more years as a main source of jobs for Honduran. He expected China and other low wage countries to lure away local investment in factories. But he was enthusiastic about the coming investment in hotels, resorts, spas, and casinos. "Tourism is our salvation." He saw the selling of Honduras to foreign countries as the only answer for a prosperous future. His plan entailed 99-year leases with no taxes to Hyatt, Marriott, and their kind. Twenty companies would be given 25 acres each. The tourist czar imagined that 37% of the money would stay in Honduras and that 97% of the jobs created would go to Hondurans.

Old and new on the Garifundi beach at Tela

The land and the workers would come from the Garifundi, the Caribs we visited one day. Their ancestors had come from Africa, via the Caribbean Islands. The Garifundi wanted to own a percentage of the resorts being built on their territory, but the government planner felt that was absurd. They didn't know how to work. He hoped the tourist centers would teach new working habits and give good training. We swam and sunned on the Garifundi beach and talked to some of the leaders of the community. They feared they were losing their culture. The schools were in the hands of the Honduran government, the children were taught Spanish and how to become good

workers, and the government was seizing land for "non-payment of taxes."

Museum, home, and matriarch in Triunfo, Garifundi

THE LENCA AND PALMEROLA

We were surprised to learn there were seven other groups of indigenous peoples in Honduras, all struggling to keep some semblance of their own culture. We sat in on a meeting of a community council of the Lenca, the largest of the groups, and heard them protest the growth of the U.S. Army presence at a near-by base called Palmerola, a base I had passed several times on previous trips to Central America. The Lenca objected to a road the US Army was building through Lenca territory. This was a humanitarian project, claimed the U.S., but do you need 4,000 sol-

Our guide César at Palmerola

diers to build a latrine or two? The Lenca didn't want the road in any case. And why was the military needed to built it?

A few days later, we visited Palmerola and were given a first-class tour of the base by the Deputy Commander. Palmerola was built to house the forward deployment of US presence in lieu of the previous regional base in Panama because treaties President Carter had negotiated would soon return Panama to the control of the Panamanian people. The army had constructed an 8,000-foot runway at Palmerola which was providing command and control for the surrounding countries and was the counter-narcotics support base for all of Central America. We brought up the Lenca's objections to the road the U.S. Army was building through the Lenca territory, and our tour guide reacted with irritation. "They're causing us a lot of trouble," he said. "Who wouldn't want a good road in place of their narrow dirt tracks?" He seemed to misunderstand completely the problem for the Lencas. As we toured the base, five huge Esso oil delivery trucks drove in. We counted eight Black Hawk helicopters, 3 Texan Chinooks, and saw where the U.S. produced its own electricity with diesel fuel. Part of the base was devoted to the Honduran Military Academy. Midnight curfew for those cadets! What better way to keep Honduras under U.S. control? Was Honduras an occupied country? How many such bases did the U.S. have around the world? Whatever the number, each was a conspicuous consumer of the world's resources, hundreds of thousands of gallons of oil not the least among those resources.

AIDS IN SAN PEDRO SULA

One day we met with the Minister of Health, some doctors and a number of nurses in the city of San Pedro Sula, the second largest city in Honduras, situated in the same valley as Palmerola. The whole area was experiencing a great outburst of AIDS. The first case had been diagnosed in 1985 (blamed on Palmerola soldiers), and by 1998 there were 10,000 cases. This meant many orphaned children and more of a burden than the medi-

AIDS workers in San Pedro Hospital

cal profession could handle. Not enough doctors and not enough drugs. The people we talked with were frustrated, able only to treat secondary infections. How to persuade a chauvinistic society to observe "abstinence, fidelity and condoms"? A kiosk, where free educational material and condoms were available 24 hours a day, no questions asked, had been built in the center of the main city square. On some shelves in that kiosk were large papier-mâché figures representing the bad guys that spread the disease, and various good guys such as condoms. We were shown a videotape of these figures in a skit put on during a championship soccer game. Sex education at halftime! No cheer leaders with pompoms at that game.

AIDS information and condom kiosk

WOMEN DON'T JUST STAND THERE

One of our last visits was to a Women's Group for Peace and Justice. The women met in a small community building in a poor barrio reached by a narrow, rugged road. A gully splitting the community was spanned by a few rickety foot bridges, a source of fun for the children and worry for their mothers. The group had been formed in 1984, in the midst of that terrible decade, to oppose "the domination of men over women, the external domination of one country (the U.S.) over another, and the domination of the rich over the poor." Their extensive program included education for women; courses in sewing, cooking, knitting, embroidery, and gardening; and a haven and counseling center for victims of domestic violence and children who had been raped. A soy project was their particular pride. The women's group taught the whole community how to plant, harvest, and process the beans, which were then sold at a very low price with recipes for their use. Two years earlier, this group had fasted until the legislature passed a law stopping the army from rounding up young boys for military

Women's Center banner
feisty Women's Group for Peace & Freedom

service. And just the previous Monday, a law they had sponsored, making domestic violence illegal, had gone into effect. I like ending my story of Central America with that ray of hope.

PART V

EPILOGUE

CHAPTER 56

A GOOD MAN GONE

Oliver Butterworth: 1915 ~ 1990

On September 17, 1990, Bud died of cancer. I accept death, I told myself, and Bud was 75, an acceptable age for dying. He had lived a full and successful, even celebrated life – certainly to the students he taught at Hartford College for Women and to the many school children whose classes he spoke to. Women still come up to me and say, "I was in love with your husband when he taught me in 1982." Or some young man will say, "Your husband came to talk to our second grade class in the 1970s, and *The Enormous Egg* is the first book with chapters I ever read." Bud fortunately didn't have much pain but gradually weakened with melanoma. During his last six months we were able to celebrate together my 50th reunion at Connecticut

Mims, Bud, Mary Jane Carpenter, Lucy Townsend, Jeannie Robinson
at Daphne Mowatt's house at Squam for the 50th Anniversary

College and our 50th wedding anniversary at Squam Lake. Friends and family streamed in during the summer to say goodbye.

The news of Bud's death reached Washington, D.C. by way of the Parmalee sisters, our nieces, Patty, Clare (Hoppy) and Cricket. For over twenty years a life-sized replica of Uncle Beazley, the dinosaur that hatched from Bud's "Enormous Egg," had stood on the Mall in front of the National Museum of Natural History. It had been made for a TV movie shown on NBC's Children's Theater in 1968. It was "a Triceratops meant for climbing," said *A Parents' Guide to Seeing the City.* You can imagine how happy we were, whenever we visited our nation's capital during those years, to see children from all over the world climbing exuberantly over our favorite character, even knowing his name because he was properly labeled. Sometime early in 1990 Uncle Beazley had been surrounded by a snow fence, preventing children from playing on him. Had someone decided he was an attractive nuisance, too dangerous to be insured? We never got a good answer. Whatever the case, the Parmalees bravely took some clandestine action to announce to the beltway world the loss of Uncle Beazley's creator. Here are some excerpts from a letter from Cricket describing their way of paying homage to their real uncle:

Dear Folks, Here is the tale of the wreath. I had been thinking Uncle Beazley should carry a floral tribute to Bud, and in fact had called up someone at the Natural History Museum and said so, but I could see we weren't going to get much action from that direction.

Then Patty came for a weekend meeting, and said she had promised people in Hartford that she would put a wreath on Uncle Beazley. So then we felt honor bound to do it.

We assembled a crack team of wreath layers, including Hoppy, Patty, myself and trusty henchman Babu (Cricket's 5 year old son.). The project had a NASA-like ring to it, since there was only a small window of opportunity, Patty's lunch break on Saturday. So Hoppy went off to the florist and got the materials. Using a base of grapevines, she wove in dried flowers, berries, seed pods and tree bracts, to make a large and autumnal wreath. I wrote out a card and sealed it in clear plastic to protect it from the elements, saying

in memoriam
Oliver Butterworth
author of "The Enormous Egg"
and creator of Uncle Beazley
d. 9/17/90

Trusty Henchman Babu and I dashed off with the wreath, the card, lots of wire, the camera and a lunch for Patty. We picked her up at the Municipal Building on U Street and headed for the Mall.

There was of course no place to park, so I dropped Patty and Babu by Uncle Beazley and circled the Mall, watching for the authorities. Patty finished assembling the wreath, studied the situation and seized the time: she hoisted the pint-sized Babu over the fence and he placed the wreath on Uncle Beazley's right horn, along with an armful of fresh asters that he laid across Uncle Beazley's broad head.

Then a moment of silence was observed, and commemorative photos were taken as several families stopped by to visit Uncle Beazley. One mother read and interpreted the card to her two sons, and a father with young children reminisced about how he used to come down to the Mall and climb on Uncle Beazley.

We didn't know what fate would befall the wreath, whether it would be immediately removed by the authorities, or whether it would be left in peace. So a week later, on a rainy Saturday night, I stopped by and was pleased to see that the wreath was still there, the card still readable in the rain.

And on the next Saturday we stopped again, Hoppy, Hugh, Babu and I. It was the morning after George [H. W.] Bush had pulled the plug on the government [because the congress had not passed his appropriation bill], and we expected the Mall to be empty, but in fact it was full of bewildered people wandering around and peering in darkened museum doors. But in response to the disappointment, a small miracle had taken place: not only was the wreath still there, as beautiful as ever, but two young adults had scaled the fence and Uncle Beazley, and were happily ensconced on his back. Seeing them, disgruntled parents from around the country began hoisting their children over the fence, and once again, climbing, sliding, and general whoop-de-doo was taking place. It seemed an entirely fitting and joyous response: the President had taken away the government so the people had taken back Uncle Beazley.

Love to everybody,

Cricket

These were the kinds of things that gave me the support I needed when Bud died. Lots of friends and a growing family kept me interested and concerned with the future.

SMITHSONIAN CHOCOLATES
Uncle Beazley

These bite sized triceratops of milk chocolate and caramel pecan were made for the Smithsonian Institution. A life-size fiberglass model triceratops, named Uncle Beazley (after a character in a child's book *The Enormous Egg*), stands on the Mall outside the National Museum of Natural History.

© Smithsonian Institution, 1987

Made expressly for the Smithsonian Institution by Harbor Sweets, Marblehead, MA.

These chocolates are hand made of the finest ingredients regardless of cost. Milk Chocolate, Sugar, 93 Score Creamery Butter, Fresh Cream, Evaporated Milk, Brown Sugar, Marblehead Wildflower Honey, Pecan Halves, Light Corn Syrup, Pure Vanilla, Salt, Soybean Lecithin and Vanillin.

SMITHSONIAN CHOCOLATES

Caramel and Pecan in Milk Chocolate
1 Piece, Net Wt. ½ oz. (14.2g)

Patty Parmalee, Babu Parmalee and Uncle Beazley on the Mall
in Washington, DC, September, 1990

CHAPTER 57

INDISPENSABLE FRIENDS

I have always needed close friends, and in my old age I rely on old timers and some young to keep me company. Many are concerned about things that concern me, and we diagnose the news together, exchange books, and even attend conferences we are particularly interested in. Here's an example: in 1995, my friend Martha Vinick and I went to a conference called 50 YEARS IS ENOUGH, where we discussed the consequences for the world of fifty years under the economic dominance of the International Monetary Fund (IMF) and the World Bank. These two institutions were formed toward the end of World War II when Western economists and other allied leaders got together at Breton Woods in New Hampshire to plan a post-war economy. Their stated objective was to bring about "development" in the Third World. After 50 years, the result of their plan has been disaster for many developing countries. We wanted to find out why.

Here's the scoop as I understand it: large development loans are pressed on Third World countries by the World Bank and the International Monetary Fund. The type of development is chosen by these lending institutions in consultation with the heads of the

Freeze friends Ada Hastings, Martha Vinick,
Flo Woodiel, Mims, Pat Wass, Sally D'Alesandro

borrowing countries, and big ticket items like dams, roads and mines are encouraged. (There's a lot of money to dispose of.) These projects often benefit, if anybody, a small segment of the recipient states. As of 1995 as many as forty percent of the projects had major problems, thirty percent were considered failures, and many had produced hugely adverse environmental and societal results. To repay the loans, citizens of the borrowing states must agree to "structural adjustments," which means privatizing their assets, giving up protective tariffs, cutting down on social programs (health, education, etc.), and taking out more loans to pay the interest on the first loans.

Because of competition from imported subsidized agricultural products (part of the structural adjustment agreements), farmers, unable to make a living by growing food for home consumption, turn to export crops. This makes them vulnerable to fluctuations in world commodity prices.

We learned that between 1984 and 1990, the net transfer of resources from poor countries of the South to rich ones in the North totaled 155 billion dollars. Here are some of the consequences: a great increase in the number of desperate people heading for the borders, a revulsion against NAFTA and CAFTA (e.g., protests in Seattle and elsewhere), a leftward political turn in the Third World, repression, increase in hunger, a widening gap in incomes, and debt, debt, debt.

Martha and I added the perceptions we gained at that conference to our world picture, having become even more aware of the centrality of economics to an understanding of world affairs.

ECONOMIC DIGRESSION

I came across a book in the 1950s titled *If Women Mattered* by a New Zealander, Marjorie Waring. She pointed out the skewed way economists measure value. Only if money changes hands does a transaction get counted in Gross National Product (GNP) and thereby accrue acknowledged worth to the larger society. The wide-spread worship of "the free market" and the demonizing of regulation, which I saw happening while at the PUCA, have taken us down another wrong road. The market has little to do with a large part of our lives – education, health care, much of foreign affairs, and religion, for instance – although we try to stuff these aspects into the free market concept.

Those of us who remember the Roaring '20s and the Great Depression know that unrestrained capitalism leads to giant monopolies, a large income gap, much corruption, an inevitable crash, and unrest. I suppose because of that experience, I have always been skeptical of a system glorifying the bottom line, encouraging the accumulation of great fortunes while marginalizing the poor. As Senator Bernie Sanders says, "Greed is not a moral value." Nor does it lead to a stable and healthy economy.

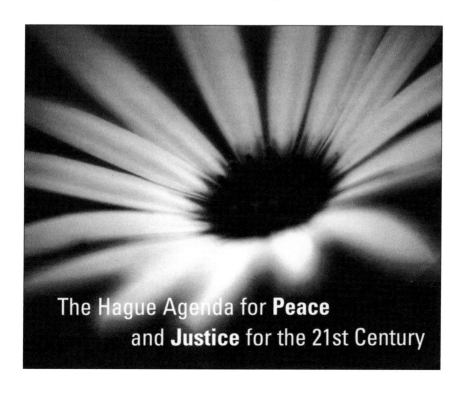

The Hague Agenda for **Peace** and **Justice** for the 21st Century

CHAPTER 58

THE HAGUE APPEAL FOR PEACE

Again in 1999, Martha and I went off together to a peace conference in the Hague, a reprise of a peace conference held there a hundred years earlier at the beginning of a new millennium that turned out to be the bloodiest century in history. Over the years a myriad of groups and governments have hunted for ways to curb the world's growing violence, including the League of Nations after WW I and United Nations after WW II. There have been bilateral disarmament agreements and treaties such as the Nuclear Non-Proliferation Treaty. Many of these agreements have been imperfectly implemented or simply ignored. Creating a peaceful world is an uphill battle, but the people we met at the Hague Conference were trying.

At one workshop, *Global Network vs Weapons and Nuclear Power in Space,* we picked up a glossy booklet titled *Vision for 2020* put out by the United States Space Command. It declared that our space forces must achieve "Full Spec-

trum Dominance." We must have "worldwide surveillance" so we can have "information superiority" while "denying an adversary's ability to gain that ability." "Space superiority is emerging as an essential element of battlefield success and future warfare." "The space area of responsibility is global and requires a combatant commander with a global perspective to conduct military operations and support regional warfighting." CINC USSPACECOM's planning should include "the prospects for space defense and even space warfare." The whole text presented an aggressive program, even while others were attempting to guarantee the peaceful use of space for all.

This booklet created quite a furor. Was the Space Command just putting out its wish list, or was its "vision" something that would be implemented? No wonder the rest of the world (particularly Russia) watches our missile defense program with suspicion. So do I.

Such trips are not all hard work and seeking solutions for global problems. After the conference, we spent a few golden days in Amsterdam, delighting in the fearless bikers, the surreal paintings on the buses, and the museums, before heading home.

CHAPTER 59

WOMEN MATTERS

In 1995 I had another chance to explore the issues of peace and justice. Early that year I went with a friend to hear Barbara Lochbinler, Executive Secretary of WILPF, the Women's International League For Peace and Freedom. WILPF, headquartered in Geneva, Switzerland, is the oldest continuously active peace organization in the world. Its 80th birthday coincided with the 4th U.N. Conference on Women, 4WCW, to be held in Beijing at the end of August, and WILPF was planning a grand celebration. First there would be six days of orientation in Finland, then 23 days on a "Peace Train" through Russia, the Ukraine, Romania, Bulgaria, on to Istanbul, back to Odessa, east to Kazakhstan, and across Central Asian China to Beijing. The train con-

tingent would talk along the way with women who couldn't attend the conference, taking their concerns along with us. What an opportunity! I paid my modest membership fee, signed up for WILPF's 80th celebration, and looked forward to new adventures.

Connecticut delegates to Beijing: Audley, Marion, Virginia and Mims

FINLAND

For six days in August about 300 of us got acquainted with each other in Helsinki and with the history of our sponsoring organization. In 1915 women from 12 countries at war and some from the still neutral United States met in Geneva to design and work for a world free from war and oppression. It was there that WILPF was born, and eighty years later it had a membership of over 40,000 women in 42 countries. Jane Addams of Hull House fame was its first president and the first of five WILPF leaders to receive the Nobel Peace Prize.

At Helsinki we were told what to expect on the train we would soon be taking and about WILPF's plans for the conference in China. Our focus was to be on ways to achieve nothing less than "a Secure and Sustainable World Society." Discussions would encompass militarism and disarmament, alternative economics and people-centered structures of government. I'm not sure I am a pacifist in the Quaker mold, but I do know "war is not the answer" to any legitimate foreign policy objective I can think of. And I am feminist enough to believe women have a nurturing role to play and thus might bring different, more pacific ideas and solutions to tense foreign policy situations if given more seats at more tables. The WILPF women I met that summer strengthened my belief, being competent, pragmatic and far-seeing.

We had time to explore Helsinki, its harbor and glorious flower market, and on August 6th we participated in a ceremony commemorating the nuclear destruction of Hiroshima: little blond children and many adults gravely set paper boats carrying lit candles afloat on an inlet of the Baltic sea.

HELSINKI TO BEIJING

August 6th was also the day we started our journey to Beijing. More passengers joined us at the Finland Station and in St. Petersburg until we numbered 232 women and 10 men from 42 countries. The train was 17 cars long with three dining cars and two all-purpose cars for workshops, etc.

A Hartford friend, Audley Green, and I were assigned to a two-berth compartment in the Blue Car about number five from the engine. The Blue Car inhabitants quickly became a community that included our two sturdy Russian attendants, Titania and Marina. They fired up the big water tank in the corridor several times a day to make us tea and were there whenever we needed them.

Titania and Marina

I still get messages from Joan Chittister, a nun who had once been a Mother Superior. We often stopped for cocktails with her and her convivial compartment mate on our way to dinner. She is a popular speaker at forums and religious gatherings, giving a feminine perspective to religious discussions. A few years ago one bishop refused to be on the same platform with her. How's that for power? And I keep in touch with Dolores from Dallas, a neonatal pediatrician who took care of the Bush twins. She served on the Texas Higher Education Commission for 6 years after returning from our Beijing fling and has lots of insightful things to say about Texan education and some of the bigwigs

*Dolores Carruth
at the Great Wall*

who moved with Bush to Washington. My roommate, Audley Green, originally from Australia, was and still is a well known concert harpsichordist.

Everyone on the train had a story to tell. I think it was Aung San Suu Kyi, Burmese Nobel Prize winner held under house arrest for many years by her political opponents, who said in a taped interview shown at the first plenary session, "Without stories it is impossible to contemplate the human condition in any sustained and meaningful way." In fact, the train trip was an orgy of women's talk. Stumbling from car to car three times a day, leaping over the noisy and shifting connecting passageways, we eagerly anticipated eating with someone we hadn't met before, hearing of their adventures and achievements.

Make Nuclear Weapons History.

NUCLEAR THREATS

Many of the workshops on the train and the meetings with women along the way dealt with issues we would be talking about at the upcoming conference. The danger of the continuing nuclear arms race and the ongoing attempts to outlaw nuclear testing were two such issues. As our trip started, France tested a bomb on a Pacific island, and 15 days into our travels, China tested a bomb under ground at Lop Nor in the Gobi desert, near the city of Urumchi, the one stop we had arranged for on the Chinese leg of our journey. The French women on the train were especially outraged at their country. In the midst of our dismay, Audley learned from her daughter how some Australians were responding. Prostitutes, legal and unionized in Australia, had voted to boycott French perfume, cosmetics, etc., and to charge Frenchmen double the going rate for their services. How's that for meaningful action! The people we met in Kiev were still struggling with the health effects of the Chernobyl nuclear plant accident, and we met similar concerns in Kazakhstan, too close to Lop Nor for comfort.

WOMEN AND THE ECONOMY

On the train and at the NGO Forum in China, I found my way to workshops and seminars run by impressive economists from Canada, India, Australia, the Netherlands and Sweden, hammering out alternative ways of looking at the economy. They talked about redefining wealth, asked what would constitute a good economic system, explored a people-centered economic and social order, and explained how women and children are particularly affected by militarism and war. Again, we talked about the impoverishment of Third World countries, especially of their women and children, by the IMF and World Bank.

Romanian War Memorial

In the Ukraine, Romania and Bulgaria, women told us neither "bureaucratic socialism nor predatory capitalism" worked for them. They were experiencing high inflation, privatization combined with layoffs and increasing discrimination against women in the labor market. In a park in Bucharest the beggars we saw were middle-aged women who had obviously seen better days. Seventy percent of the unemployed were women, we were told, of whom 25% were engineers. They had no social security, no benefits for the previous work they had done. In another Russian city we discovered a sweat shop employing younger women and talked with them about their working conditions through knee-high half windows open to the sidewalk until a supervisor closed the windows, cutting off contact. Back on the train and later in the Beijing workshops, we talked about experiments in alternate ways of coping with the alarmingly swift changes taking place in that part of the world as it was assimilated into the global market.

VIOLENCE

We would hear much testimony about violence when we reached Beijing. Stories from women we met along the way prepared us for what was to come. Listen to Zina who ran a child-care organization in Kiev. She joined us there and rode with us for several days until we reached Odessa, telling us about her husband, a well-known young scientist who wanted to go to the West (Was it to Switzerland?) to do some research. His requests had repeatedly been denied by the Soviet authorities until one day, about a year before the USSR collapsed, his wish was granted. He was ecstatic, packed up, kissed Zina farewell and took off for his plane. At the airport he was shot and killed before he could board. Zina shed no tears when that government fell. Unfortunately, she also explained that the

Mims and Zina from Kiev

position of women under the new Ukranian government was deteriorating as we had found in Romania.

Two young women, peace envoys from Croatia and Bosnia, met us in Bulgaria and described their countries' situations. It is hard to be pacifists in countries at war, they said – those who make war are not good at making peace. Women must be an equal part of decision-making if there is to be a peace that lasts. They weren't sure women would make a real difference, but see what has happened with men at the helm! Women could hardly do worse.

In Istanbul we were entertained at a women's center called The Purple Roof. Turkish women were contending with a conservative trend in their country. Their participation in governmental and societal affairs was being curtailed, but although the women we met seemed subdued, they were persevering. The center was not only a meeting place for women artists and activists but also a safe shelter for abused women.

The European part of our trip ended in Almaty, Kazakhstan, where Bud and I had spent several days in 1971. It's an attractive cosmopolitan city near the border with China. In 1995 it was struggling with health concerns from exposure to nuclear fallout from the USSR testing site in the Kazakhstan hinterlands and from a site in China. The women we talked with were also worried about their new president, who wanted to change their new constitution so he could be president for life. He's still there.

WE CROSS INTO CHINA

ngo forum on women *beijing '95*

211 East 43rd Street Suite 1500
New York, NY 10017 U.S.A.

The transfer from our familiar, rather dowdy Russian train to a Chinese one at the border was difficult – even hazardous. Instead of drawing up parallel to the new train at the station, the Russian train was forced by the Chinese to let us off some distance away. We had to clamber down an eight-foot slope, carrying our luggage, walk across a field and then scramble back up to a shiny new train standing in the station. Remember – one of us was blind, another was on crutches, several of us in our 80s. The Chinese from the station and the new train crew had been told not to help us. Why such animosity?

We had run into similar Chinese official attitudes earlier. Some of us, unable to get visas for China in our home countries, were told to try again in Helsinki. There, the Chinese Embassy dragged its heels until the very last minute. At Odessa we had been told our train couldn't enter China as agreed upon, so we had stayed an extra day in Odessa, wandered across southern Russia on a route never before traveled, stayed longer in Almaty than planned, and eventually were allowed to cross the border. Then for five days we hurtled across China as fast as their modern train could take us. No stop at Urumchi! We paused twice at isolated stations where we were allowed to walk up and down the platform for about ten minutes, prevented by guards from straying and from contact with any chance native travelers.

The Chinese train was spandy new but not comfortable. We had to double up, four to a compartment, and we had no Titania and Marina. Instead, we were attended to by a young man and a young woman in army uniforms packing guns! The first morning on the new train, our friend Joan, the former Mother Superior, opened her compartment door just as they were marching by. I heard her say with incredulity, "What the hell are you doing here?" In the first few days we were very cold or much too hot, while our attendants played games with the thermostat. Finally, while they were out of our car, I went back to their quarters, found the thermostat, and put it in the middle range. Their game was up and fortunately those two were soon reassigned. One other attempt at harassment: our WILPF organizers were told that the train crew would serve only two meals a day although arrangements had been made for three. Perhaps WILPF contacted our Embassy at that point? At any rate, three meals it was!

The magic had gone out of the trip. We still enjoyed getting better acquainted with our new and old car mates and spent hours watching out the window at the unrolling scenery: distant mountains, flat plains, Gobi Desert, remnants of The Great Wall, goat herders, tethered camels foraging in the dust, a group of grinning boys hoping to sell us melons if we slowed down enough. We zoomed past Xian where, in 1987, Bud and I had seen the excavation of sculptured soldiers, horses and chariots, and had watched them emerge from the earth. This was not the time for sight-seeing. On August 30 we arrived at Beijing station and were met by a familiar face from home, Helen Raisz. And, of course, there were the usual welcomers who gave us hotel assignments and plans for the next eight days at the NGO Forum.

CHAPTER 60

HUAIROU

A little clarification: there were *two* overlapping United Nations women's conferences. One was for officials like First Lady Hillary Clinton and Madeleine Albright, representing governments, and another, the Non-Governmental Organizations Forum, was made up of social organizations from all over the world. These NGO's are formally accredited by the UN and can attend UN sessions in New York to keep track of that world body, which makes decisions affecting us all. It is this connection that enabled NGO's to be an integral part of the UN women's conference, where women talked together about the reality of their lives and proposed solutions to their needs.

Earlier, China was eager to gain prestige by hosting 4WCW – previous conferences had been held in Mexico, Denmark, and Kenya – but after China's bid was accepted, the Tiananmen Square uprising had fed China's paranoia. Also, China may not have understood the implications of the NGO Forum part of the conference. Imagine their dismay at finding they were making arrangements for 30,000 self-selected watchdogs, women at that, to spend a week describing discrimination and repression and proposing solutions to world problems! That would explain the attempts to withhold visas and the harassment on the train – and what happened to the organizers of 4WCW.

In June of '95, those organizers had been told they couldn't have the NGO Forum in Beijing, where they had spent months mapping out places for Forum activities, but would have to move it 32 kilometers outside the capital to Huairou. They had until September 1st to make the changes. A shuttle bus service had to be arranged and 57 rooms and 69 tents set up for workshops and seminars. There had to be areas for telecommunications, the press, a marketplace, an auditorium and stage, and a parasol area for sitting and eating. Food had to be ordered to feed over 30,000 people at least two meals a day for a whole week! Yet the transfer was ready on time. What organizational abilities! WILPF had a prominently placed Peace Tent, and that became our home base in Huairou.

LOOK AT THE WORLD THROUGH WOMEN'S EYES

Korean Women vs Violence

was the theme of the NGO conference, and we did. Some people have asked why have women's conferences anyway? The answer: such conferences indicate a recognition that discrimination against women is wide-spread and that we all have a stake in how women live around the world. "It's not just a women's question but it is the survival question of the 21st Century."

On the issue of violence, one of the most egregious examples came from a group of Korean Comfort Women who had been sex slaves to the Japanese military from 1932 to 1945. They had been taken prisoner, kept in caves in China, servicing 30 to 50 Japanese soldiers a day. At the end of the war the caves were bombed, some of the women were forced to commit suicide, and others were killed aboard ships on the way home. About 1000 survived and forty years later, some of them whose anger was overcoming shame told their stories for the first time at Huairou. Domestic, tribal, social, and religious abuses of women – we heard it all. This sounds grim, but instead it was cathartic, like Greek tragedy.

Women's forum hears stories of abuse

Another group had brought a clothesline on which women who had been victims of domestic violence hung T shirts. It was very long. We learned that domestic violence is the leading world-wide cause of death for women between the ages of 14 and 44. In light of these testimonies, we decided that improving the status and lives of girls and women is the key to building a more secure, peaceful world and the way to combat poverty and social disintegration.

I continued to go to workshops on economics, learning how women were organizing locally for economic justice. In other workshops, we talked about environmental degradation, discovering what women in other countries were doing to protect their forests, water and land – the earth on which their lives depended. Much of the work was aimed at finding a sustainable future. As for the effects of globalization, brought about by the international institutions formed and dominated by the industrial nations, "the question is not whether women are better off as a result of World Bank programs, but whether they can survive them at all." It was also agreed that none of the goals of women at the 4WCW are attainable by wars and the monopolizing by armies of the world's resources.

WILPF PEACE TENT

Conflict resolution and training, peace education, and disarmament were the main topics at our tent all through the week of the Forum. Women came to tell about the moral, social, and deep cultural costs of militarism, the devastation for women and children in conflict areas and occupations. "Don't give us military solutions to problems in our countries. We want non-violent alternatives." We were visited by The Women In Black, Israeli and Palestinian women who once a week stood together back in their homeland to show that peace is possible in their part of the world. One day we took some symbolic action, marching around our tent and declaring it the first nuclear-free zone in China. While the official representatives to the conference in Beijing talked about ameliorating the effects of war on civilians, the NGO forum in Huairou talked about understanding and eliminating the *causes* of war to achieve a *durable* peace.

WILPF in the Peace Tent also discussed developing a framework of a people-centered and just economic and social order. A group of women from Canada had with them copies of a Canadian women's budget their WILPF Sector had produced.

TIBETAN EPISODE

One day there was more excitement than usual. China, trying to downplay its aggressive attacks on

Women's Meeting Demands That China End Meddling

its neighbor, had denied visas to Tibetans wanting to attend the Women's Conference. However, some Tibetan women had come as members of other delegations, and there was a Tibetan tent where a documentary about the Chinese/Tibetan conflict was shown. In every workshop I sat in on, there was a person (often a man) observing the proceedings – taking notes. On the third day of the Conference, the Tibetan documentary was about to start when the "observer" dashed up and attempted to grab the DVD. There was a scuffle, the woman operator holding fast, the Chinese man tugging, many other hands grasping for it until suddenly it disappeared. A WILPF friend had extricated it from the melee, quickly slipped it into her back pack and left the room unnoticed, leaving the others still hunting.

That was the last straw. The Congress officials met with the Chinese authorities and threatened to close the whole conference down unless the Chinese "note takers" were withdrawn and the Forum organizers were allowed to be in charge within the Huairou Forum boundaries as had originally been agreed upon. A black eye for China was avoided. There was no more harassment, no more spying.

China vows to relax security at forum

ANY GOOD RESULTS?

The participating states made written commitments to encourage women's literacy and find money for shelters for abused women, and they agreed that women's rights are human rights. Don't laugh! This had not been an accepted idea earlier. Our government pledged, among other things, more participation for women and more attention to women's health. President Clinton subsequently formed the President's Interagency Council on Women, which was to be "gender sensitive," to be sure legislation and social actions were first tested for their effect on women and girls. It was soon after this that various U.S. states established Permanent Commissions on the Status of Women.

Today in our country there are many more women decision makers: congresswomen, senators, governors. Internationally, the idea of the Grameen Bank has spread, giving small amounts of credit to women to start small businesses, enabling women to subsist. Jody Williams from Vermont received the Nobel Peace Prize for achieving the International Land Mine Treaty in 1998, and there has been more attention paid to the detrimental effects on women and children of environmental degradation and economic distortions. Were these all the fruit of the 4WCW? The four world conferences certainly shone light on women's situations and needs. And the networking and understandings gained at Huairou and on the Peace Train are still fermenting.

GOING HOME

We flew to New York by way of Helsinki. I sat beside a Connecticut friend who had caught a terrible cold – dripping nose, sneezes, hacking cough. A young corporate type sat on her other side, and after hours of my friend's contagion, I felt I should at least acknowledge the situation. I caught his eye and found myself saying, "Don't worry about her, it's just tuberculosis."

"Oh" (he was quick on the uptake), "I was afraid it was something serious."

A bit of wit went a long way to brighten a long, dreary, cramped and anticlimactic flight home.

International Herald Tribune

PUBLISHED WITH THE NEW YORK TIMES AND THE WASHINGTON POST

Women Talk Back

China's ludicrous effort to restrict demonstrations at the United Nations conference on women broke down almost as soon as nongovernment participants assembled on Thursday at a site 40 miles from Beijing. Women accustomed to fighting for their rights were not about to be intimidated by the bureaucrats and security guards of a Communist police state.

There is no place for censorship at an international conference like this. The women know that. The Chinese do not. If the Chinese fail to lift the restrictions entirely, the participants should make enforcement of them as exasperating to the authorities as possible.

Originally, China ordered public political activities confined to a small area of the forum site and prohibited any criticism of Chinese policies and practices. But on the forum's first day, an overflow crowd of 4,000 women crowded around a movie theater that showed the Burmese Nobel laureate Daw Aung San Suu Kyi on videotape denouncing her country's ruling junta and all other authoritarian regimes. A Tibetan women's group also managed to screen its videotape after security officers unsuccessfully attempted to confiscate it.

Meanwhile, Amnesty International displayed images of female political prisoners, including two held by Beijing — Gao Yu, a prominent Chinese journalist, and Phuntsog Niydrou, a Tibetan nun serving a 17-year sentence.

After the Amnesty group deliberately marched outside the area allotted to demonstrations, Chinese authorities retreated, announcing that the less restrictive rules used by the United Nations would apply throughout the forum site.

More tests are sure to come, with the main conference opening on Monday in the heart of Beijing.

China's leaders remain determined to prevent discussions about individual rights and social and political change from seeping into their own tightly repressed society.

Coverage by the official Chinese media has been highly selective. But having sought the international prestige of playing host to this conference, Beijing is obliged to drop its attempts to censor the participants. Instead, it should let its own people benefit from the ideas and experiences that will be discussed at the meetings.

At first, China saw its role in the conference as a way to advertise its recent economic gains and its determination to take a more active place in international affairs. That seemed even more important after human rights problems cost China its chance to stage the 2000 Olympics.

But later, Chinese leaders began to panic about what might happen as tens of thousands of experienced political activists and representatives from the world's press descended on Beijing.

The clumsy and repressive steps that followed reinforce the view that the Olympic site selection committee made exactly the right call. UN authorities, for their part, should have stepped in earlier to challenge China's approach to conference planning.

It makes good sense to hold the Fourth World Conference on Women in a country that is home to one-fifth of the world's women — provided those women get a chance to hear and see the proceedings.

— THE NEW YORK TIMES.

CHAPTER 61

ONE MORE ADVENTURE

In the spring of 2000 a friend of mine hosted a Hartford area Connecticut College alumni meeting. The guest, Roger Brooks, a professor in CC's Department of Religion, described a June archeological seminar in Israel that he and a colleague offered to undergraduates and to anyone else in the college community interested in that significant slice of our world. Thirty-four years earlier, we had hoped to include Israel in our family's year of wandering, but because of the hostility at the time, planes from Egypt were not allowed to land in Israel. Here was another chance.

At age 82, was I too old for such an expedition? I thought I could manage but would the trip's organizers agree? After his talk, I spoke to Professor Brooks about the possibility of joining the seminar, acting as sprightly as I could. He suggested I apply. I did, was accepted, and began to prepare myself for exploring another history and another culture. I poked around for some sound sources to study and, among other things, discovered Karen Armstrong, a prolific author and religious scholar with a deep understanding of Jews, Christians, and Muslims. She had once been a nun but now describes her own religious thought as a mixture of all three monotheistic beliefs. Her books have been called "vital," "balanced," and "insightful." I found them so.

I started with her *Jerusalem, One City, Three Faiths* and continued on through her *The Battle for God* and then *Holy War, The Crusades and Their Impact on Today's World*. By June when I joined the CC Summer Seminar at El Al's New York terminal, I had some background in the complicated country of Israel. There were about forty of us, the majority undergraduates with courses on Israel's history and religions under their belts. A few were mothers of students, eager to be a part of their children's adventures.

A group of Hasidic seminarians from Brooklyn shared the plane with us, closing their eyes in horror when thrown into contact with the skimpily dressed girls in our group. On the way to our Jerusalem hotel we stopped at the Biblical National Park where we picnicked on biblical foods, scythed some wheat ready for reaping, worked an olive press, and picked myrtle to make fragrant sachets. Before we even unpacked we were transported back into biblical times. From then on, we spent every day digging up the past, experiencing the past, living the past – the geography and stories of the Bible.

Here are the excavated walls of David's City, built around 1300 BCE, and here the Gihon Spring as described in *Chronicles 1 and 2* and *Samuel* in the Old Testament. There are excavations of Solomon's Temple as seen in *Kings*. There is where Jesus was born, where he held the Last Supper, where he appeared to his disciples after he was crucified. In

Tunnel to the Temple Wall

~379~

our first few days we concentrated on early Jewish history and evidence of the various empires that had ruled the Middle East – Jebusites, Assyrians, Egyptians, Romans. We passed Jericho and the caves where the Essene's *Dead Sea Scrolls* had recently been found. We swam in the Dead Sea, drove in Jeeps through the Sinai desert along the old Nabatean spice route, and dined with some Bedouins in a large communal tent.

One day we drove to Masada, where Herod had built an impressive palace and where, in a fortress on a near-by plateau, the Jews had held out for three years against the Romans until their situation became untenable. Then they had killed each other rather than become slaves of their enemies. Until recently, all Israeli army recruits had been inducted in a ceremony at Masada, a symbol of Jewish indomitable will. However, it was also a place of defeat. Now Israeli soldiers are inducted at the Temple Wall, a place that signifies a more glorified future.

The Western Wall

We went through a recently excavated tunnel that took us along the Temple Wall, as close as one could get to Jerusalem's most sacred spot. On Thursday night, we watched worshipers at the Western Wall: men with various shaped beards and hats and robes praying and reading the Torah. Some young Hassidim performed what looked like courtship dances, maybe wooing some Jewish girls in the roped-off audience section.

~380~

EVERYBODY'S HOLY GROUND

Mixed in with Jewish sites were Christian churches: one in Bethlehem, not far from Jerusalem in Palestinian territory. It marked the manger where Jesus was born. Just beynd it were fields where shepherds still kept their flocks! It was clear that the Kings who are said to have brought gold, incense and myrrh didn't have far to travel. The territory is so small and its neighbors are so close! We had to stop at a check point before entering Bethlehem. The Palestinians we passed looked much poorer than the Israelis on the other side, and they didn't look or smile at us as we passed by.

Back in Jerusalem we saw where Jesus and his disciples ate their last supper together – how long ago? Well – yesterday! We walked through the Garden of Gethsemane, and followed the Via Dolorosa and the Stations of the Cross. Nearby was the elaborate Church of the Holy Sepulchre built by order of Constantine's mother, Helena, in the 4th Century. It contains Jesus's tomb and a marble slab on which Jesus's body was presumably placed and from which he rose from the dead. (I had trouble believing the story of that marble slab.)

At the Holy Sepulchre Church the rivalry of the various Christian sects was all too evident. Who "owns" the story of Jesus's death and resurrection – Armenians, Greek or Latin Orthodox, Ethiopians, Syrian Christians, Copts, Roman Catholics? They all lay claim to the oversight of that church and place. At the moment there was a truce, with various sections of the church and different times of day assigned to each denomination for their prayers and ceremonies. However, certain entrances and areas are jealously reserved for the exclusive use of one or another of these religious groups. The battles of the past are ever present.

The conflicts in the Jewish community were on exhibit too. In Jerusalem at the Temple Institute, run by the Third Templists, we were shown blueprints and some artifacts collected for a new temple planned for the Temple Mount. That site, presently occupied by Al Aqsa and Dome of the Rock mosques, is sacred to Muslims as well as Jews. Our Israeli guide, Rouven, came out from the meeting with the Third Templists visibly shaken. "If those people ever managed to carry out their plans, we'd have the worst civil war you can imagine!" Three months later, Prime Minister Sharon with a number of

Israeli police climbed onto the Temple Mount, provoking a strong response from the Muslim Palestinians and incidentally bringing an end to Connecticut College's annual Israeli seminars.

I lost my skepticism in Galilee. Looking out of the Church of the Beatitudes in Capernaum over the Sea of Galilee onto a wide expanse of fields, you could easily imagine a multitude gathered to hear Jesus preach the Sermon on the Mount: "Blessed are the poor in spirit . . . blessed are the meek . . . blessed are they which do hunger and thirst after righteousness . . . blessed are the peacemakers . . . ." – lofty concepts even if they were written and given their poetic form long after they were spoken.

Wherever we went we walked on excavated streets, marveled at excavated walls, explored excavated places like King David's Tower and the

King David's Tower, with Chihuly glass sculpture

Connecticut College archeology

Western Wall tunnels. We dug out and helped sift rubble from burial caves at Beit Guvrin that had been destroyed in 40 BCE. In the Galilee area we saw the remains of Peter's house and a beautiful mosaic floor in the ruins of an ancient synagogue. The largest dig was of a Roman city at Sepphoris. There we met a group of American students who were spending their summer expanding discoveries that already included an amphitheater, other city buildings and, again, some grand mosaics. In Athens and Rome, Egypt or England, tourists are shown the sites of earlier gods and monuments to earlier victories, but the

Greeks no longer believe Apollo will give them a helpful prophesy, nor do the Italians expect to rebuild the colosseum. In Israel, however, each stone, each tile, each cobble re-inforces someone's faith, confirms someone's claim to ownership.

Sometimes the past wasn't so long ago. At the Holocaust Museum at Yad Vashem we were reminded of tragedies that happened in my lifetime. There was the stone commemorating the slaughter at Babi Yar, where Bud and I had paid our respects in 1971 during our month in the Soviet Union. And there an array of mirrors, reflecting flickering flames of five candles, sent thousands of lights out into what looked like eternity, a heart-wrenching memorial to the million and a half children killed by the Nazis.

At Megiddo (Armageddon) some of us took the same route down the cliffs that the zealots took to escape from the Romans. Here, we were wrapped in the future as well as the past: according to *Revelations*, Armageddon is where the final war before the Rapture will be fought.

SIDE TRIP

On our sixth day, our bus drove us to the Allenby Bridge. We were checked out by Israel and in by Jordan as we walked over the border to a Jordanian bus that would take us to Petra, one of the archeological wonders of the world. I didn't know about Petra and was overwhelmed by that Nabatean city carved out of red sandstone walls in the deep canyon of Wadi Araba. Tombs, temples, amphitheater, market place, fort, baths – all cut into the rock. Most spectacular was the Treasury, an exact copy of a Roman building, reproduced from blueprints Nabateans had presumably seen in Alexandria, the trading end of the Nabatean spice route.

We walked through the Siq from our hotel past the market and the Treasury and on to the Forum Restaurant run by Bedouins. After lunch, Roger asked who would like to ride back to the market in a mule-drawn wagon. I spoke up for a camel. So three of us rode some not-very-happy lumbering beasts about a mile, satisfying my long-held desire to really go somewhere by camel. A mile sufficed.

We returned to Israel by way of the Wadi Rum, crossing the border at hot hot Aqaba on the Red Sea.

Treasury Building, Petra

CHAPTER 62

THE GROWING FAMILY

THE MICHAEL BUTTERWORTHS

Michael and Carol came back from California in 1971. Carol has become a top-notch paralegal. Mike spends weekdays in New York City, a systems analyst and much else, keeping CBS's polling section honest. He still reads everything he gets his hands on, and remembers it, so he's a gold mine of information.

Carol, Beth and Mike at Mt. Vernon College

Olivia and Lily

BETH

Mike and Carol's daughter, Beth, is creative, gregarious and a good mother. She studied interior design and graduated from Mt. Vernon College in Washington DC. She and her husband Marc Daitch, a great father, have two daughters – Olivia, nine years old, and Lily, five. Olivia is a great reader like her grandfather, and both children are confident travelers who know how to find fun things to do wherever they are.

One year, Natasha, Kate's oldest, and Beth wandered together for a month in Europe. They returned best friends and decades later are best friends still.

TIMOTHY ET CETERA

Tim and Sue's marriage lasted ten years, and ten years after that Tim married Kay Kloppenburg. They live on a farm in Chesterfield, New Hampshire, where they have an orchard, grow Christmas trees and harvest timber, produce enough maple syrup to carry all of us through the year, and preserve vegetables for the winter from a thriving garden. Kay is a gifted Special Education teacher, and Tim does what farmers need to do, dabbles in desktop publishing, and now, as a New Hampshire State legislator, is headfirst into politics.

BROOK

Tim and Sue's daughter Brook, our first grandchild, was taking dictation from Bud, typing on his old Royal typewriter as he struggled to finish another book two days before he died. Several days after his memorial service, she asked me when I expected her to leave. What a boon for me to find she wanted to stay! She substituted in the West Hartford schools that year and worked nearby another year, teaching drama at Miss Porter's School. We had seen her act at age 13 in Moliere's *Imaginary Invalid* and watched her in many college

Brook, Mimi, Kay, Tim and Ibby in Atlanta

plays, so I wasn't too surprised when she made the big time in Washington, becoming an Equity actor.

Brook and her husband, Benjamin Newland, have recently moved to Dubai where Benjamin's law firm is opening a branch office. They and their three children – Isabel, Miranda and Benjamin, now ages 7, 5 and newborn – come back to the States for the summer.

BEN

Tim and Sue's second child, Ben, is a musician. When he was fifteen, he spent the winter with Tim and Kay in Granada, Spain, where he acquired a guitar and had some training in playing it from the American ex-pat flamenco devotee downstairs. However,

Lateef, Ben and Brook

Ben is essentially self-taught and now plays with several bands. Like many musicians Ben has found it a tough career, but now in his 30s he is married and is supplementing his income working with children in an after-school program.

LATEEF JACKSON

In the late 1980s Tim and Kay brought into our family Lateef Jackson, a twelve-year-old, our ninth grandchild. He graduated from the University of North Carolina in Charlotte where he now lives with his wife Melissa. Besides having careers in computer science and finance, they rehabilitate old buildings, creating affordable housing. When we are with them, they take good care of us elders, are adventurous and fun.

In January of 1991 and again a year later, Tim and Kay took some of us camping in Tortola, one of the British Virgin Islands. We snorkeled along the reefs just off the beach of our campground and in the seas surrounding Virgin Gorda. I found myself swimming with a Black Margate or a Goatfish or becoming a part of a school of Grunts or Angelfish. I had to remind myself I was a different species and couldn't really join their graceful swooping dances in and out of the coral reefs.

Visions of Tortola: five-year-old grandson Cody and a child from a neighboring tent, scared when Tim's reading of *Treasure Island* got too graphic ("That's another Tortola. That's not *my* Tortola," the little neighbor girl reassured herself); the treasure hunt following a map we found in a bottle floating off our beach; exuberant Schery a few months before her debilitating accident. These were wonderful diversions at a time when I needed diversions most.

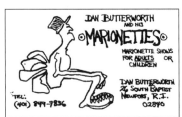

DAN'S CLAN

At the end of the 1960s and the Vietnam War, Dan found a job as a puppeteer's assistant and later became a master puppeteer himself. In June of 2004, at a gala evening celebration, Dan, elegant in a tuxedo, was presented with a Pell Award for contributions to the arts. We marvel at the beauty of his marionettes and his continual creative imagination.

Dan's wife, Beverly Blood, is an artist, too, and has more creative skills than she uses while working on prototypes for various toy companies. She and I spent a good bit of last summer together, banishing any feelings of loneliness on my part.

They and their two children, Teal and Cody, our youngest grandchildren, live in a barn with long ropes for swinging across their large open hayloft living room. Dan built stairs to a bedroom, a kind of shelf, perched like a bird's nest part way up one of the walls, where Teal has a bed and a study.

TEAL

Teal shone at Connecticut College, where I proudly presented her with a diploma in June, 2005. Everybody seemed to know her: "Oh. You're Teal's grandmother!" In her first post-college year, Teal tried her luck in San Francisco. She found a job and three other girls to join in an affordable living arrangement. I think she'll do all right.

Teal and friend Nikki
at Connecticut College

CODY

Four years younger than Teal, Cody once had a formidable temper, but now, six feet four inches tall and a superior athlete, he is unusually gentle and kind. He is a Sophomore at the University of Rhode Island, interested in engineering and much else.

Bev, Dan, Cody in RI; Chris Brooks
and band on Dan's stage; Teal and Dan

AND THEN THE VALDEZES

Kate and Natasha

Kate and Fernando's marriage lasted 23 years. When we visited them in Guadalajara in 1970, they were expecting their first child. Kate had a cradle but not much else. We shopped together (in a foreign language, remember) for needed equipment – clothes, blankets, etc., – and we met the obstetrician Kate had little confidence in. We could see much of the support system a new mother needs wasn't there. When we said goodbye at the airport, the expression on Kate's face was so bleak, I kept my composure until out of sight and then sobbed much of the way home. Natasha was born in February, a healthy contemplative child.

The Valdezes bought land in Ciudad Del Sol, a little town not yet wired for telephone service, built a house for themselves, and had two more children: Scheherazada, four years younger than Natasha, and Eliott another four years later.

When Natasha was twelve, the family moved to West Hartford where Fernando got jobs as an auto mechanic and Kate taught Spanish and found employment for laid-off Latino farm workers. After the Valdez marriage unraveled, Fernando returned to Mexico. Today, Kate lives a five-minute walk away from me. She has a business of her own called All Purpose Cleaning, is involved in the lives of her three children, and has a close friend who is a union organizer, now very much a part of our family activities.

NATASHA

Natasha is sensitive, serious, affectionate and adventurous. She maneuvered her way through her teens in West Hartford and graduated from the University of Minnesota. After working three years in Spain, she returned to the fold or at least to Boston, where she met a Navy medic, Carl Palazzotto.

Brook and Natasha in Lucerne

Natasha and Carl

They married and now live in West Hartford, where Carl, too, grew up. They now have two children – Maximilian, born in 2007, and Alexis, born in 2010.

When Natasha was ten, Bud and I took her and her cousin Brook, then fourteen, to Europe for a month – an unsophisticated girl who had not heard of Shakespeare or Gilbert and Sullivan with a worldly-wise Hanover, New Hampshire, high school student who had starred in a grown-up play. They soon joined forces, enjoying the trip while finding new ways to torture their grandparents.

SCHEHERAZADA

Kate and Fernando's second child, Scheherazada, born in Mexico in 1975, is a vivacious, pretty, dark-haired girl who flirts with every male she meets. In February of 1992 the kind of life she dreamed she'd have came to an end in a car crash on South Main Street in West Hartford, less than a mile from her home. She had gone to the movies. On the way home, she and her best friend, Vanessa, were offered rides by Vanessa's brother, and the nightmare of all parents became real. Steve slid sideways off the road, hitting a tree near the back door where Schery and Vanessa were sitting. Vanessa died a week later and Schery awoke from a four-and-a-half-month coma to find she had lost her best friend and the ability to talk. She still can't speak except by signing, a new language those around her quickly learn, and spends much of her time in a wheel chair, but she can take care of herself, given enough time. She regained her sense of humor and a remarkably happy spirit.

Natasha, Schery and Teal;
Dale and Schery

In spite of her condition, she is an integral part of family affairs, even at Squam where Tim organized the family to build a board walk connecting her sleeping cabin with our main cabin. She "swims." She and her partner Dale Wakeley joined us in Greece last April, where in a dull moment on a boat tour along the coast of Mount Athos, she gestured to a monk on the ship to pose with her for a picture. Not even an austere monk can refuse Schery.

On August 5, 2006, she and Dale, a magician, musician, poet and computer programmer committed themselves to each other before a large caring group of friends and families at the Friends Meeting House in West Hartford . Theirs was a unique Catholic/Quaker wedding.

ELIOTT

The third Valdez, Eliott, was four when he moved to Connecticut and started nursery school at the Friends Meeting House. He didn't have much English but made up for that by doing lots of hugging. His teachers called him their Latin lover. He needed a school that didn't require him to sit still, but he stuck with the West Hartford school system and graduated. He then spent three years in Arizona, studying massage therapy and working at a sports center. There, he helped young people with their homework and showed them how to live healthy lives. He returned to Connecticut because, he says, he missed so many family happenings. Here, he has found a similar job, helping youngsters with their schoolwork while teaching them some good physical fun. He's the fireworks man on the Fourth of July, with an assist from his girlfriend.

Eliott is a speedy, graceful skater and a terrific dancer. Kate and I once urged him to audition for an acting job with a friend in California and he was encouraged, but you need ardor as well as talent. That was our dream, not his.

CHAPTER 63

A WIDER CIRCLE

Two other families have melded with ours over the years, turning us into a tribe more than nuclear families. My brother Doug, his wife Betty, and their four boys spent many Thanksgivings and Christmases with us at Sunset Farm and many summers at Squam Lake. There, on the other side of our point, they built a camp facing east and the rising sun, a few minutes away from our Squaw Cove compound facing west. The two families joined almost daily in outdoor adventures until the Brooks children found far-flung work and their parents grew unwell. The Brooks brothers, now numbering three since the youngest, Donald, died in a motorcycle accident, get together on Squaw Cove for a week each summer. They have been joined by their newly discovered half-sister, Toni Gorman, and Donald's family. Toni and her husband, Patrick now add excitement to our summer and Thanksgiving festivities.

It seems that the Brookses have inherited a religious gene as well as a musical one. Alan is an ordained Buddhist, Ken is a born-again Christian minister, and Toni has earned her doctorate in Theology. This could have led to schisms, but so far, family trumps ideology.

The Brooks Family

We consider Bud's sister Dinny's family a part of our immediate clan too. We have seen little of the Parmalee boys because of Mac's untimely death and the rarity of Charley's forays east, but we keep in close touch with the three sisters. Patty, the oldest of the three, chose to go to school in Vermont while her family lived in Utah, and we happily acted as surrogates. She is an activist. Her latest triumph was organizing a group that saved from development a forested area in upper New York State, where she now lives: *Save the Ridge!* She is an iconoclast whose bluntness shocks, amuses, or elicits "Right On." China, her daughter, grew up in Manhattan, vacationed during childhood with her Chinese father's clan in California, and she blogs. We count on seeing them for Thanksgivings and summers at Squam.

The middle Parmalee sister, Clare, is a sculptor, a photographer, a superior gardener specializing in orchids, and the owner of two intelligent birds. She has chaired the Washington branch of Habitat for Humanity.

Cricket, the third sister, writes unusually well, is a professional storyteller, a collector of stories, and the mother of Joe, a student at Reed College. She keeps in touch with us at family gatherings, showing up in Wilmington, Delaware, for an opera version of *The Enormous Egg*, or at a cousin's wedding shower. All three sisters have lovely voices, and Clare has organized a monthly evening for singing music lovers.

Bud and Mims with Clare, China and Cricket Parmalee

Butterworths and friends head for Wilmington and the Enormous Egg opera.

I still live a few hundred yards away from the house where Bud grew up in a community started by his father. Not far off is stepsister-in-law Lucy. She and her sister Jeannie are the kind of friends who can be counted on to help out when needed, and whose children I'm in touch with and care about.

Paul and Elizabeth's children: Harry, Lucy, Dinny, Bud and Jeannie

WE KEEP IN TOUCH

At Thanksgivings as many as thirty-five of us sit down in our not very large living/dining room to a banquet of whatever specialties people want to bring. I provide the turkey. We find out what has happened to one other since we last met and discuss our future hopes and plans. And of course many of us re-une at Squam during the summer.

During the past decade I've rented places in Europe for a few weeks: in Murren, Switzerland, in 1997, and on the coast of Wales near Fishguard two years later. In 2003 we stayed in a converted Tuscan monastery and finally last April, 2006, at a b&b in Sarti, southeast of Thessaloniki in Greece. We not only revel but do exciting things together: I have another motive. In case one of my grandchildren decides to run for President, I want her to have sampled cultures other than the Tijuana tourist mecca on our border.

China, Mike, Patty, Mims and Kate in
Mürren, Switzerland;
Bev and Cody in Wales;
Kate, Natasha and Schery in Tuscany

CHAPTER 64

SUMMING UP

For sixteen years I have been living alone, losing a warm companionship with someone close who shared ideas, adventures, and responsibilities for household maintenance and financial decisions, but gaining an independence and privacy I've come to cherish. Some of my friends are worn out caring for a failing partner, even resenting the continuing burden of catering to an ever more needy spouse while they are at an age when they can barely take care of themselves. These are not choices for us to make...

In the early '90s, when my brother's Parkinson's Disease worsened, he and his wife, Betty, moved to a retirement home in Bloomfield, Connecticut; and I watched a difficult ending. For a while we again celebrated special events and did things together until their health deteriorated. Doug was for some time idolized for his good looks and prominent scientific career. He wrote poetry, too. But he had to struggle harder and harder to make the last

Doug and Betty Brooks

decades of his life meaningful. He had often demanded much of his family, and now he needed Betty's help in setting up his "office." He needed her help in filing this and finding that. He needed to get something copied or to organize a reading of his poetry – right away.

Betty had never learned to protect herself from such demands, and she couldn't do so at that late date. Although not gregarious, she had a knack for forming genuine friendships. I know of three good, caring friends she bonded with during her time in Bloomfield, but they all died too soon to give her any sustained comfort. I think Betty dreamed of having a few years of freedom from the responsibilities she couldn't slough off, but it wasn't to be. Doug died first in the spring of 2004 and Betty followed five weeks later.

In time, the images of the last long illnesses and deaths of those you love give way to recollections of earlier days – particularly the joyous ones: Carpenters' Christmas greening parties, our annual holiday square dances, winter trips to Squam, summer island picnics, climbing in the White Mountains, picking mountain cranberries and lakeside blueberries, sharing the day's adventures at dinner around our round table. Just living with someone with a creative mind and a love of life.

Jim and Mary Jane Carpenter

CHAPTER 65

AND OLD AGE

How to describe this final Act of my life? Aches and pains? Walking less steadily? Eyes failing? Sometimes lonely? Yes. And vigiling every Saturday in West Hartford Center, holding signs against the Iraq War, against Bush and his administration, and for universal health care and the reestablishment of constitutional rights.

Flo Woodiel and Mims

Several of us started Saturday morning vigils long before the Iraq invasion. Friend Martha Vinick was the instigator. Flo Woodiel, wispy white-bearded Jack, and I were there at the beginning. We could hear the drum beats for war with Iraq although everybody knew it was Saudi Arabians, NOT Iraqis, who flew the planes into the towers and the Pentagon on 9/11. We doubted the presence of WMDs. A number of friends and strangers have joined us: poet Dave from Pax Christi; angry José from Trinity; former SDS member, politically savvy Lynn; Southern Connecticut University Professor Chengiah from South Africa; singers Nancy and Jerry; friend Paul, long-time worker on sustainable

> UNPROVOKED PREEMPTIVE STRIKE – WHAT HAVE WE BECOME?

energy matters, to name a few. And the Clarke Allens from Glastonbury show up faithfully with hand-made signs for us all.

This week's anger is directed at Congressional Democrats. Why hasn't Pelosi stopped the war yet? They have been in power since January! Impeach Bush! Stop funding the war! Every

Weekly Saturday vigil in West Hartford

TORTURE
BREEDS
TERRORISM

day more people are dying, more people are becoming refugees. I argue that the votes aren't there yet. The margin is too thin. We've got to change more minds. Remember we weren't even able to unseat pro-war Senator Lieberman here in Connecticut in the '06 election.

Here's s typical series of events in my life:

• I go to a meeting to hear our Congressman, John Larson, explain the actions Congress is taking to stop the war, but his audience isn't satisfied. When a questioner mentions impeachment, the group erupts in loud approval. I, too, clap loud and long. Congress is accumulating evidence of the Bush administration's "crimes and misdemeanors" through its investigations, but pressure from us must provide necessary support.

• I revel in a weekly Sunday walk in "The Reservoir" with Kate & Steve, Natasha & Carl, Beth, Olivia & Lily, Lisa, Flo, Eliott and three dogs. We ooh and ahh over the sonogram image of Palazzotto fetus. Miracle! I am slowing down and my legs ache by the end of the three-mile hike.

• In the afternoon I write a Letter to the Editor of the *Hartford Courant* about the Larson meeting. (It never gets published.)

• Mike comes by on his way back to New York and his job with CBS. I give him a sandwich and some cider in exchange for information about his polling work and a good political discussion. Yes, he'll be here for Easter and will go to Florida for Lateef and Melissa's wedding in July, and probably to

Florence in September.

• I take an aerobics class at Cornerstone pool, the last for the season.

• We have our monthly Freeze Ladies' pot luck dinner at Roz Spier's in Glastonbury. Good talk as usual, ranging from religious beliefs to news of our offspring to the struggle within the Democratic party. How to stop the Iraq war when there is no agreement on how soon and how far we want to get out. We friends, having worked for years to achieve an end to the nuclear arms race, are pragmatists. Democracy is slow.

• Great Decisions at Stella Johnson's in Simsbury. Chapter on Global Warming.

• Kay calls to report on Florida trip where she and Tim met Lateef, Melissa, and Melissa's family.

• I take the originals of Bud's *First Blueberry Pig* to a printer to produce a new edition.

• Friend Martha calls from Florida. I miss her and am worried about her health.

• I have a long talk with Mary Jane. She can no longer take care of 93- year-old Jim, is exhausted and psychologically wrung. We make a date for lunch.

• I hear from Tim, our New Hampshire legislator. He is debating and voting on many exciting and important bills: the death penalty, same sex marriage, minors' notification of parents before abortions, expansion of gambling. He has made his first speech, supporting a resolution to get out of Iraq. We talk about tickets for Florida in July, summer arrangements at Squam, and dates in September for Florence, but have to cut our call short so he can tend to the maple sap boiling in his sugar house.

• I go with Flo to Real Artways to see a film on Ralph Nader, with an hour-long discussion with Nader himself thrown in. We arrive early and find crowds ahead of us – standing room only! So many familiar faces! "Hello, Mims, I haven't seen you since the Duffey campaign." "Hi, Mims. I last saw you when we were working for (Gene) McCarthy." Nader, his sister and mother are there, and Bill Curry, with his sister and mother – old friends.

The main issue of the evening: were Nader's runs for President in 2000 and 2004 ego trips, making him a spoiler, or serious attempts to make the elections more meaningful? We also talked about what had to be done to preserve democracy: proportional representation, instant run-off, get money out of elections, encourage third parties… I remember attending a forum in 1948 when four candidates vied for Connecticut's fifth district Congressional seat: a Republican, Democrat, Socialist, and Communist. Soon after that election, the Communist Party was outlawed and the Socialists disappeared, silencing arguments and proposals from the left. The result has been a skewed political scene, a power shift to the right.

Well there's a start.

And it's spring – my 89th! The weather has been cold and rainy, but the days are longer and the sun is warm when it shines. The world is turning forsythia yellow and willow green. The skunk cabbages are up and my neighbors' hillside of daffodils is in full bloom. Red cardinals and purple finches flash through my yard, hunting material for nests. Tree frogs and red-eyed vireos have formed noisy choruses of avid procreators. The times, though perilous, are bursting with historical significance The pigeons seem to be coming home to roost for the destructive Bush administration and, though I am "feeling my age," I'm still full of wonder at "the grand pageantry of life."